GREAT JOBS

FOR EVERYONE 50+

GREAT JOBS

FOR EVERYONE 50+

Finding Work That Keeps You Happy
and Healthy . . . and Pays the Bills

Updated Edition

KERRY HANNON

WILEY

Creative director: Scott A. Davis
Cover design: Lesley Q. Palmer
Photograph: Elizabeth Dranitzke

Published by John Wiley & Sons, Inc., Hoboken, New Jersey.
Published simultaneously in Canada.

AARP produces print and e-books on a range of topics. Visit AARP.org/bookstore.

For general information on our other products and services or for technical support, please
contact our Customer Care Department within the United States at (800) 762–2974, outside
the United States at (317) 572–3993, or fax (317) 572–4002.

Wiley publishes in a variety of print and electronic formats and by print-on-demand. Some
material included with standard print versions of this book may not be included in e-books
or in print-on-demand. If this book refers to media such as a CD or DVD that is not included
in the version you purchased, you may download this material at http://booksupport.wiley.
com. For more information about Wiley products, visit www.wiley.com.

ISBN 978–1–119–36332–3 (Paper)
ISBN 978–1–119–36334–7 (ePDF)
ISBN 978–1–119–36333–0 (ePub)

Printed in the United States of America.
10 9 8 7 6 5 4 3 2 1

*For my siblings Michael, Pat, and Jack, who make
a positive impact on the lives of others every day.*

Contents

Contents

Part II The Great Jobs Workshop

Acknowledgments

I've been privileged to have a distinguished cadre of colleagues, experts, and fellow travelers on the road to creating this updated edition of *Great Jobs for Everyone 50+*. Each one has honed my methodology for the best pathways to navigate the workplace today for experienced workers.

What a difference five years makes. Since the first edition appeared, I've spent countless hours meeting with, interviewing, studying, and speaking to audiences of people over 50 who are either keen to find a job or share their messages of job hunting success and optimism with me.

This new edition reflects the latest knowledge and experience I've gleaned along the way. As with any book project, there are several individuals who I must recognize in this public forum to show my genuine appreciation for their grace and support.

I owe boundless gratitude to the experts who gladly offered thoughtful guidance. These include Encore.org's founder, Marc Freedman, and the nonprofit's vice president, Marci Alboher, author of *The Encore Career Handbook,* an essential tool I recommend to those seeking a second act for the greater good.

Other pros I admire and whose work I deeply value include Chris Farrell, Ruth Finkelstein, Paul H. Irving, Elizabeth Isele, Susan P. Joyce, Beverly Jones, Mark Miller, Dorian Mintzer, Maggie Mistal, John Tarnoff, Mark S. Walton, and Betsy Werley.

My "Great Jobs" column, which has appeared at AARP.org since 2010, has benefited in recent years from the vision and skilled editorial gifts and guidance of Tara Coates, Rick Levinson, James Henderson, Kimberly Palmer, and John Burgess.

My deep gratitude to my agent, Linda Konner, of the Linda Konner Literary Agency, whose savvy publishing wisdom and belief in my work has propelled my mission of empowering individuals to do more with their career and personal finances—now and for the future.

Acknowledgments

My thanks to former John Wiley & Sons editor, Tula Batanchiev Weis for greenlighting this revamped edition, helping me shepherd several of my previous books, including *Love Your Job: The New Rules for Career Happiness*, through the publishing maze, and always trusting my work.

Special thanks to Jodi Lipson, Director of AARP's Book Division, who meticulously shaped this book to bring forth the kind of plain-speaking job help that 50+ workers are pursuing.

Without Julie Kerr's patience and smooth editing chops, these chapters might never have attained this new coat of paint and smart presentation. Kudos, Julie, you made the ride stress-free.

I send a heartfelt thanks to Susan Cerra, Wiley senior production editor, and James M. Fraleigh, copy editor, who diligently pored over my manuscript with an eye for detail and smoothly polishing the prose.

A salute to AARP Art Director Lesley Q. Palmer and Creative Director Scott A. Davis, who produced a handsome design for the book jacket that exudes the energy of what readers will find inside.

On a professional and personal note, Richard Eisenberg, the managing editor of PBS's NextAvenue.org, is one of the finest editors and innovative thinkers I have ever worked with. His kindness and humor make it a publishing journey with meaning.

I also want to thank A. J. Campbell of CoSynergy.com, my web designer and social media consultant.

On a personal note, my own great job is made possible by the support and inspiration of the following board members of Kerry Hannon, Inc.:

To the Bonney family—Paul, Pat, Christine, Mike, Caitlin, Shannon, Garrett Goon, and Piper, too—for always welcoming me with open hearts and a wagging tail (in one case).

To the Hannon family—Mike, Judy, Brendan, Sean, Conor, Brian, and Emily—for inspiring me with your genuine examples of the meaning of helping others and giving back along the way.

To my brother, Jack, for being the calm, clear voice of solutions whenever I call for help; and my sister-in-law, Charmaine, for the love you spread.

To the Hersch crew—Ginny, David, Corey, and Amy—and the Hackels—Stu, Sue, Cassie, and Eric: Through the bond of family ties you provide endless rays of encouragement and laughter.

Acknowledgments

To Tom and Cindy Goutman, proprietors of the Goutman International Hotel and Spa in Naples, Florida, your oasis among the palm trees provided the right place and the right time to complete this manuscript without distraction. And for Cindy, your observation to me that "not every job will have deep meaning, or change the world. Nor is every job one that allows you to follow a passion . . . but what every job must be is an adventure" is one that resonates.

To Jonelle Mullen, my friends at TuDane Farm, and Caparino Z for helping me clear my head and learn from the enchanted world of horses.

To my cherished childhood friend, Marcy Holquist, for being there as my artistic and personal touchstone.

A heartfelt embrace to my mother, Marguerite Hannon, for being my cheerleader for decades as well as a wonderful public relations steward.

Finally, my husband, Cliff, for your love, friendship, and unflappability. Thanks are just the tip of the iceberg,

Of course, without Zena, our Labrador retriever and the quintessential road manager, I would be adrift.

About the Author

Kerry Hannon is a nationally recognized expert and strategist on career transitions, personal finance, and retirement, She is a frequent TV and radio commentator and is a sought-after keynote speaker at conferences across the country. Kerry focuses on empowering yourself to do more with your career and personal finances—now and for the future.

She has spent more than two decades covering all aspects of careers, business, and personal finance as a columnist, editor, and writer for the nation's leading media companies, including *The New York Times, Forbes, Money, U.S. News & World Report,* and *USA Today.* She has appeared as a career and personal finance expert on *The Dr. Phil Show,* ABC News, CBS, CNBC, *NBC Nightly News,* NPR, and PBS.

Kerry is currently a columnist and regular contributor to *The New York Times,* a contributing writer for *Money* magazine, AARP's Jobs Expert and Great Jobs columnist, a contributing editor and Second Verse columnist at *Forbes,* and the PBS website NextAvenue .org's expert and columnist on personal finance, wealth management, and careers for boomer women.

Kerry is the award-winning author of a dozen books, including *Getting the Job You Want After 50 For Dummies; Love Your Job: The New Rules for Career Happiness;* and *What's Next? Finding Your Passion and Your Dream Job in Your Forties, Fifties and Beyond.*

Kerry lives in Washington, D.C., with her husband, documentary producer and editor Cliff Hackel, and her Labrador retriever, Zena.

Follow Kerry on Twitter @KerryHannon, visit her website at KerryHannon.com, and check out her LinkedIn profile at www .linkedin.com/in/kerryhannon.

Introduction

When Dane Peters was 65, he retired as head of the Brooklyn Heights Montessori School in Brooklyn, New York, but he wasn't ready to stop working altogether.

It wasn't about money—although having income to cover some day-to-day living expenses and travel was an incentive. (He and his wife, Chris, a retired schoolteacher, had a cruise in Alaska and a longboat tour in France on their immediate travel bucket list.) Work, Peters says, gave him his "own sense of identity," and he wants to hang on to that. Plus, he wants to give back to others who could benefit from his decades of experience.

"I wanted to stay in the game and support independent schools with my expertise," he says, "but I didn't want the pace of a 70-hour workweek."

To see if his services as a consultant might be in demand, he took on weekend consulting assignments *before* retiring. Happily, he discovered a niche. He now chooses when he wants to work—normally one or two jobs a month.

Today, he leads a life of consulting, volunteering, caring for grandchildren, and enjoying leisure time. "It's my trifecta," he says. "Paid work, giving back, and relaxation." He calls it "consulteering." The biggest challenge is time management, he says: "How many gigs I will take on and how much volunteering my wife and I can realistically do."

Money, Mental Engagement, and Meaning

Not everyone is in a financial position to work just one consulting gig a month. Some of us need or will need to keep working full or part time for the income. The reality is that many people aren't financially secure enough to retire. When I speak to audiences of people over age 50 around the country looking for job-hunting advice, I see the palpable fear in their eyes that they will outlive their money. They might.

Nearly half of families have no retirement account savings at all, according to a report by the Economic Policy Institute, the independent, nonprofit think tank that researches the impact of economic trends and policies on working people in the United States. The median savings, or those at the 50th percentile, may be a better gauge. The median for all families in the United States is just $5,000, and the median for families with some savings is $60,000.

According to a recent survey by the Employee Benefit Research Institute (EBRI), a sizable percentage of workers say they have no or very little money in savings and investments. Among workers providing this type of information, 47 percent report that the total value of their household's savings and investments, excluding the value of their primary home and any defined benefit plans (a traditional pension where an employer ponies up the money and promises you a certain payout after you retire), is less than $25,000. This includes 24 percent who say they have less than $1,000 in savings.

"Even people with retirement savings see earning a half-time income as a safety net," says Beverly Jones, author of *Think Like an Entrepreneur, Act Like a CEO*, who advises 50- and 60-somethings as a career coach at Clearways Consulting in Washington, D.C.

Let me remind you of the four money-wise reasons to stay in the workforce as long as you can:

1. You can still contribute to retirement plans. The more earning years when you can build savings in a defined contribution plan like a 401(k) or an Individual Retirement Account (IRA), the better off you'll be in terms of retirement security down the road.
2. The pay can also help provide a cushion to allow you to delay tapping into Social Security until age 70. You can claim benefits as early as age 62, but by holding off until your full retirement age (currently age 66), you'll receive 100 percent of your primary insurance amount; every year that you delay beyond that, until age 70, adds an additional 8 percent annually.
3. You can refrain from dipping into existing retirement funds. The longer you work, the longer you delay tapping these funds, which can continue to grow.
4. Working can provide income to pay for health insurance until you're eligible for Medicare at 65. Fewer employers are

offering their retired workers medical benefits, and those who do are ramping up the amount retirees must contribute to the cost of coverage. Even better, you might find a job that offers you access to a health plan. The income can also help with medical bills not covered by Medicare.

But like Dane Peters, people 50+ want more from a job than just income, says Dorian Mintzer, a retirement transition coach. "They want to build social connection, mental engagement, and meaning into their life," she says. "It's an important part of how they define themselves, and they don't want to totally give it up."

"Growing old in the 21st century is not what it was in the 20th," says Marcie Pitt-Catsouphes, director of the Center on Aging & Work at Boston College. What's different now is that baby boomers are either continuing to work much longer, or approaching work not as an afterthought but as a pillar of their "retirement" plans, as oxymoronic as that sounds.

The vision of people 50+ spending their retirement years gardening, golfing, and lounging on the beach is out. Meaningful work is in.

Today's 60-year-old might reasonably plan to work at least part time for another 15 years, figures Marc Freedman, founder and CEO of Encore.org, a nonprofit that promotes second acts for the greater good. "That changes the entire equation about what you want to do, what's possible to do, and whether it is worth investing up front for additional education," he says.

I like his thinking. To me, it's exciting, inviting, and empowering, providing that you enjoy what you're doing. Continuing to work helps people feel more relevant and needed and less isolated. And research shows that besides giving us meaning, work keeps our brains sharp—the old "use it or lose it" axiom—and our bodies healthy:

- Working tends to keep people physically active, socially connected, and mentally challenged—all things known to help prevent mental decline, according to the researchers at INSERM, the French government's health research agency.
- Work may even help stave off dementia. A large study by INSERM of nearly half a million workers in France suggests that delaying retirement means people may be at less risk of developing dementia, including Alzheimer's disease.

- For each additional year of work before retirement, the risk of getting dementia is reduced by 3.2 percent, according to Carole Dufouil, a scientist at INSERM.
- "Mental Retirement," a 2010 paper by economists Susann Rohwedder of RAND and Robert Willis of the University of Michigan, reviewed data from the United States, England, and 11 European countries. They concluded that retirement significantly hampered the cognitive ability of people in their early 60s.
- Scholars have reported that workers with routine jobs may find cognitive benefits if their employer offers variety and training for their jobs. For example, in studies of older workers' productivity at a Mercedes-Benz truck factory and a large German insurance company, economist Axel Borsch-Supan and colleagues at the Munich Center for the Economics of Aging found that older factory workers were as productive as their younger peers, when offered variety or training in their work.
- Volunteering and paid work produce better physical and mental health, says Linda Fried, a founder of the Experience Corps (a nonprofit enterprise now run by AARP that brings people age 50 and over into elementary schools) and a dean of Columbia University's Mailman School of Public Health.

Now in my mid-50s, I can't imagine not working in some form as a writer well beyond age 67—the age I can start receiving full Social Security retirement benefits. I've been passionate about writing since childhood. I've been tickled to make a living at it. And as I grow older, I appreciate that it's flexible work I can do from home, with my Labrador retriever, Zena, at my feet, or anywhere I can carry my laptop computer.

The Value of Older Workers

While working longer is better for employees, it turns out it's also better for employers. Those I've interviewed say that they find that workers age 50 and older are more loyal and aren't as likely as younger workers to job jump. They are reliable and dependable. And that lower staff turnover benefits the bottom line. The costs of high turnover are tangible. Finding, hiring, and training a new employee is a costly venture.

Employers also tell me that they value older employees because they have an ability to make quick decisions and solve problems based on their knowledge and overall life experience. They have superior communication skills, both written and oral. Importantly, they have the ability to serve as mentors.

In a global and fast-paced workplace, many employers don't have time to waste while a younger worker gets up to speed. Companies are realizing that it's often wise to seek out and hire experienced workers. Believe me, you're on the cusp of a sweeping change in workplace demographics. And leading the charge is the boomer generation.

Baby boomers are also better educated than previous generations of older workers, making them much better able to compete for positions, according to Harvard economists Claudia Goldin and Lawrence Katz.

They found that a large fraction of women, in particular, is working a lot longer, past their 60s and even into their 70s. In fact, the U.S. Bureau of Labor Statistics (BLS) projects that by the end of the 2010s, about 20 percent of women over 65 will be in the labor force.

"Women's increased participation beyond their fifties is a change of real consequence," according to Goldin and Katz. "Rather than being an increase in marginal part-time workers, the higher labor force participation of older women consists disproportionately of those working at full-time jobs. Women are remaining on their jobs as they age rather than scaling down or leaving for positions with shorter hours and fewer days.

"From my work with Katz, we find a strong increase in employment among the most highly educated of those women older than fifty-five and for those who are in managerial and professional occupations—even if their financial security appears to be reasonable," Goldin told me. "Higher levels of employment for women older than fifty-five years also appear to be among those who are healthier and whose occupations are the most rewarding and least physically taxing." (This echoes the survey conducted by Elizabeth Fideler for her book, *Women Still at Work*.)

Catherine Collinson, president of the Transamerica Center for Retirement Studies and the Transamerica Institute, told a U.S. Senate Special Committee on Aging hearing that her organization's surveys found that only 42 percent of women workers say they are building a large enough nest egg to retire without financial worries, compared to 55 percent of men.

"Women age 50 and older—especially unmarried women—face extreme financial risks and potential poverty in retirement," Collinson told me when I interviewed her for a Next Avenue article. Many women Transamerica surveyed say they plan to work until age 70 or later—or don't plan to retire at all.

"Work can provide important resources for women—such as a sense of meaning and purpose, a positive identity, and a social network—in addition to financial benefit," says Colorado State Assistant Professor Gwenith Fisher, who has been studying when and why people retire. Fisher was on a Future of Work and Retirement panel I moderated at Columbia University's Age Boom Academy.

Moreover, Fisher concurs with what I mentioned above: "Continuing to work is also associated with cognitive and health benefits: Research that has studied patterns of cognitive functioning has shown that working in jobs that involve thinking, problem solving, and creativity is related to less cognitive decline, and retirement is also linked to earlier mortality, even among people who did not retire due to their health."

Of course, men can enjoy these benefits by working longer, too.

Yes, There Are Jobs

Landing a job after 50 does take research, soul-searching, and swagger. It's not an easy skate. I know that and so do you. So do organizations like the AARP Foundation, whose Back to Work 50+, for example, connects workers 50 and older with the information, training, and support they need to get back into the workforce.

The openings are there, though. You may wind up doing lots of different jobs in your 50+ years. You may want a job for a season, for a few years to gradually unwind into retirement, or even for a few hours a week. Then, too, you may be looking for a job that really does turn into a full-blown second career.

I also wouldn't be surprised if you test a number of different kinds of jobs to find what you really shine at or want to do in the years ahead. You may even strategically build an income stream from a tapestry of work you enjoy and are skilled at doing. After taking a hard look at the numbers and talking to older workers,

I've discovered that things are actually far better than the national conversation might indicate.

Let me put things into perspective.

Older job applicants do get hired. It typically takes longer for someone over 55 to land a job than someone younger, according to the BLS, but the current unemployment rate for people over 55 is 3.5 percent; it's 4.9 percent for those age 25 to 34 and 4.8 percent overall.

Among 65- to 74-year-olds, labor force participation is predicted to hit 32 percent by 2022, up from 20 percent in 2002, according to the Bureau of Labor Statistics. For those age 75 and up, the rate will jump from 5 percent in 2002 to 11 percent in 2022.

Meanwhile, as the U.S. economy swings from physically stressful manufacturing jobs to service positions, there are more jobs in which using your mental skills and tapping your knowledge and experience are in demand. That translates to more opportunities for older workers. "We have more older-worker-friendly jobs now than we used to," according to David Powell, an economist at the nonprofit policy-research organization Rand Corp.

At a time when many employers are complaining about a scarcity of skilled workers, older Americans have much more work experience than younger ones. "When there is a shortage of skilled workers, older workers get jobs," says Nicole Maestas, an economist and associate professor of healthcare policy at Harvard Medical School.

According to research by Matthew Rutledge, an economist at the Center for Retirement Research at Boston College, the jobs are often a mix of high-skilled service work (managers, sales supervisors, and accountants) and low-skilled service work (truck drivers, janitors, and nursing aides). But, unfortunately, Rutledge found that the types of jobs that favor older workers pay 6 to 11 percent less than ones favoring younger workers.

Still, when I ask older job applicants how they'd feel about working for less money than in the past, I often hear something that may surprise you.

Many aren't looking for high-pay, stressful management positions on the frontlines. I know this depends on your age and the kind of work you do. Moreover, a worker in their 50s may have different work goals than someone in their 60s. But in many instances, regardless of age, I have found that pay is not as much of a deal breaker as you might think.

What they want mostly are flexible hours and a sense of autonomy. Better still, they say, they'd love to work for a business or nonprofit whose mission they believe in and where they feel they can use their talents to make a difference.

For these people, rewarding and flexible work are worth far more than a paycheck. In fact, according to a 2016 FlexJobs survey of more than 1,000 respondents aged 50 and older, work flexibility is the most important factor in evaluating a job prospect. The survey said that nearly a quarter of respondents would take a 10 or 20 percent pay cut if they could telecommute, for example.

"Older workers have reached a point where they realize that, while money may be important and necessary for them to make, it's not the first consideration they pay attention to when trying to find a job," Sara Sutton Fell, CEO and founder of FlexJobs, told me. "Workers nearing retirement age often have a strong understanding of their priorities."

Deciding What (Else) You Want Out of Work

What motivates us to work and what each of us calls a "great job" is as individual as we are. "Different flavors of ice cream," as my sister Pat likes to say. But I beg you: Try to find a job you love.

For my book, AARP's *Love Your Job: The New Rules for Career Happiness*, I interviewed hundreds of workers about what made them love their jobs. Most people say they're driven by the people they work with, the opportunity to keep learning and growing, or the mission or cause of their employer's services or the products it makes. Sometimes they say they love the travel opportunities.

Yes, money matters, but don't get locked into a must-have salary. When searching for jobs and comparing offers, be sure to account for other benefits, including the following:

- **Flexible workday:** Half of employers are willing to offer flexible arrangements, such as working part time or job sharing, to their most skilled and experienced workers, according to a Bank of America/Merrill Lynch survey of 650 human resources executives.
- **A healthy work-life balance:** Three in five people interested in a second career midlife say it's very important that the job leaves free time for things they want to do, such as travel, education, or engagement in other activities they

enjoy, according to a report by Encore.org. Indeed, many of those interested in encore careers appear eager to mix fewer hours of work per week with more years of work in total. A flexible schedule may make working a few more years more palatable.

- **Meaningful work:** As I discussed earlier, meaning can be as critical as money. More than 25 million Americans 50 to 70 years old are eager to share their skills, passions, and expertise in encore careers that address social needs, typically in education, healthcare, human services, and the environment, according to a study by Encore.org and Penn Schoen Berland.

- **Opportunities to interact with others and stay productive:** A Pew Research Center survey found that working for non-financial reasons, such as job enjoyment or the desire to be productive, increases with age.

- **Learning opportunities:** Employers are increasingly tuning into these enticements. So while they worry that they may not be able to meet your salary expectations, they're increasingly offering training and education opportunities.

How to Use This Book

In these pages, you will discover the ultimate guide to great jobs, where to find them, pay ranges, and qualifications needed. I'll give you the action steps to take to find a job that works for you.

I've divided this book into two sections.

In Part One, "Great Jobs," I provide eight chapters that set out the best jobs for you. And there are plenty of them to peruse. In this second edition, there are nearly *twice* as many jobs as I listed in the first edition five years ago.

Categories run the bases from a large section on part-time jobs—because followers on social media, listeners, readers, and audience members told me that is what they're seeking in many cases—followed closely by work-at-home jobs. I expanded these chapters significantly in this edition. Other chapters are more specific, such as those on nonprofit jobs, jobs for educators, and healthcare jobs. I canvass jobs in a range of industries from transportation and energy/utilities to federal jobs, healthcare, and technology, as well as skilled trade and manufacturing.

As AARP's Jobs Expert, I have developed this material through extensive reporting and interviews conducted for my "Great Jobs for Retirees" column that appears monthly at AARP.org. The pressing need to find these kinds of jobs is evidenced by the more than one million visitors who click on the columns each month to find job suggestions and insider advice. Quite frankly, that's astounding to me.

There's something here for everyone, a job hunter's smorgasbord. No, this is not the master list of every job under the sun, but you'll discover plenty of ideas to spur your imagination about how you can make the most of your talents to create work that, well, works for you.

You'll find lots of professional occupations and some that may require retraining and adding a degree or certificate. And you'll also find a large selection of the jobs geared for someone who wants a little income but doesn't want to do much heavy lifting.

You will find that many offer flexible schedules—a week, a month, a few months a year, or even on-again, off-again contract work—which means that three weeks at the lake house in the summer is still possible. If you want full-time work, many part-time positions hold that promise.

Each job description follows this format: the nitty-gritty, pay range, and qualifications needed, with a smattering of job-hunting tips tossed in. A handful of broad-based jobs may fall under two different categories. Some jobs, of course, may be too physically demanding for some (but not all) of us in this age group, say, home health aide or even a retail cashier, which require lots of time on your feet.

Pay ranges vary widely from employer to employer and city to city and by your experience. They are listed here as a guideline. Jobs are listed alphabetically, so don't be put off by the random jump from a professional full-time position to a more casual part-time retirement one that will let you earn some extra cabbage for your slush fund.

In Part Two, "The Great Jobs Workshop," I deliver the professional advice and strategies I've been doling out as a career transition strategist and as a retirement and personal finance expert and journalist for more than two decades. Most recently, I've been fortunate to reach out to job seekers through my work as a columnist for *Forbes, Money* magazine, *The New York Times,* and PBS Next

Avenue. Some of the material here has been tested out there first. It has allowed me to get a conversation going with thousands of people to see what kind of advice they want and what really helps.

My tips also stem from the worries that I hear from audience members when the lights come up at the end of one of my keynote speeches, or when a listener calls into a radio talk show where I have been a guest to ask a question, or when someone calls or e-mails for one-on-one career guidance. These shout-outs for advice convinced me that there's a blazing need for this kind of straightforward career guidance.

I have designed this section so you can dip in and out of the chapters as they apply to your situation. You'll find tips on resume writing, what you need to know to land a job at a nonprofit, how to use social media to discover this new chapter of your work life, and much more. Explore. While not every chapter will speak to your situation, I'm confident that you will find the direction you need right now.

Throughout, you'll find websites, job boards, and books to help your search.

■ ■ ■

At the very heart of it, I wrote this book to help you find the work you love. The rest will follow.

Bottom line: Brush off that resume. Let's go job hunting!

GREAT JOBS

■ ■ ■

*G*reat. That's a word that fascinates me.

We all know what it means to have a great time. You can have a great time at a Bruce Springsteen concert, at a friend's 50th birthday party, or on a Caribbean vacation. But can you have a *great* job?

Is there work that's really great? You bet. But what constitutes greatness is up to you to interpret and define in context to your own life.

For me, it's something I lose track of time doing. Something that, well, doesn't feel like work. It doesn't have to be a passion, but it's nice if it is. It should be something that adds to your life—whether it's a financial or psychological boost.

In the next eight chapters, I will take you down that path of discovery, showing you great jobs available to you. This is not, however, meant to be the definitive listing of jobs, but rather ones I've selected that may simply get you pondering positions you've never considered.

The goal is to open your mind to possibilities, to widen your view of work, to take down the bumper rails and allow you to explore a wider lane of options. Don't worry, you'll still be able to roll a strike.

You'll meet people who are looking for a new job for a slew of reasons. Some have retired and are working in part-time jobs they take real pleasure in—jobs that help build their bank account until they no longer need, or want, to work. You'll meet those who may have left one career but have set off on another one with just as much determination. And you'll meet people who have lost their jobs and moved on to work that is rewarding—and pays the bills.

Most of the people I've interviewed for this book told me that flexibility is *the* essential ingredient in a job. It's the ability to work from home, part time, or for just a few months a year, that they're after. As a result, I've geared several chapters to jobs in that category. The lion's share of these jobs, however, can easily ramp up to full-time schedules, if desired.

The salary ranges I've listed are just that—ranges. Depending on your skills, where you live, and your previous work experience, what you might get paid could be quite a bit higher. I've used these figures to give you a general idea. Qualifications, too, will vary from employer to employer. The details I suggest are standard in many occupations, but everything is open to poetic license, in my view.

So I encourage you to read through all the jobs I have profiled (listed in alphabetical order) to see which ones capture your attention and fit with your personality and skills. Be creative with your job search; be willing to experiment, to try something new, to be humbled by being a beginner again. Use this time to open your mind to possibilities.

There is an underlying theme here: A great job is not just something you imagine. It is something you not only *want* to do, but that you *can* do.

Great Part-Time Jobs

■ ■ ■

A part-time job is just that, a few hours a day, a couple of days a week, a month, or even a stint of several months. The jobs I've listed in this chapter tend to be available year-round and most can be ramped up to full-time positions, depending on your financial needs. The key to landing a full-time job is often getting your foot in the door.

But if the possibilities listed here aren't quite what you're after, keep reading. In the chapters that follow, you might find a job that you can negotiate for part-time duties. In today's job market, anything is negotiable. So don't be afraid to ask.

The reality is that after stepping away from a full-time job, many people still find that not only does work provide a much-needed paycheck and an ability to continue to save, but it gives them a crucial identity. So if you can afford to go part time, you can find a job that gives you satisfaction while you enjoy a more flexible schedule and have time for other things that make a difference to you and bring joy.

Consider Sue Walbert, who retired in her early 60s from her position as head librarian at Fauquier High School in Warrenton, Virginia, but wasn't ready to quit working altogether. "I was okay with the idea of retiring, but I didn't want to not work at all," she says. "And I definitely wanted to keep my earnings going."

Her initial solution: a part-time job at the school library. Walbert arranged to clock in two days a week through a job-sharing arrangement with a colleague who also wanted to cut back on hours. The sweetener: her preretirement hourly wage and pay for sick and personal days.

Then she picked up work as a part-time bookkeeper, helping out with monthly billing for a local horse boarding and training business. "I've always been good with numbers, so I enjoy it," she says. Finally, she added to her repertoire tutoring for homebound kids who cannot go to school for some reason (usually an illness or injury), and picked up work administering SAT and ACT tests.

After John Kerr retired from a long career in public broadcasting at age 65, he went on to scratch "his latent itch in conservation," he says. "I found an amazing encore job as a seasonal park ranger in Yellowstone National Park—something I have done for the past 12 summers. It is an absolute ball. I feel useful, I learn new things, I work with amazing people, I help steward America's First National Park. It complements and adds to everything I have done before, and I get paid for doing it."

Kerr is paid at the government's GS/05 level, as is the norm for "Seasonal General Rangers" in Yellowstone, which is currently $15.52 an hour. During the season, which runs May through September, he works a 40-hour week, plus overtime and small extra pay for special days and duties. All told, Kerr makes roughly $13,000 per season. There are no fringe benefits. He pays his own travel to and from the park from his home in New England, and he rents his own cabin just outside the park's Northeast Entrance. He could opt to stay in the park's shared housing, at a favorable rate, but he prefers to have his own place.

"This place continues to be magical, inspiring, and absolutely beautiful, as well as vast and completely awesome," he says.

These two people have each found a unique way to make money without the full-time constraints holding them back from savoring their new stage of life. If you're like me, their stories have sparked some ideas of ways you can start planning what you might like to do, too.

Resources at Your Fingertips

AARP has a wealth of resources to help get you thinking about what you might be interested in and where to find work you will love.

I recommend beginning your research at aarp.org/work, a hearty cache of information about full- and part-time work. AARP also has a job board at AARP.org/jobs, and AARP Foundation's Back to Work 50+ (aarp.org/aarp-foundation/our-work/income/back-to-work-50-plus/) connects workers 50+ with the information, training, and support they need to get back into the workforce.

Many of us have the good fortune to be living more years and in generally better health. That gives us more choices for how we want to spend those years, including working as long as we want to, where we want to, and the way we want to.

These are a few additional websites that can also help you find part-time work year-round.

FlexJobs.com lists jobs in more than 50 categories, from business consultant and translator to project manager and small nonprofit executive director, with a range of scheduling arrangements. To get the full listings, the basic fee is $14.95 for a month.

RatRaceRebellion.com, specializing in work-at-home part-time jobs, scrutinizes its postings to ensure legitimacy and delivers them in a free e-newsletter. You'll find a variety of positions, from customer service representatives to freelance writers. Many pay under $20 an hour, but you can find some higher-paying ones.

TempAndPartTimeJobs (careers.tempandparttimejobs.com) is good source for temporary and part-time jobs for retirees and boomers. This is a board run by the same people who now own and operate the site Retired Brains.com.

Upwork.com and **Guru.com** list freelance opportunities in fields such as Web development, graphic design, and business consulting.

Now let's pull out some of these great part-time jobs for you to consider. Pay estimates vary based on such factors as experience and where you live.

Accountant/Financial Manager

The nitty-gritty: Duties include preparing financial reports, processing payroll checks, invoicing, and tracking down delinquent accounts. Some firms will ask you to monitor checking and savings accounts and track credit card bills, too. If you have the qualifications, you may be in charge of helping to prepare annual tax returns. Many of these positions are virtual, but some are on-site as well. Employers run the gamut, from start-ups and small businesses to churches and local nonprofits.

Pay range: The U.S. Bureau of Labor Statistics (BLS) reports that the hourly wage for accountants and auditors is between $19.90 and $57.18 and above, depending primarily on experience and industry.

Qualifications: A degree in accounting or business is helpful, but not required. The most common certification is certified public accountant (CPA). The American Institute of Certified Public Accountants administers the exam. CPAs are licensed to offer a range of accounting services, including tax preparation. Other skills to have in your kit: knowledge of financial and accounting computer software such as QuickBooks. Familiarity with Word and Excel is expected.

Adult Education Teacher

See Chapter 6, page 126.

Alumni Event Planner

The nitty-gritty: Multitasking can take on a whole new meaning in this position. Colleges constantly stage get-togethers. This is detail-oriented work that requires lots of behind-the-scenes labor leading up to a major event, such as a class reunion or campus academic conference. So there's plenty of work organizing these events. It's a job that requires lots of behind-the-scenes logistical work. You could be scheduling speakers, drafting a program agenda, registering guests, coordinating transportation, and setting up audiovisual equipment. You might handle contract negotiations to book off-campus venues and hire outside parties such as photographers, musicians, or florists. Now and then you might take the show on the road to alums in their hometowns.

The hours can really pile up as the big day approaches and during the event itself, which is often on a weekend or evening.

Payrange: $11.61 to $35.08 per hour, according to PayScale.com.

Qualifications: It helps if you're an alum. A bit of gray hair can be an asset too. Alums who go for the menu of offerings (reunions, lectures, workshops, etc.) tend to have graduated some years ago rather than recently, so you may be age-appropriate. Strong communications and computer skills, especially in word processing and database managing, are nonnegotiable. Ease with computers, including social media such as Facebook and LinkedIn, and a knack for managing a budget. Experience in hospitality, catering, or public relations will help. Some colleges offer continuing education courses in event planning; the Events Industry Council offers the Certified Meeting Professional (CMP) credential, a certification for meeting and convention planners.

AmeriCorps VISTA Summer Associate

The nitty-gritty: This position gets you involved with the needs of your community. You'll engage in projects such as tutoring at-risk children or managing a volunteer network.

The VISTA summer associates program in Indiana, for example, matches you for work with nonprofit organizations, including Big Brothers Big Sisters, Mother Hubbard's Cupboard, and United Way. The summer associates project in Florida operates summer camps for at-risk kids in kindergarten through eighth grade.

Pay range: VISTA summer associates receive a biweekly living allowance cumulatively totaling about $2,200 and varying by location. At the completion of service, you may elect to receive either a $1,230.69 education award or a cash stipend.

Qualifications: There is no maximum age. Skills in communications, community organization, leadership, and teamwork are valued. All applicants must be U.S. citizens or legal permanent resident aliens. Expect a background check.

Job hunting tips: Go to my.americorps.gov to search for AmeriCorps VISTA opportunities. Under Service Terms, check the Summer box. You can also find postings on Indeed.com. To learn more, go to nationalservice.gov/programs/americorps/join-americorps.

Amusement Parks

The nitty-gritty: Amusement and theme parks are for the kid in all of us. There's an array of positions—from ride operators and ticket takers to waiters and souvenir T-shirt vendors. There are also openings in security patrol, custodial work, repair, and grounds upkeep. If you have a flair for showbiz, you might even score a role as a dancer or storyteller. Drawbacks: The summer heat in some locations and hours on your feet.

Pay range: $8 to $15 an hour. Employees typically can get free tickets for friends and family. There may be discounts on food and beverages, merchandise, and hotel stays.

Qualifications: Hiring managers seek experience in the jobs being sought. That said, your upbeat personality will be a vote in your favor. Plan for background checks and drug tests.

Job hunting tips: Look for job fairs sponsored by the theme parks in your region and visit their websites. For example, Kings Dominion in Doswell, Virginia, has a list of openings such as first-aid helper, games attendant, and theater usher. You can also search websites such as CoolWorks and JobMonkey.

Athletic Coach/Umpire/Referee

The nitty-gritty: Check into coach, referee, umpire, or scorekeeper posts, in high school programs, various youth and amateur leagues, parks departments, recreational and church leagues, and soccer clubs. Expect plenty of time standing, and for outdoor sports, prepare for the elements. Travel is usually part of the job, but it's probably a scoot across town. If you're blowing a whistle, you better brace yourself for the possibility of verbal strip-downs (parental ire).

The hours fluctuate widely by sport and organization. Coaches can figure three hours or so for late afternoons, five days a week, plus weekend days in season. Umpires, referees, and scorekeepers usually work two to three hours per game. Figure on once a week for two or three games in an afternoon or evening.

Pay range: High school coaching salaries vary widely by sport and geography and size of the student body. These positions may be for the season or the school year. You might search Salarygenius.com for average annual salaries in your town. Umpires and referees generally can make $30 to $70 per game.

Qualifications: You need to be good with children, possess moderate physical fitness, and have an overall knowledge of the game. Specific education, training, and licensing requirements for coaches and officials vary greatly by the level and type of sport. Some entry-level positions for coaches require only experience gleaned as a participant in the sport. Umpires and referees usually are required to attend a training course and pass a test. You can gain experience by volunteering for intramural, community, and recreational league competitions.

If you have a hankering to umpire, check out your local umpire association. For American Legion high school games, contact your local division and attend a certifying clinic. There are one-day refresher classes and full courses with several sessions, plus an American Legion exam. Some leagues require that certification be renewed periodically. You may need to pass a background check and applicable drug tests. Ask your local high schools, parks departments, recreational and church leagues, and soccer clubs if they offer a club-certified referee or umpire class. For soccer, you might need FIFA certification.

For additional resources, contact the National Association of Sports Officials (naso.org).

Athletic Event Ticket Services

The nitty-gritty: Team spirit counts. If you live near a college or university, these openings tend to pop up during fall and spring semesters. You don't have to dress up as the mascot, but you'll be the one juggling urgent ticket requests from well-heeled donors, eager alumni, university staffers needing a last-minute favor, students, and die-hard fans. The work may be by phone, internet, regular mail, or in-person at a customer service window. The key is a knack for solving the customer's troubles fast. You must also be up to speed on rules—national ones or your own university's. You might supervise interns and student workers. Be sure to clear your weekend social schedule for home games.

Pay range: $10 to $20 per hour.

Qualifications: A background in customer service, administration, and clerical duties; strong oral and written communication skills; basic computer skills.

Ballparks

The nitty-gritty: If you're a baseball fan, working at the stadium can be a dream. You may get free tickets to games when you're not on duty and free team-logo shirts. Major League Baseball teams and their vendors around the country hire ballpark tour guides, box office attendants, cashiers, groundskeepers, ushers, and ticket takers. There are openings, too, for suite attendants, in-seat servers, and concession stand workers. Some positions require standing for long stretches and enduring the unpredictable elements that Mother Nature tosses out.

Pay range: Generally from $8 to $11.50 an hour. Food and beer vendors who work the stands might pull in a minimum of $8 an hour, with tips and commissions possibly taking it to $25.

Qualifications: Training is usually provided. But remember that even though this is a sporting event, it's also entertainment. So hiring managers look for people who are personable, enthusiastic, and at ease kibitzing with fans. Background checks may be performed.

Job hunting tips: Tap into your hometown team's website for openings. Team-by-team contact information can be found at baseballjobs.teamworkonline.com. Also, look for your city's team-sponsored job fairs, which typically are held early in the year. Minor league teams also hire for the summer and have job fairs. Check out PBEO.com, the official employment service of Minor League Baseball. Batter up!

Bartending/Waiting Tables

The nitty-gritty: Smile though your feet are aching. Food and beverage service positions are in high demand particularly during the end-of-year holiday party season. From restaurants to local pubs to private parties, typically a wide variety of places are hiring for the holiday season.

Patience, a good memory, and organizational skills are part of the job. It goes without saying, of course, that an amiable persona, charm, and an uncanny ability to smooth ruffled feathers of disgruntled customers are expected. A certain level of physical fitness is required.

Expect flexible schedules. Nights, weekend, and lunch times can peak during the weeks before New Year's.

Pay range: Of the $16.59 bartenders earn per hour on average, more than half comes from tips, according to PayScale.com. Waitstaff: $8.08 to $17.14 plus tips, according to the BLS.

Qualifications: A pleasant personality and an ability to banter with customers are essential. Math and memorization skills come in handy, too. Past experience is helpful, but other positions where you've worked with people even as a volunteer are worth noting. Personal and professional references are valuable calling cards.

If you're considering bartending, especially as a post-holiday part-time job, you might enroll in a bartender training school that offers two-week programs.

Job hunting tips: Before you apply for jobs as waitstaff or bartender, do your reconnaissance as a customer to see how the staff dresses and get a feel for the venue and menu.

Blogger

See Chapter 2, page 70.

Bookkeeper

The nitty-gritty: In small businesses, bookkeepers handle a full sweep of financial recordkeeping. You might take care of purchasing office supplies and processing payroll. Other duties can include establishing and maintaining inventory database systems, tracking accounts receivable and accounts payable, maintaining checking and savings accounts, producing financial reports, following up on delinquent accounts, and overseeing audits and reviews. According to the BLS, bookkeeping, accounting, and auditing clerk employment is expected to grow by 11 percent between 2012 and 2022.

The hours vary by business; they are frequently limited to one week mid-month and one at the end of the month for invoicing or bill-paying functions.

Pay range: Generally $11.58 to $24.76 per hour, according to PayScale.com, but $50 or more is possible, depending on advanced training.

Qualifications: A degree in accounting is desirable; being a CPA is best. Relevant experience or formal training in accounting/auditing services is a plus. But experience with managing a broad range of financial matters for a company, nonprofit, or other organization can qualify you. This skill transfers seamlessly from one industry to another. Other key skills: data entry, and being detail oriented and adept with financial and related computer software.

Job hunting tips: Check out the American Institute of Professional Bookkeepers (https://www.aipb.org/) for job listings. The group also offers a bookkeeper certification, as does the National Association of Certified Public Bookkeepers (nacpb.org). Community colleges and universities in your area are good places to look for continuing education offerings. New York University's School of Professional Studies, for example, offers a diploma in bookkeeping. A high school degree or a GED is required.

Tuition for the two-semester course: $2,200. Networking with local business groups, industry associations, or Rotary clubs for leads is probably your best approach.

Bridge Tutor

The nitty-gritty: Teaching newcomers or those who haven't played in years how to play bridge can take some patience. Demand for teachers is on the rise, as bridge is in the midst of a revival. According to the American Contract Bridge League—the game's official governing body—25 million Americans over the age of 18 know how to play. And roughly 3 million players hit the card table at least once a week at a nearby club or online (games.aarp.org/games/bridge/). Even those who have been playing for years often are looking to up their game and improve as well as get a tune-up on bridge etiquette. Your job is to make bridge enthusiasts not only enjoy the game, but also build their skills and turn them into smart, confident card players. The hours when you set your lesson schedule are up to you.

Pay range: Rates vary, but $30 for a class is typical. At BridgeTeacher.com in Maryland, the instructor charges tuition for a course of six classes of $175 paid at the door.

Qualifications: Contact a local bridge club to make acquaintances and offer your services to potential students. The American Contract Bridge League (acbl.org) offers accreditation programs. The program can be taken online. The site also has a searchable list of bridge clubs around the country to help find one near your winter escape. The American Bridge Teachers Association (abtahome.com) and Betterbridge.com also offer resources.

Call Center Tech Representative

See Chapter 5, page 118.

Campground Worker

The nitty-gritty: If you're spending time on the road with your RV, this is a great way to earn money along the way.

At campgrounds, parks, marinas, and resorts, you may be able to take on flexible work in exchange for a free or discounted campsite, vehicle hookup, and perhaps a paycheck. Jobs run the gamut from guest check-in and rental management to handyman fix-its and retail sales.

Pay range: There are a variety of arrangements in this semi-barter prospect. Pay is typically $7 to $12 an hour, but compensation is usually a combo of such things as campsite access, wages, store discounts, and laundry allowance.

One option is an unusual Amazon program that recruits workers for seasonal peaks from nearby camping grounds. Amazon CamperForce pays up to $11.50 an hour, with time and a half for overtime. Benefits include paid campsite fees and a completion bonus. Be aware that working in an Amazon "fulfillment" facility can be noisy, difficult work. Expect a lot of lifting and time on your feet.

Qualifications: Past experience in the type of work helps. Expect on-the-job training if necessary. Go to Workamper News (workamper.com) to track down jobs on its bulletin board. Many campgrounds post jobs on their own sites; have a look, too, at CoolWorks (coolworks.com).

Car Transporter

The nitty-gritty: If rolling down long open highways catches your fancy, then delivering vehicles up and down the East Coast can pay your way to a warm weather getaway of your own. Busiest months are December and May, but departures and returns are staggered. In peak-demand periods you can snap up deliveries in rapid succession. You'll quickly get up to speed on shortcuts and construction detours, and maybe accrue frequent flier miles in the process. Long hours on the road can take a physical and mental toll, so stopping to stretch and rest is a must.

It's possible to find seasonal driving jobs with a professional service, but drivers who want to work only in snowbird season may find it easier to drum up clients by word of mouth. Try posting flyers at senior centers, retirement communities, assisted-living facilities, libraries, pharmacies, and grocery stores. Build up a roster of repeat customers.

The hours: Expect to drive eight hours a day, but this is negotiable. Most one-way trips, however, can be done in two to three days.

Median pay range: This fluctuates widely, but a base pay of $200 a day, plus gas and tolls, is the ballpark.

Qualifications: A spotless driving record and impeccable character references. It helps if you know how to change a flat and have a working knowledge of car mechanics. You'll need a GPS and a cell phone to stay on course and connected to clients. Plus, be prepared to have some company on your way. Cars heading south tend to get crowded with precious cargo such as fragile personal belongings and even family pets.

Caterer

The nitty-gritty: As a caterer, you're the power behind the scenes at events ranging from small birthday brunches to office holiday parties and blowout weddings and bar mitzvahs. You might be in charge of menu planning, food preparation, and setup. Time management skills will come in handy.

Pay range: Generally $8.56 to $17.66 per hour, but it can run up to $20, plus tips, according to PayScale.com.

Qualifications: While food is the core of this job, you must also have a knack for event planning and keeping to a budget. You might bolster a loyal corps of clients by offering your service gratis, charging for the cost of food alone in exchange for a professional reference. If you haven't worked in a restaurant kitchen, consider moonlighting at one.

Community colleges typically offer cooking classes, and culinary arts schools can sharpen your food preparation skills. Consider hanging out a shingle as a personal chef.

The American Culinary Federation (acfchefs.org) certifies personal chefs, in addition to other types such as sous chefs or pastry chefs. Certification standards stress work experience and formal training. Minimum work experience for certification can range from six months to five years.

Certification, however, is not a requirement in the food industry. Keep in mind, though, if you're working as a caterer, you will most likely need a certificate in food safety and sanitation (depending on municipality/jurisdiction, but almost all in the United States have this requirement).

Cruise Liners

The nitty-gritty: If you've got your sea legs and are up for a little adventure, a cruise line job can be swell. Some cruise ships hire married couples, so if you're escaping the cold with your partner, you both can set sail. Leading cruise lines, such as Carnival Cruise, Disney Cruise Line, Princess Cruises, and Royal Caribbean International Lines, hire across a full array of jobs, including hosts, cruise directors and staff, disc jockeys, performers, swimming and other instructors, and shore excursion staff. Also needed: pursers, photographers and videographers, wait staff, bartenders, cabin stewards, cooks, bakers, cleaners, gift-shop attendees, beauticians, medical staff, massage therapists, fitness instructors, and engine room technicians.

Tight quarters for accommodations can be a squeeze. If you're solo, you may share a small cabin and a bathroom. Plus, you will be afloat in all types of weather. If you suffer from severe seasickness, perhaps you can land one of the liner's landlubber jobs. Long hours can be a drawback—12 or 14 hours a day, seven days a week, typically for a period of six months.

Pay range: Deckhands typically should hold a high school diploma or equivalent and may work in seasonal to full-time capacities, earning up to $1,800 a month, depending on the cruise line. An activity coordinator may earn up to $1,400 a month. Tipped personnel like bartenders and waitstaff can earn $1,500 to $4,000 per month (including the tips). You get free accommodation and food and book some great gratis travel to boot.

Qualifications: Experience in the hospitality industry is essential for many of these openings. If you have an expertise in a particular area, say, personal finance and investing or technology, or you are an author, journalist, or college professor, you might be able to land a gig as a paid lecturer.

Most employees will be required to pass a course on work safety and first aid. The most important job qualification, however, is good language skills—you must speak English effortlessly, and if you're multilingual, even better. Your passport must be current.

Job hunting tips: When applying, it's best to target a specific job. Check out the cruise lines' website career sections for more details; apply directly to the cruise line by following the instructions on the website for the specific position being offered to avoid scams. Bon voyage.

Dietician and Nutritionist

See Chapter 4, page 102.

Eco-Landscaper

The nitty-gritty: Gardening is not for wimps. It's mostly outdoor work in all kinds of weather. From a purely physical perspective, it means bending, squatting, lifting, and pulling—unless you can hire a brawny assistant to handle those chores. The goal of building these types of "sustainable" gardens is generally to create landscaping that's cheaper to maintain over time, a lofty environmental goal. To do it right, you'll be able to make money-smart choices based on a deep understanding of native plants. Beauty is in the eye of the beholder, so you'll work closely with your clients to create a space that works best for them and the environment.

Pay range: $12.30 to $15+ an hour, according to PayScale.com; $50 to $90 an hour is possible, depending on experience. Most landscapers opt for a flat rate for an initial design, and then add hourly fees for execution and maintenance.

Qualifications: Understanding of horticulture, including a wide-ranging knowledge of plants and diseases. Drafting a design by hand is generally accepted, although some clients might want to see a computer design via CAD software. You might consider taking a Master Gardener class to boost your resume. The Ecological Landscaping Association holds an annual conference with workshops and educational sessions. The site provides links to seminars and events held around the country.

Many community colleges and universities offer certificates and degrees in sustainable landscape design. George Washington University's program, for instance, is offered on a series of weekends, and there is an annual landscape design career fair. Check out garden centers in your locale for classes and certificate programs. In Pittsburgh, for example, you can earn a certificate in sustainable horticulture at Phipps Conservatory and Botanical Gardens. The Association of Professional Landscape Designers offers certification to members who have at least four years of experience and submit three projects they have completed for review.

Event Planner

The nitty-gritty: Must love putting on a party. You'll need the creative and organizational chops to coordinate logistics smoothly and professionally with a keen eye to all the devilish details. Event planners are the architects behind annual association gatherings, big birthday bashes, weddings, and fundraising events such as 10K charity races and silent auction black-tie dinners.

Employment of meeting, convention, and event planners is projected to grow 10 percent from 2014 to 2024, faster than the average for all occupations, according to the BLS. Job boards such as FlexJobs and CareerBuilder, for instance, currently list hundreds of openings in this category.

Pay range: Hourly pay ranges from $11.31 to $36.50, according to PayScale. Annual salary ranges from $28,993 to $73,488.

Qualifications: There's no must-have degree or certification for this position. Some universities and community colleges, however, offer degree and certificate programs in event management. George Washington University in Washington, D.C., for example, offers an event management certificate. You might also consider the Certified Meeting Professional credential (conventionindustry.org).

If weddings are your thing, check out the websites of the American Association of Certified Wedding Planners (aacwp.org) and the Association of Certified Professional Wedding Consultants (acpwc.com).

Fitness Trainer

See Chapter 8, page 154.

Food Critic/Food Blogger

The nitty-gritty: You're a foodie and you're bursting with writing talent. Blend these to produce articles, blogs, and reviews that give diners the inside scoop on food quality, décor, and service at the hot restaurants, gourmet boutiques, and farmers' markets of your community. Keep in mind that if you're starting from scratch, you won't make a lot of cabbage, at least initially. There's lots of competition out there. But if you steadily build a following, you can generate income from ads on your page.

You can also make money by selling merchandise directly—from books to T-shirts. Sign up for Google AdSense (google.com/adsense), which allows Google to place ads on your website, determined by your blog content. You get paid a small fee each time someone clicks on an ad. With an Amazon Associates affiliate program (affiliate-program.amazon.com), you can create an online store for Amazon products, and get paid an advertising fee when someone makes a purchase through your site's link. Chitika (chitika.com) is another income stream to consider.

Pay range: As a freelance food critic for a media company, you might command 50 cents to $1 a word. An in-house food critic might make $39.95 an hour according to Salaryexpert.com, or a blogger $17.95 an hour, according to Indeed.com.

Qualifications: Success stems from a savvy knowledge of the culinary arts and having something to say . . . with chutzpah. You'll need top-notch writing skills. Photography and computer skills are obligatory, and journalism experience is ideal.

Food Stylist

The nitty-gritty: A picture is worth a thousand words when it comes to marketing food. As a food stylist, you'll work closely with chefs, food retailers, editors, restaurant owners, and photographers. Your job is to artfully pose food to make it look delectable whether it's in a display case, on a plate, or in an ad or online posting. Can you say eye candy? While there are full-time positions, freelancing is the norm.

Pay range: Hourly rates vary, but an experienced freelance stylist can earn $450 to $850 per day.

Qualifications: It's best to have logged some time in a commercial kitchen. You must be au courant with food styling trends on websites, blogs, and magazines.

Consider classes at a culinary institute, and volunteer to work with an established stylist. A degree in photography or design will give you a leg up. Go to CulinarySchools.org's roster of programs near you or online tutorials.

Front Desk Clerk/Night Auditor

The nitty-gritty: Whether it's a boutique hotel or an RV park and campground, guests come and go at all hours of the night and day. The basic drill: Meet and greet with a smile. Check guests in and out, access their reservation in the computer system, run their credit card, assign rooms, hand over keys, and answer questions on hotel services. You'll even dole out directions. You'll be expected to answer telephones and schedule reservations.

But the underbelly is when something goes wrong. A reservation can't be found; there's a dispute over charges; the air conditioning in the room is on the fritz. That's when patience and a cool head prevail. Some employers combine these desk clerk duties with bookkeeping, so be clear about what you are ready to tackle. If you have a knack for numbers, you might have a bit more to offer doing double duty as a night auditor who can balance accounts and perform overnight bookkeeping chores.

The hours: Seasonal and part-time schedules of 20 to 30 hours a week, or four days a week, are common. Availability to work evenings, weekends, and holidays is usually required. Overnight generally means availability from 11 pm to 7 am.

Pay range: $7.88 to $13.68 an hour, according to PayScale. More is possible depending on advanced degrees, bonuses, and overtime.

Qualifications: Hotel or retail experience is a plus, but on-the-job training is the norm. Each hotel or motel has its own reservation and billing systems. Most important, employers are always on the lookout for someone with a customer service sweet spot. A degree in accounting is desirable for night auditors; being a CPA is best. Relevant experience or formal training in accounting/auditing services is a plus. Your room is ready!

Gift Wrapper

The nitty-gritty: When it comes to wrapping special gifts, you need the creativity to make a present alluring. Much of the pressure comes from having a customer standing in front of you while you try to cut, fold, and tie a bow with precision. Some things you can't rush, but you do need to move rather swiftly with nimble fingers and not too much wasted paper. These wrapping table positions are usually found at gift shops, department stores, or booths in shopping malls. In-store jobs track shopping hours. For distribution center jobs, night shifts apply.

Pay range: The range is typically $8 to around $13 an hour, according to Glassdoor.com.

Qualifications: The ability to fold and wrap paper so it's taut and neat around a package, plus a knack for deftly twisting ribbon in ways that the typical customer can't fathom. This skill is generally self-taught, but you may be given crash on-the-job training with a few test packages. Some community colleges offer classes that teach the art of gift wrapping.

Job hunting tip: Search online job boards for "gift wrapper associate" and stop by or contact the human resource department at nearby stores.

Green Building Consultant

The nitty-gritty: If you're genuinely interested in building a postretirement or second act career with a green bent, it's worth the time and effort to head back to the classroom. In general, a background in architecture, engineering, and construction will provide a firm foundation. Older buildings in particular are getting serious facelifts. States, counties, and cities are offering incentives targeted for green building projects. You probably need a grasp of (or the burning desire to learn) the technical aspects of building construction, say, the nature of leaky windows, the best ways to use natural lighting, energy-efficient heating and air-conditioning systems (HVAC), plus water-smart features such as low-pressure faucets and toilets.

Pay range: Hourly rates can run from $35 to $150+, according to Indeed.com.

Qualifications: The Leadership in Energy and Environmental Design (LEED) organization offers a certification program that leads to a credential as a green building specialist. That's your calling card to offer strategic advice on a wide range of building projects. The Green Building Certification Institute provides information, as does its parent organization, the U.S. Green Building Council (usgbc.org).

Job-Hunting Help: How to Find a Green Job

As many as 3.5 million "green" jobs will be created by 2028, forecasts the U.S. Conference of Mayors. If you have a passion for the environment, or are thinking of pursuing a full- or part-time job that is eco-friendly or environmentally focused, here are some tips from Joel Makower, executive editor of GreenBiz.com:

Check out these job hunting sites: GreenBiz.com, Greenjobs.net, Idealist.com, and SustainableBusiness.com all have information on green jobs.

Search keywords. Three words companies will list in online green job descriptions are "energy," "efficiency," and "waste." Also search the words "environmental," "green," and "nonprofit" in the jobs section of the big online job boards.

Network. Join a discussion group for environment and green careers or green business on LinkedIn.

Troll green conferences. There's a cornucopia of green forums and conferences around the country that can be tracked down with a basic query to a search engine. GreenFestivals.org, for example, lists upcoming events around the country.

Contact nonprofit environmental groups. Ask whether local nature clubs or national and global advocacy organizations have any openings. Some may be volunteer or board positions, which can be a great way to get in the door for a paying job.

Corporate jobs are harder to find, however. Groups like the National Association of Environmental Managers (naem.org) are a good resource. And then there's the growing world of "social enterprise," which can be nonprofit, for-profit, or a hybrid. The annual SoCap conference (social-capitalmarkets.net) is a good way to get the lay of the land.

Go back to school. Check in at your local community college or university to see whether they have any environmental job fairs or lectures. Attend Earth Day events. You'll meet everyone from entrepreneurs and advocacy groups to local utility representatives and solar installers. Talking to them about job opportunities will give you great firsthand information.

Stay put. While the mayors' report indicates green job growth in large metropolitan areas like New York, Los Angeles, and Washington, D.C., cities like Pittsburgh and Boston also make the list. "There are as many jobs open in the middle of country as there are on the coast," Makower says. In Detroit, for instance, there's lots going on with the Great Lakes and clean water and revitalizing the manufacturing economy. Think start-up companies making wind turbines and electric vehicle batteries, and more.

Hairstylist

The nitty-gritty: Customers inevitably want a change: to look more professional, more youthful, or just want a "do" that fits their lifestyle. The job demands precision and fashion sense, listening skills, and sometimes barber-chair psychotherapy. The essence of the job is shampooing, cutting, coloring, and styling. The job can take a toll on you because you spend so much time on your feet, bending forward, and using your arms to wash and rinse your client's hair. Demand for hair coloring, hair straightening, and even adding hair extensions has ramped up in recent years, a trend that's expected to persist over the coming decade. If you work as an independent contractor—as about half of all stylists do—you'll need to keep detailed records for tax purposes. Juggling clients can be tricky, especially when someone calls with a last-minute request. The key is a gracious smile and an ability to make each customer feel special and, well, happy. Employment of hairdressers, hairstylists, and cosmetologists is projected to grow 10 percent from 2014 to

2024, faster than the average for all occupations, according to the BLS.

Pay range: $7.58 an hour to $25.17 and up, plus tips. A typical cut and color can easily top $120 per appointment. No one really charges by the hour, of course. A basic cut and shampoo can start at around $19 at a Hair Cuttery in Culpeper, Virginia. Tips of 10 to 20 percent are standard. Everything changes if you run your own salon. A typical cut and color can easily top $200 per appointment in a big city.

Qualifications: All states require hairdressers to be licensed. Qualifications for a license vary by state, but generally a person must have a high school diploma or GED and have graduated from a state-licensed barber or cosmetology school. Some states have reciprocity agreements that allow you to transfer a valid cosmetology license. State licensing board requirements and a list of licensed training schools for cosmetologists may be obtained from the Beauty Schools Directory. Word-of-mouth marketing makes or breaks your success as a hairdresser.

Job hunting tip: You might consider a niche clientele service. A friend of mine started her hair stylist business by serendipity. She regularly visited her octogenarian mom at the assisted care home in Pittsburgh where she was living. While there, she would shampoo and style her mother's hair, and cut it when necessary. She also would do her makeup for outings. Other residents started requesting her services and insisted on paying her a fee. After her mother passed away, she had a business card made, obtained her license, and launched her own mobile beauty shop. She has continued making visits twice a week to where her mother lived in her final years and is steadily building her business and adding other senior clients both aging in place at their homes and in assisted care, 50+ communities, and hospices.

Handy Jack/Handy Jill

The nitty-gritty: If you tackle this as a self-employed, fix-it-up service, figure on a smorgasbord of odd jobs that range from tightening loose door handles to repairing running toilets. It can be a mix of woodworking, plumbing, electrical, and even painting projects. You'll find more structured opportunities with building owners who hire part-time workers to perform basic maintenance. This is one job, even on a part-time basis, that requires a certain level of fitness and stamina. You'll also want to be on a first-name basis with the manager of your local hardware store!

If it's your own business, you can call the shots, even working weekends-only. Part-time schedules for building maintenance will depend on the owners' needs. Some employers might prefer to have you on call for emergencies, while others might like to have you on-site and available to residents during specific hours.

Pay range: $12.07 to $43.80 an hour, and sometimes more than $50 for certain custom work.

Qualifications: Be competent in various aspects of home improvement, have your own tools, be self-motivated, and have good customer-service skills. Some states may require you to have a contractor's, electrician's, or plumber's certificate, depending on the project. And clients might require you to be licensed, bonded, and insured.

Job hunting tips: If you want to formalize your business, tap into the U.S. Small Business Administration (sba.gov) under licenses for help on how to get started.

Holiday Decorator

The nitty-gritty: Do you have a passion for decking the halls with boughs of holly—or blue and silver Chanukah streamers? This job calls for creative flair and a way with bows and bulbs. You'll be making and setting up holiday decorations and displays. You might need to tap into your electrical smarts, too. Sometimes a touch of brawn and a strong back is required if you're responsible for moving large poinsettias, picking up boxes of ornaments, setting up Christmas trees, or stringing lights outdoors. You might have to clamber up ladders to get to rooftops and high trees if offering outside decorating services. Expect to get your hands dirty.

Demanding clients and last-minute flourishes can be a little nerve-racking. Jobs range from adorning large offices and retail shops to hotels, restaurants, and private homes.

The hours are potentially long and variable, but expect brief stints, November to early January. Some late-night and weekend work are required for installation and dismantling.

Keep in mind that there are actually many different types of holiday decorating, including New Year's, Valentine's Day, St. Patrick's Day, Easter, Fourth of July, and Halloween, to name a few.

Pay range: $8 to $20 per hour, but varies widely.

Qualifications: Past holiday decorating experience is a plus. Floral designer training helps. If you've got a knack for this type of work, a good attitude, and a willingness to learn, many florists and decorators will gladly train you as you go.

Many vocational schools and community colleges award certificates and degrees in floral design. You'll learn the basics of arranging flowers, including the different types of flowers, their color and texture, cutting and taping techniques, tying bows and ribbons, and proper handling and care of flowers. The American Institute of Floral Designers offers an accreditation examination.

Job hunting tips: Check with local florists and floral departments at grocery stores and event planning firms for openings.

If you're confident in your own decorating panache, you might opt to start your own business. You can land clients through word of mouth. Ask friends and family to help spread the word. For starters, decorate the homes or offices of a few friends or family members gratis or at a bargain price. You'll be able to build up a portfolio or website with display pictures to show potential clients.

Six Steps to Landing a Holiday Job

'Tis the season to earn a little extra money on the side.

Getting hired part-time during the holiday season can be easier than finding work at other times of the year.

Opportunities exist for a variety of positions including gift wrappers, salespeople, shipping clerks, and call center reps. Try these six steps to find employment that's well suited to your skills and interests:

Stop by for a face-to-face. Many retailers offer online applications, but it's best to meet the manager in person.

Offer future help. If you think you might want to extend your hours after the holidays, or be willing to work during other hectic times of the year, tell the manager during the interview. It could sway the job your way, since employers are looking for ways to trim the cost of future hiring and training.

Be flexible. Holiday jobs mean adding and cutting hours at a drop of the hat, depending on the ebb and flow of demand during peak periods.

Network. Kick off your job search by checking with friends already working in places that typically add holiday workers.

Go where they know you. Check for openings at establishments where you are an existing customer.

Don't wait for a help-wanted sign. If there are shops or restaurants where you'd like to work, drop by during an off-peak time and meet the manager or assistant manager.

Human Resource Manager

The nitty-gritty: As a company hires more employees, tasks such as recruiting, benefits administration, payroll, and employee relations all become vital to building a top team. Someone who knows employment law and practices, as well as recruiting and employee-screening techniques, can save a business time and prevent potential personnel issues.

Pay range: A typical range is $34 to $57 per hour, according to Salary.com.

Qualifications: Many professional associations offer certification programs. Although certification is usually optional, some employers prefer or require it. Check out the Society for Human Resources Management for educational offerings.

Librarian Assistant/Aide

See Chapter 6, page 129.

Limo Driver

The nitty-gritty: Limo drivers can find work year-round, but their dance card fills up during prom and wedding season from April to June. Routine duties include keeping the car shipshape each day. You'll help passengers into the car, hold open doors, and provide umbrellas if it's raining. Loading and unloading heavy luggage can call for some strong muscles. Other drawbacks: Driving for long periods can take a mental toll, especially in crowded city streets. Then, too, remaining seated for several hours at a time isn't as easy as it sounds.

For weddings and proms, drivers are busy from April to June and usually book in three- to five-hour increments. Proms are evening and night shifts. Weddings vary from morning to night bookings. Other trips are often booked by the hour.

(If driving is your thing, you might look into driving for Uber or Lyft. More than half of Uber and Lyft drivers are 51 or over, according to a recent survey. Uber says 80% of its "partners" drive fewer than 35 hours a week in its 20 largest markets; more than half drive one to 15 hours each week.)

Pay range: Pay can range from $7.82 to more than $20.24 per hour, according to PayScale.com, though figures vary widely depending on experience, where you live, the number of hours worked, and customer tips.

Qualifications: Most limo companies provide on-the-job training. A good driving record is vital—no more than two moving violations in the past five years, and no reckless or drunk driving violations. If you're 70 or older, insurance restrictions might be a stumbling block. Patience, punctuality, and level-headedness are de rigueur. A basic understanding of auto mechanics can also be useful. To spruce up on your driving skills, check out at AARP's Driver Safety Program.

Manicurist and Pedicurist

The nitty-gritty: These professionals typically work out of salons or spas, taking care of nails. About 3 in 10 are self-employed, the BLS reports, which means they run their own businesses. The job requires a high level of customer service and patience, as you are sitting in close quarters with clients and often chitchatting while you trim, buff, and polish. The job outlook is strong, with the BLS predicting a 10 percent rise in jobs between 2014 and 2024.

Pay range: The average pay in this industry is approximately $10.98 per hour, according to PayScale.com. Hourly rates range from $8.82 to $24.09, not including tips.

Qualifications: Manicurists and pedicurists must go through state-approved programs and then pass a state exam to receive a license. (Connecticut, however, does not license manicurists.)

Medical Assistant

See Chapter 4, page 104.

Move Manager

See Chapter 8, page 157.

Nursery Worker

The nitty-gritty: It's all about getting dirt under your nails, tending plants, and answering customers' gardening queries. More physically demanding tasks may require cutting and stacking sod, staking trees, packing plants to fill orders, and digging up or moving shrubs and trees.

Pay range: $7 to $10 per hour according to JobMonkey.com.

Qualifications: Training is on the job. It helps to know the difference between an annual and a perennial, or course, and what plants do best in the shade versus the sun. You might consider taking a Master Gardener class to boost your resume, or take classes in soil science or horticulture. You might also become a member of the American Nursery and Landscape Association.

Office Manager

The nitty-gritty: This position is generally at the core of a company. It can easily morph into a full-time post if you're looking for one. You're often in charge of administrative tasks ranging from bookkeeper and office supply manager to salesperson. You could find yourself recruiting new employees, handling employment paperwork, scheduling vacations, and even running recycling programs.

Pay range: $11.87 to $24.18 per hour, according to Salary.com. For higher-level operations management, $50+ per hour.

Qualifications: Nothing trumps prior experience in a similar high-paced job. A strong work background that demonstrates managerial chops and ease with juggling a variety of roles is what this position comes down to. The business owner wants to instantly feel that things are being turned over to a capable pro who can keep the trains running on time. The International Facility Management Association offers a competency-based professional certification program for administrative services managers that's worth exploring.

Package Delivery

The nitty-gritty: You don't have to bear the responsibility of a full-time driver, but UPS and FedEx add thousands of part-time and temporary helpers and package handlers for their drivers during peak delivery period from Thanksgiving through New Year's. It can require lifting and moving boxes, plus a smile for the customer if they happen to open the door. Hours can range from full eight-hour shifts to part time, depending on where you live.

Pay range: $9 to more than $14 an hour; tips and bonuses are possible. Data from Glassdoor shows that the average UPS driver earns $27.46 an hour, but can range to $35, while the typical FedEx delivery driver salary is $16 an hour, with an upper level of around $25 an hour.

Qualifications: You should be somewhat spry to handle the physical aspects of this job. At UPS and FedEx, there's typically a written test to gauge communication skills that may be called on when you come face-to-face with a customer. And some training is provided.

Job hunting tips: Check the big delivery company websites online for openings.

Park Service Employee

The nitty-gritty: Each year the National Park Service as well as state and local parks hire temporary and seasonal employees. You might be in charge of basic tasks like collecting fees at the entry gate, answering visitor questions, and passing out maps and brochures. With a little homework, you might find yourself teaching brief educational programs about the park ecosystem from bear habitats to flora and fauna. Those of you with a fit physique might step it up with trail upkeep responsibilities or guiding tours.

Parks with lodges hire part-time employees to accept reservations, provide concierge-type information, check in guests, and perform other booking functions. Other responsibilities may include maintenance and office work, equipment rental, housekeeping assistance, food and merchandise sales, fee collection, and other general support services.

These types of positions are usually available at most parks and forests and wildlife management areas. There are also guest service and hospitality jobs at park stores and restaurants via Aramark, a national firm that provides facility and concession management under authorization of the National Park Service.

State parks, too, pump up rosters during the tourist months. State park jobs include collecting fees, issuing permits and passes, and directing traffic. Community parks also need help with managing recreational activities such as softball, volleyball, craft programs, and summer day camps.

You might also find jobs at touristy gift shops and restaurants near the parks.

Pay range: National Parks: $12.75 to $31.78 an hour. You might opt to work as a National Park Service volunteer, too, where your only pay may be free housing or a pad for your RV.

Qualifications: Training is provided for most jobs. A knack for working smoothly with park visitors of all ages may be the most important criterion. A teaching resume or public speaking skills help. Expertise in a particular field—such as history, botany, or geology—can get you in the gate. If you're interested in pursuing a nature guide job, then flora and fauna identification skills are a must.

Job hunting tips: Keep in mind that if you actually work for the National Park Service and not one of the outside vendors, you will be applying for a federal government job. You may be subject to a security background check. The best way to find a job at a National Park is to go to each park's individual website, or USAJobs.com, and click on Employment Opportunities. For a state park opening, check with your state's division of parks and recreation.

Personal and Home Healthcare Aide

See Chapter 4, page 110.

Personal Assistant

The nitty-gritty: Name it and you might be asked to do it: organize bills, papers, and appointment calendars; accompany someone to doctor appointments; pay bills; handle laundry duties; run errands; cart around children; walk the dog; track and file medical bills and insurance payments; make meals; shop for groceries. The list of to-dos will depend on your client's needs. In essence, you're a one-stop shop. You might be hired by adult children who live out of the area to be their eyes and ears, and keep track of how their parents are doing. Your hours will be flexible and depend on your client's needs.

Pay range: You can probably charge hourly fees that range from $9.88 to $24.73, according to PayScale.com.

Qualifications: There are no formal training courses or certifications for this business. You might need to be physically fit to handle some requests you'll get. People with Alzheimer's will need special attention, so some nursing or caregiving skills are useful. Emergency medical technician training might come in handy. If you'll be behind the wheel, you'll need a driver's license in good standing. All in all, the key is building trust and being patient, flexible, and reliable. You may be asked to be bonded for the client's protection if you will be providing services in someone's home. Many clients will request a background check and references.

Job hunting tips: Advertise your services in community newspapers, online neighborhood listservs, Craigslist, even bulletin boards in apartment buildings, retirement or adult community residences, grocery stores, and libraries.

Pet Concierge

The nitty-gritty: Pet owners are heading off on vacation—and they need you. If it's a canine client, you'll do walking and maybe ball tossing, so fitness is a requirement. Some dog owners look for people to stay at their homes or take the pooch into their own homes. Cats and smaller charges usually require a daily visit for feeding and litter cleanup.

Pay range: The charge for a single visit to a pet ranges from $10 to $22. A daily half-hour walk typically runs $20. Expertise with administering medications pays a bonus.

Qualifications: While there are no required certifications, a love of animals and experience with pets is essential. Still, if you're interested in getting certified, you can. The National Association of Professional Pet Sitters (NAPPS) offers an at-home certification course online. If you're going to turn this into a regular business, you may want personal liability insurance and possibly business insurance and bonding coverage, too. Associations such as the NAPPS, Pet

Sitters Associates, and Pet Sitters International offer access to plans.

Job hunting tips: Pitch yourself on your neighborhood list-serv or on TaskRabbit. Local pet shops may allow you to post a notice in their store. Play your cards right, and work may expand. For Ilene Wellner, dog walking services started by word of mouth, has grown in seven years into her own pet care business called Dog Gone Walking in Wynnewood, Pennsylvania, a Philadelphia suburb. She's got a team of 10 to 13 dog walkers overseeing 30 to 50 dogs a day. Her employees include chefs, musicians, writers, nurses, and plain old animal lovers and pet owners.

You can also consider signing up with a national franchise operator like Fetch! Pet Care. Or look for local pet-sitting services in your neighborhood newspaper.

Pet Groomer

The nitty-gritty: Primping a pooch (or cat) runs the gamut from bathing to nail trimming and brushing, to cleaning ears and clipping coats. You've got to be detail-oriented and love the down and dirty work. It takes some stamina, too; the work can include kneeling, bending, and lifting. The result is worth it when you tie that bright bow on a collar and see the owners' smiles when their pal rushes out to greet them. You might work out of a kennel, pet shop, your own home, or even a mobile grooming van.

Pay range: $8.86 to $20.59 an hour, according to PayScale, but an experienced groomer might earn $25 to $30 an hour. Tips are an extra perk and will vary.

Qualifications: Although pet groomers typically learn by training under the direction of an established groomer, they can also attend one of 50 state-licensed grooming schools, according to the BLS's *Occupational Outlook Handbook*. The length of each program varies depending on the school and training offered. The National Dog Groomers Association of America offers certification as a groomer and can provide a list of state-licensed schools.

Product Demonstrator

The nitty-gritty: Don't be shy. This is "meet and greet" show time. Talk to people with snappy banter and product know-how. You boldly step right up to a shopper and say with a friendly, earnest smile, "Would you like to try our apple cider?" You're not actually selling the elixir, but you're getting folks in the buying mood.

Demonstrators are typically standing or walking, and it can be fairly fast-paced. This is not a job for the couch potato. Think Energizer Bunny™. Prepare to pass out food samples or product coupons or brochures. Performances might be on tap if you're assigned to demo a blender or new software program, or you could be asked to try your hand at in-store cooking. You might face some grunt work—setup and cleanup, as well as bringing the goods to and from the stores. Extra bonus: tantalizing tidbits at your fingertips. During holiday crunch times, evenings and weekends are the norm.

Pay range: $11.55 to $19.91 per hour, according to Glassdoor.

Qualifications: On-the-job training to glean sales techniques is standard fare. Smooth public speaking and communication skills and an outgoing personality will serve you well. This is a performance in many ways, so you'll want to channel your inner entertainer. Humor and friendly chitchat attract customers.

Past jobs in retail, sales, or customer service make it easier, but any volunteering or public speaking experience is noteworthy on your resume.

Job hunting tips: If you know a shop, even a "big-box" store, that uses demonstrators near you, stop by and ask if the store does the hiring directly. If so, put in your application.

You might also ask an in-store demonstrator during a break how he or she got the job. Some companies pay a bonus for bringing in a new worker. If the store uses an outside agency, get the contact information. If you're interested in a specific product, go to the company website to check for openings and apply online. Kiosk operators in malls sometimes hire part-time product demo help. Pump it up.

FlexJobs Identifies 10 High Paying Part-Time Professional Jobs

FlexJobs, an online service for professionals seeking telecommuting, flexible schedule, part-time, and freelance jobs, has identified 10 flexible high-paying professional-level jobs.

"Part-time work is sometimes associated with less professional, lower-paying jobs, but, as this list indicates, that isn't necessarily true," says Sara Sutton Fell, founder and CEO of FlexJobs.com. "The opportunities for high-paying part-time jobs span industries and positions, while still offering competitive salaries.

"The flexibility professional part-time jobs offer provides workers the opportunity to practice within their chosen profession and maintain their skills, without the time commitment of a full-time role and a massive disruption to their income."

Each of the 10 jobs on this list is geographically varied and meets the following criteria:

- The job is a part-time position, requiring less than 40 hours per week
- The job is professional level, requiring advanced experience and education
- The job's pays at least $50 per hour, which, in a full-time role, would equate to at least $104,000 annually

Director of Operations

Pay Rate: $50 per hour for 12 to 20 hours per week
Description: Will create policies, implement procedures, and provide staff leadership. Business-focused BA/BS, 8+ years' similar experience in an operational position a must.

Jazz Music Instructor

Pay Rate: $51.05 to $78.75 per hour
Description: Temporary opportunity with a part-time schedule. Will instruct courses in jazz music. Must have a master's or bachelor's degree in music, humanities, or a related area. Requires professional experience teaching jazz.

Curriculum Writer

Pay Rate: $50 per hour
Description: Education professionals with experience in curriculum writing will find a variety of part-time, temporary positions to assist educational institutions and organizations with curriculum development, writing, and adaption. These jobs seek people who have excellent teamwork skills and who work well under deadlines.

Dentist

Pay Rate: $65.65 to $86.69 per hour ($136,548 to $180,324 annually)
Description: Part-time opportunity providing dental care services for correctional facilities. Requires current state licensure and proficiency in all aspects of general dental care.

Clinical Pharmacist

Pay Rate: $54.69 to $71.58 per hour ($91,000 to $119,000 for 32 hours per week)
Description: Clinical pharmacists are needed for a part-time opportunity to provide clinical pharmacy services to patients. They address the needs of nursing personnel regarding drug disposition and usage. Bachelor's degree is required.

Controller

Pay Rate: $50 to $60 per hour for 20 to 25 hours per week
Description: Part-time, telecommuting role with a flexible schedule. Real estate accounting, general accounting, real estate tax, and supervisory experience required. Must have QuickBooks knowledge.

Software Engineer

Pay Rate: $60 to $73 per hour
Description: Develop and support application as well as back-end system. Debug systems and perform programming enhancements. Support SQL-based reporting. Write codes. Pays hourly. Five-month, short-term contract. Possibility for extension or conversion.

Financial Consultant

Pay Rate: $50 per hour
Description: Part-time, temporary assignment lasting six months. Will manage the month-end close process, review and oversee reconciliations and payroll, review financial statements, and manage and coach finance staff. Position may become permanent.

Government Contracts Attorney

Pay Rate: $50 per hour
Description: Needs eight years' experience in government contracting and a JD for this part-time, short-term, remote job. Advise the company on a range of matters such as contracts, disputes, compliance issues, and auditing.

Mobile Developer

Pay Rate: $65 to $70 per hour

Description: Engage with a development and architecture team to design, code, and implement an iOS application that will be used in a customer-facing role. Must have 2+ years of experience and solid JavaScript skills. Six-month contract.

FlexJobs also identified the top 35 companies hiring part-time remote workers in 2016, as well as hot categories for flexible jobs that can pay over $50,000. Firms hiring include Aetna, AT&T, Dell, IBM, Kaplan, Kelly Services, Robert Half International, and United Health Group.

Project-Based Consultant

The nitty-gritty: This requires top-level expertise and self-starter initiative. Most independent contractors parachute in to problem-solve or work on a specific project. You might work for an intense period, then take time out for several weeks or even months. Small and fast-growing companies looking for experienced employees who can tackle a range of duties are great sources of work. Drawbacks include slow payments at times, and projects that run longer than expected or don't begin on schedule. This line of work is best for those who aren't afraid to jump into the deep end and start swimming fast.

Pay range: $32.67 to $113.43 per hour, according to PayScale .com, but can exceed $300 an hour depending on your industry and expertise.

Qualifications: Consultants with a track record in finance, management, healthcare, and information technology are sought after, but even more esoteric areas like art appraisal can fall under this job description.

Job hunting tips: The trick to landing a project is tapping fearlessly into your professional network. Past employers are a good first stop when you're looking for a consulting gig. Contact ex-colleagues and clients for help finding great opportunities. For leads, you might get involved with the local Rotary or a regional small business association.

Recruiter

The nitty-gritty: This position is perfect for a "people person" with a deep network of industry contacts developed over decades. For instance, if your career has been in banking, healthcare, or IT, you'll have an understanding of what certain jobs demand and where to look initially for candidates. But be warned: These days, you must also be nimble, searching social media sites such as LinkedIn for potential candidates.

Lots of schmoozing—in person, by phone, and virtually via Skype and similar video apps—is an integral part of the recruiting process, so strong interviewing skills are a given, along with an enthusiastic, self-motivated work personality. Aside from possessing a flair for razzle-dazzle salesmanship, you'll analytically examine resumes to pinpoint qualified candidates who meet job requirements, which requires an expert no-nonsense eye for detail. You'll also need to rely on your instincts to decide if a job candidate has that intangible ingredient for which the employer is searching. Some travel may be required.

Pay range: Recruiters can earn an hourly wage of between $12.10 and $29.94, according to PayScale. That said, many recruiters are paid on commission and bonuses, based on a percentage of the annual salary for the job placed.

Qualifications: There are no specific degree or certification requirements. A bachelor's degree in business administration, human resources, or a related field, or equivalent experience, can be a plus. It's crucial, though, to be conversant in the field for which you're recruiting. Even if you have no related professional experience, a background in customer service or sales can work in your favor.

Repairperson

See Chapter 8, "Medical Equipment Maintenance and Repair," page 156.

Resort Worker

The nitty-gritty: Resorts from the Puget Sound to the Jersey Shore fill all shapes and sizes of jobs as they ramp up for the summer months. There are also opportunities in the winter season at ski resorts or resorts in warm climates like Arizona or Florida. You might find work ranging from ranch hand to concierge, massage therapist to front desk agent, parking valet to room cleaner. Be mindful of the physical demands of some service jobs.

Pay range: Anywhere from $7 to $15, generally, plus tips or discounts and other perks.

Qualifications: Experience and licenses are requisite for particular jobs (such as yoga instructor or boat mechanic). But skills needed for entry-level positions (such as retail sales or slicing and packing pounds of fudge) can be picked up swiftly.

Job hunting tip: If at first you don't succeed, try, try again. These businesses typically have higher-than-average turnover, according to the outplacement firm Challenger, Gray & Christmas. An employer that did not hire you initially might need more workers a few weeks later. Search where others do not. Behind-the-scenes jobs often are not as sought after by teen job seekers. Offer to work evening shifts.

Restaurant Greeter

The nitty-gritty: Meet, greet, and seat customers with a smile. Keep an eagle eye on the ebb and flow of the dining crowd as you nimbly make adjustments so everyone feels special. You're the first impression a visitor gets of the restaurant, so a positive vibe is key—even though you'll be on your feet for long stretches of time and the atmosphere can be chaotic.

Pay range: Generally $7.33 to $11.66 an hour, but varies widely by size and popularity of the venue, according to PayScale. com. Perks: free food and employee meal discounts.

Qualifications: Prior experience is not always required. What is required is a genuine gift for making people feel welcome and ready to spend. You'll need the cool to deal with those inevitable times when a table of guests lingers over coffee while hungry patrons wait impatiently for a place to sit down.

Tip: During the holiday season, or in popular snowbird towns or summer vacation getaways, there's often a swell in openings during the peak periods.

Retail Sales Cashier

The nitty-gritty: Cha-ching. Smoothly staffing the cash register is one of the most important jobs in the store, especially during the holiday season. While there's a great vibe when people are in the gift-buying spirit, it's often repetitious work. You'll need a grasp of basic math, keen attention to detail, and stamina to be on your feet for hours. At some shops, you'll fold and box items, too, and you might handle returns and exchanges.

Basic duties include entering charges for all items minus the value of any coupons or discounts; and taking payment in cash, personal checks, and gift, credit, and debit cards. Requesting additional identification from the customer or calling in for an authorization is standard procedure. Scanners and computers make the job pretty perfunctory, but some registers require price and product data to be entered by hand. Depending on your shift, you might have to open or close registers, which can include counting the money and separating charge slips, coupons, and exchange vouchers.

Forgo fashionable shoes and pony up for comfy footwear. Practice saying, "Did you find everything you were looking for?" The hours are variable. Plan on working evenings and weekends.

Pay range: Pay can range from $7.75 to more than $12.47 an hour, according to PayScale.com.

Qualifications: Cashiers need little or no previous experience, although that helps. Training is generally on the go with a more seasoned co-worker. Department and chain stores might offer a short training course to get you up to speed on customer service, security, the store's policies and procedures, and cash register operation. Employers generally run a background or credit score check to make sure you're trustworthy to handle money. You should be at ease with financial transactions and basic computer commands. Remember—the customer is always right.

Retail Salesperson

The nitty-gritty: It should come as no surprise that the heart of this job is having the customer at hello. You need to connect quickly with people in a warm manner. You're there to help them find what they're looking for, and that might mean a little sales razzle-dazzle, product demos, and know-how of certain model features. It's possible that you'll be asked to reel off financing options if it's a big-ticket item.

In addition, you'll need to be at ease at the cash register and when packing up purchases. Depending on your shift, you may have to open or close cash registers, which can include counting money and separating charge slips, coupons, and exchange vouchers. In addition, you may stock shelves, mark price tags, take inventory, and prepare displays. Since you'll be on your feet for long stretches, it makes sense to spring for a pair of comfortable shoes. During holiday crunch time, plan on working evenings and weekends.

Pay range: Pay can range from $8.12 to more than $14.54 an hour although bonus and commission pay is possible.

Qualifications: Previous sales experience helps, but it's not a deal breaker. Greenhorns can apply. Expect on-the-job training by a more experienced employee. This can be on the fly at this frenzied time of year. Don't be shy about asking questions. In department stores, training programs are more formal. Topics often include customer service, security, store policies and procedures, and cash register operation. Insider knowledge helps. If you're hawking computers, a sense of the technical distinctions between products is vital. People skills are de rigueur. Employers might run a background or credit score check on you to make sure you're trustworthy. Best arrows to have tucked in your quiver: patience and persuasion. Employers might run a background or credit score check on you to make sure you're trustworthy.

Retail Worker

The nitty-gritty: This position differs from a retail salesperson since it is not focused primarily on demonstrating the features of a product. Big chains and boutiques add part-time workers during the holiday or high-vacation seasons. There can be a range of tasks from running checkout to stocking shelves. While there are a variety of retail positions that can be as basic as greeting customers and folding sweaters, most have a physical aspect to them. You need to be prepared for bending, stretching, lifting, and walking around without plopping down in a chair for long periods. Plus, customers can be demanding, so cool demeanors come in handy. The underlying incentive: discounted merchandise. Sweet sale-o-rama.

Pay range: Pay can range from $7 to more than $19 an hour, including commissions. Upscale shopping areas will usually pay top dollar.

Qualifications: Previous sales experience helps. If you're new to the game, on-the-job training is standard. Each store operator has its own way of selling and running things from security procedures to customer service peccadilloes, so even old hands have a learning curve. It helps if you have a passion or familiarity with the goods you are selling. Enthusiasm is infectious and opens wallets. Top-notch people skills are the underlying ingredient to making this a good fit for both you and the employer. One caveat: Expect a background or credit score check on you to make sure you're trustworthy.

Retirement/Life Coach

The nitty-gritty: In the topsy-turvy job market of recent years with downsizings and early retirements, the uncertainty of what to do next can be overwhelming. This is where you can step in. Keen listening skills and a clear sense of how to encourage people to find their path is your job. You help clients identify what motivates and inspires them and gently show them ways to suss out how they want to contribute or find meaning in their lives. You might counsel on whether they should go back to school or start a business. This position can combine life coaching and job coaching. The work is a process and takes someone who is patient, intuitive, and good at coming up with creative solutions and action steps.

Pay range: $50 to $400 an hour.

Qualifications: Career and life coaching is a self-regulated industry and an emerging profession. Many coaches have been doing it for years without adding professional designations. If you have a corporate background in human resources, counseling, even teaching, this might be a natural next step for you. To learn more about certification, go to the nonprofit International Coach Federation (ICF). This is the only organization that awards a global credential, which is held by more than 4,800 coaches worldwide. ICF-credentialed coaches have met stringent educational requirements, received specific coach training, and achieved a designated number of experience hours. Some coaching courses are offered online, while others consist of a few workshops. More intensive programs run over the span of a few semesters and may combine online and classroom study.

To learn more about life coaching, consider reaching out to someone already doing that job to learn more about how they started their practice via the Life Planning Network (lifeplanningnetwork.com), a national association of professionals from diverse disciplines who help those planning and transitioning to their next phase of life. You can search for a Life Planning Network consultant in your town on the site. You might check into programs such as the Coaches Training Institute, New Ventures West, or the Rockport Institute. Be sure to check your local colleges for course listings. Duquesne University and Georgetown University are two schools that offer coach training programs. Tuition ranges widely from $1,000 to more than $10,000. The tuition for the professional coaching course at New Ventures West, for example, is $12,400.

Sales Representative

The nitty-gritty: Marketing and sales are the heartbeat of a small business. But as the company expands, it's tricky. If the owner's time is spread too thin, he or she has trouble devoting enough time to continually pump up new business and follow up on leads. An energetic and skilled salesperson adept at cold-calling, networking for new clients, and keeping existing accounts happy can keep things rolling while the owner focuses on big-picture strategies. This can be grueling work if you're thin-skinned, especially when it comes to cold calling. So slip on your persuasive shoes and polish up your confidence and composure. It's meet-and-greet time.

Pay range: $9.77 to $20.90 per hour, according to PayScale. com. Most positions are structured with base pay plus commission.

Qualifications: Business owners look for candidates who know their market, have experience in their industry, and have established relationships and contacts. Experience with "customer relationship management" software such as Salesforce.com may help. According to the BLS, many people in this occupation have either the Certified Professional Manufacturers Representative (CPMR) certification or the Certified Sales Professional (CSP) certification, both offered by the Manufacturers' Representatives Education Research Foundation. Obtaining these credentials typically involves completing formal technical training and passing an exam.

Second Home Property Manager/Concierge

The nitty-gritty: In general, you prepare homes for their owner's or guests' arrival and close them up when they leave. The duties may include grocery shopping to stock the pantry, checking on the condition of the home's interior, inspecting for pests, running water in faucets, checking that all the kitchen appliances are in working order, flushing toilets, testing smoke detectors and air conditioners, opening the pool, and checking the condition of screens. You set the house temperature and pool heater to the desired temperature just prior to the snowbirds' arrival. You can accept packages they send in advance. You might open the home for house cleaning services, pest control services, and maintenance workers. You also provide end-of-season house cleaning and shutdown. You might also offer your services for getting an accommodation ready for rentals, by getting the place prepared for the intake of weekly guests and turning over the house for the following week's guests.

While you might seek out a seasonal job at an existing property management firm, this is a good one for entrepreneurial self-starters. You can extend your undertaking to provide a variety of maintenance chores from plumbing to electrical and painting projects throughout the months. You might offer your services as an errand runner or airport driver to ferry guests to and from the airport.

This is not a job for slackers. You'll need to be in reasonably good physical condition and adept at fixing things fast, or know whom to call who can. And don't forget the fresh flowers on the table—always a nice touch.

The hours: If it's your own business, you can call the shots, but it will depend on your client's needs. Part-time schedules for condo, townhouse, or retirement community maintenance vary. Some employers might prefer to have a handyman on call for emergencies, while others might like to have you on site and available to residents during specific hours.

Median pay range: $10 to $20 an hour, but can be $60+, depending on your area.

Qualifications: Be knowledgeable in home repair, have your own tools, be self-motivated, and possess good customer-service skills. You will probably need to be bonded and have liability insurance. Laws vary by state. Some clients who don't know you personally may require a background check. Clients who vouch for your dependability are the keys to opening doors.

Job hunting tips: To build this business will take some selling on your part. Word-of-mouth will be your best means to drum up customers. This is a referral business, after all.

You might start with pitching your services to your neighbors in your winter haven, or market to northern connections who have second homes. Some real estate management firms, retirement communities, and timeshare communities hire part-time workers to take on this advance prep and handle routine maintenance during the winter months.

Shipping Clerk

The nitty-gritty: Around the holiday season, the big package shippers such as UPS and FedEx need your helping hands, but the small boutique around the corner selling hand-dipped chocolate-covered candies might, too. This behind-the-counter position calls for skill at fitting the right box or envelope to the item being shipped. Other duties: Explaining the various shipping methods and rates to customers, knowing how to pack an item so it arrives intact, taking inventory, stocking shelves, weighing packages, entering computer data, applying proper insurance coverage, affixing labels, working a cash register, and arranging pickups and accepting deliveries.

Plan on spending a good bit of your time upright and on the move. You might have to lift boxes up to 55 pounds. Remember: Bend at the knees. Flexible and partial shifts during the rush season.

Pay range: Hourly wages range from $9 to $15 based on experience and employer, according to Glassdoor.

Qualifications: Computer literacy and retail experience staffing a cash register can come in handy. Background check is standard for most positions.

Shuttle Bus Driver on Campus

The nitty-gritty: If you like to drive, climb aboard. During the busy fall and spring semesters, the demand for university transportation ramps up, and driving jobs are plentiful. You cruise the campus byways on university transit wheels. The routes are clearly set, and you keep to a regular schedule. You might occasionally have to give directions or help someone on or off the bus.

Heavy traffic is not usually a problem unless it's a city campus. Bad weather can make road conditions dicey. If you drive the night shift, your riders might get a little exuberant. You'll usually be the one in charge of checking the tires, lights, and oil.

Pay range: $12.25 per hour on average, according to Indeed. com. Range: $8.50 to $20.06 per hour.

Qualifications: You must have a commercial drivers license (CDL) in good standing and undergo some short training that will include a driving course and practice of various maneuvers with a bus. The qualifications for getting a CDL vary by state, but normally include both knowledge and driving tests. Your vision and hearing will be checked, too. States have the right to withhold a license from someone who's had a CDL suspended by another state.

Skin Care Specialist

The nitty-gritty: Maintaining healthy, glowing skin is not just a luxury treatment for the well-to-do. As aging boomers shell out for treatments, the employment of skin care specialists is expected to grow 12 percent from 2014 to 2024, according to the BLS, faster than the average for all occupations. "The desire among many women and a growing number of men to reduce the effects of aging will result in employment growth. Good job opportunities are expected," according to the BLS.

Department stores hire sales clerks to assist customers with skin care selections. Spas, health clubs, beauty salons, and even medical offices are also hiring. Skin care specialists and aestheticians recommend products and can perform procedures such as waxing and electrolysis or give pore-cleansing facials. Providing head and neck massages might be in your tool kit, too. Traditionally, this has been a female-centric job, but men shouldn't shy away from this growing field. It's no longer unmanly to go for a facial.

Pay range: $11.89 to $17.74 an hour, according to BLS.

Qualifications: Skin care specialists usually take a state-approved cosmetology program that can cost several thousand dollars, according to the nonprofit American Association of Cosmetology Schools. An aesthetics program focuses primarily on learning how to perform facials, waxing, and reflexology and makeup application is usually less expensive. Some schools offer scholarships and financial aid. After completing an approved cosmetology program, you'll need to take a written and practical exam to get a state license. Licensing requirements vary by state. For details, contact your state board. You'll find jobs posted online, but seeking out local businesses is your best bet.

Social Media Specialist

See Chapter 5, page 120.

Spring Training Staff

The nitty-gritty: Spring training camps for Major League Baseball teams in Arizona and Florida have a range of possible positions: ushering, selling programs, fielding ticket inquiries, working concession booths, running cash registers in the team merchandise shop, and juggling other customer service duties. Teams may hire drivers to transport players and staff to and from the airport.

Some jobs require more expertise than others. Seasonal sales assistants take an active role in marketing and special promotions. IT analysts are called upon to make sure wireless networks and computers run smoothly for press and players. While duties might be mundane, the chance to work alongside a World Series ring bearer is anything but.

The hours: Vary by team and demands of the job.

Pay range: From $7.50 to more than $10 an hour.

Qualifications: Qualifications will depend on the post, but on-the-job training is standard in most cases. A valid driver's license and a fluency in Spanish might be necessary. Bestselling advantage: love of the game.

Job hunting tips: To learn more, go to Major League Baseball's website, click on the link to your favorite team's website, then click on Job Opportunities. You can also try contacting the training camp office directly.

Tailor

The nitty-gritty: Sewing like a pro is a nifty mixture of sharp hand-eye coordination and artistic flair. The job boils down to dexterity and details. And, truth is, for many people, simply threading a needle is maddening. Old-fashioned sewing has become a fading art even though the demand for someone who can perform the job with panache has been in steady demand. It requires a built-in precision to cut and measure fabric. Altering or repairing clothing and creating custom garments demands an inner focus and patience. Sewers may also tap their talent to make handcrafted items from quilts to placemats, napkins and table runners. You might find work in a dress shop, department store, or dry cleaner, but nearly half of all seamstresses and tailors are self-employed, according to the BLS. Reality check: Our hands and eyes are not as strong as they once were, so take a good physical inventory to be sure you are up to the task.

Pay range: $9.44 to $19.76 per hour, according to PayScale.com.

Qualifications: Informal, on-the-job-training is standard for those working in a shop or store setting. Sewing is a solitary task, but to keep the customers coming back with pants to be hemmed, dresses to be taken in, or buttons to be sewn back into place, you'll need to pull out those people-pleasing talents, too.

If you take to heart the age-old advice that it feels good when you make someone else feel better, you might want to consider one of these jobs. They offer flexible hours and can be on a full- or part-time basis.

Tax Preparer

The nitty-gritty: To prepare annual income tax returns for individuals or small businesses, you typically will want to be an enrolled agent with the Internal Revenue Service. Your job is to help filers avoid penalties, interest, or additional taxes that could result from an examination by the IRS.

Expect to book plenty of hours between January and the April tax deadline, particularly if you sign up with a tax preparation firm.

Pay range: $7.25 to $36.55 per hour, according to Indeed.com.

Qualifications: A degree in accounting is helpful, but not required. Computer use is mandatory. You are required to use IRS e-file if you prepare 11 or more returns. Under new IRS rules, any individual who, for compensation, prepares or assists in the preparation of a tax return or claim for refund must have his or her own Preparer Tax Identification Number, which costs $50 per year. Check with the IRS (irs.gov) for more guidance. Next, you must pass a competency exam—mandatory for most, but some certified public accountants and others are exempted—to become an IRS registered tax return preparer. Additionally, you must take continuing education courses.

Job hunting tips: Large tax firms—for instance, H&R Block and Jackson Hewitt Tax Service—hire thousands of tax preparers each year to come on board from January until May 1. You usually need to take the firm's income tax course in the fall to prepare. You apply via individual stores. Refresher courses are offered each season. To get your toes wet, you might start by volunteering with the AARP Foundation Tax-Aide Program (aarp.org/taxaide). It can offer good experience for those who want to graduate to a paying tax preparer job. Bean counters should apply.

Teacher's Aide

See Chapter 6, page 132.

Tour Guide

The nitty-gritty: If you're a history buff, or a born educator, this might fit you to a tee. You need to be at ease talking to groups of tourists and have your facts and anecdotes at the ready. You might lead visitors through points of historical interest in your hometown or give personal tours of, say, a local winery or pretzel factory.

Pay range: Hourly wages of $9.04 to $20.52, according to PayScale.

Qualifications: The most in-demand skill is a knack for captivating an audience. Employers might require you to pass a written exam of knowledge of specific locations and city history. Some community colleges offer short-term courses in tour- and travel-related occupations. The Certified Tour Professional certification is offered through the National Tour Association.

Think too about the not-for-profit Road Scholar program (roadscholar.org), which offers 5,500 "learning adventures" in 150 countries and all 50 states. If you become an ambassador for the program, you promote it through speaking engagements. Your compensation is credits toward participation in those adventures.

Meet a Tour Operator

After retiring from a nearly 38-year career at Amtrak, Paul McKenna spent a year working to get a captain's license, CDL, and fulfill other requirements to be a ConDUCKtor for the Boston Duck Tour. At the age of 60, he set sail on his second career. The ConDUCKtors narrate and educate in an engaging way while recounting historical details about Boston, as the Duck passes by landmarks and attractions. It's a seasonal position, of course, and part-time schedules are available.

Pay rates for Captains range in the tourism industry from $15 to $25 per hour depending on the vessel. Tipping is a factor in many of these jobs such as water taxis, fishing charters, and various tour boats. "I'm looking forward to a fun job showing off the city of Boston and its rich history," McKenna told me.

Travel Agent

The nitty-gritty: If you think that travel agents are passé, you're mistaken. Even with the proliferation of online booking sites, growing numbers of travelers want the human touch. Agents are particularly helpful on special trips, say, a honeymoon, or an adventure travel getaway. And who doesn't long to have someone to text or e-mail to help you find another flight if theirs's is canceled or delayed, The result is an uptick in agents setting up their own home-based businesses, says Erika Richter, spokeswoman for the American Society of Travel Agents (www.asta.org).

You'll spend a fair amount of time on the phone and doing online research, so this job requires patience, an unflappable demeanor, and attention to detail. It helps to have your own lust for travel, which allows you to add the secret ingredient of insider knowledge.

One possible perk: gratis trips of your own to evaluate hotels, resorts, and restaurants for potential clients.

Pay range: Annual salaries range from $25,484 to $55,364, according to PayScale.com. Hourly wages range from $10.70 to $22.34. Travel agents, however, who work independently, are often paid on commission by airlines, hotels, and resorts for the bookings. It's not unusual to charge additional fees to customers for your time. Then, too, some charge fees up front and then remove them when the client books the trip.

Qualifications: In general, no agent license is required. However, community colleges often offer technical training and continuing education classes for agents. Coursework covers the ins and outs of computer reservations systems, marketing, and regulations for international travel. A few colleges offer full degrees in travel and tourism.

The Travel Institute (thetravelinstitute.com) offers training and professional certifications. The International Air Transport Association (iata.org) has a program for "travel and tourism professional" as well as "consultant." The Cruise Lines International Association (cruising.org) meanwhile, offers its own certifications.

Travel Nurse

See Chapter 4, page 114.

Tutor/Counselor

See Chapter 6, page 132.

Veterinary Technician

See Chapter 4, page 115.

Waste Reduction Consultant

The nitty-gritty: If you're a recycling devotee, you'll revel in the chance to help companies and residential communities reduce waste. Show that your efforts save money and you've won a convert to your cause. Consulting opportunities can be found in both government offices and private companies. Waste consultants may also be called recycling consultants or waste reduction coordinators. Consider specializing in a certain area, such as paper or food. You'll of course need data to back up your efforts. Don't be fooled into thinking everyone is on board with green initiatives.

Pay range: Income levels vary widely by employer and location. Consultants' pay range: $13.72 to $16.60 per hour, according to PayScale.com.

Qualifications: It's a smorgasbord. Knowledge of recycling programs from previous work, even on a volunteer basis, shows you know what you're talking about. You'll need clear communication skills to explain what the program is all about and why it matters. Sales chops will help you persuade people to actually stick with it. Project management ability will ensure that your program runs smoothly. Accounting basics will prove that it's worth an employer's while. The National Recycling Coalition offers webinars on a range of recycling topics and more. Some states now offer recycling certification programs via local colleges. Rutgers University, for example, offers a 21-day New Jersey recycling certification program.

Web Strategist

See Chapter 5, page 124.

CHAPTER 2

Great Work-from-Home Jobs

■ ■ ■

Returning to work is an economic necessity for some and a personal choice for others. Either way, the prospect of long commutes and annoying co-workers can be off-putting. A good compromise might be to find a work-at-home job without returning to the 9-to-5 grind.

The good news is the growth of technology makes it easy to work from anywhere. As well, more companies connect at-home workers with employers, increasing your chances of landing a work-at-home position.

If you've set your sights on a work-from-home job, you might go straight to a company you would like to work for and see if it hires remote workers. A good place to start is the career section of the company's website. There are also sites like FlexJobs.com and Remote.co that are focused on legitimate work-from-home jobs and prescreen each job and employer to be certain they aren't scams.

From 2016 to 2017, FlexJobs analyzed over 100,000 job listings to find the industries looking for professionals to fill remote, flexible-schedule, or freelance positions. The survey found that five industries in particular saw a jump of 20 percent or more in listings for these types of remote or flexible jobs.

Mortgage and real estate: Companies like American Advisors Group, Homeward Residential, and Zillow have recently recruited for remote jobs in mortgage and real estate. Job listings include positions for mortgage loan officers, underwriters, and mortgage processors.

HR and recruiting: Aon Hewitt, IT Pros, and Xerox have recently recruited for remote jobs in human resources and recruiting.

Companies are looking for workers to fill postings as recruiters, human resources specialists, and human resources managers.

Accounting and finance: Large financial institutions like Ally Financial, Citi, and Wells Fargo have recently recruited for remote jobs in accounting and finance. Postings include openings for accountants, bookkeepers, and auditors.

Pharmaceuticals: CVS Health, Pharmaceutical Product Development, and Thermo Fisher Scientific have recently recruited for remote jobs in pharmaceuticals. Postings include openings for pharmacists, clinical research associates, and account managers.

Education and training: K12, Kaplan, and other education companies are recruiting for remote jobs in education and training. Popular job postings include online tutor, adjunct faculty, and virtual teacher.

WORK-FROM-HOME JOB BOARDS

aarp.org/jobs
flexjobs.com
glassdoor.com/index.htm
jobspresso.co
remote.co
retiredbrains.com
skipthedrive.com
virtualvocations.com
weworkremotely.com
workingnomads.co/jobs

Beware of Scams

Working at home has a nice ring to it—sometimes, too nice. Work-at-home scams have been around for decades, but in the past few years, the Federal Trade Commission has seen the number of complaints nearly double.

Two glaring red flags: jobs touted via e-mail that promise to pay more than you ever dreamed, and firms that charge you a fee to obtain more information about a job. "Payment for the privilege of working is rarely acceptable, in our view," says Christine Durst, an internet fraud and safety expert and cofounder of RatRaceRebellion.com, a website that screens job leads on home-based jobs.

Other tips include:

- Check for complaints with the Better Business Bureau in your area and the area in which the company is headquartered. You'll also want to verify the company with your local consumer protection agency and state attorney general. For free information on work at home consumer issues, visit the FTC consumer information site at ftc.gov.
- Just because there aren't complaints doesn't mean the company is above board. Devious companies may settle complaints, change their names, or move to avoid scrutiny. It's a good idea to enter the company name with the word "complaints" into a search engine to see if anything appears.
- Ask what specific tasks you'll have to perform, whether you will be paid by salary or commission, who will pay you, and when and how frequently you'll be paid.
- Never give any financial information like bank account or credit card numbers over the phone or online until you have done your research.
- Ask what the total cost to you will be, including supplies and equipment.
- Be wary of overstated claims of product effectiveness, exaggerated claims of potential earnings, and demands that you pay for something before instructions or products are provided.
- Be wary of personal testimonials that never identify the person so you can't investigate further.
- Get answers to your questions in writing.

Source: Federal Trade Commission.

That said, there are legitimate work-at-home jobs in customer service and other fields, but you'll need to do legwork to avoid scams. Here are jobs to consider:

Blogger

The nitty-gritty: Most bloggers make very little per month. Little wonder. There's lots of competition out there for eyeballs. By early 2017, there were 335.5 million Tumblr blogs, and WordPress users were producing about 73.9 million new posts and 49 million new comments each month, according to WordPress.com.

It is possible, though, to break through. An income stream comes from steadily building a following through referrals and generating income from the ads on your page. You can also make money by selling merchandise directly— from books to T-shirts. You can sign up for Google AdSense (google.com/adsense), which allows Google to place ads on your website, depending on your blog content. You get paid a small fee each time someone clicks on an ad. With an Amazon Associates affiliate program (affiliate-program. amazon.com), you can create an online store for Amazon products, and you get paid an advertising fee when someone makes a purchase through your site's link. Chitika is another income stream to check out.

How much income they produce varies by blog. Developing traffic flow (and money) to your blog is time consuming. You can't just come up with a few pithy posts on a whim every so often and expect visitors to show up with any consistency. It takes discipline. Use Facebook, Instagram, LinkedIn, Google+, Pinterest, Snapchat, and Twitter to get the word out.

It's tough to measure how long it takes someone to write a post of around 800 words. It might take three or four hours. The real money-hungry bloggers log full-time schedules of 40 hours or more a week managing their blogs. While that's heavy duty, you should plan to blog at least three times a week. You also need to keep tabs on the business side— managing display ads and product sales adds up to a few hours a week.

Pay range: The majority of bloggers make less than $100 a month from their sites. But the opportunity is there to earn more. Some bloggers produce more than one blog, which antes up income. There are bloggers who pull in more than $100,000, but they're the exception.

Qualifications: At the heart of it you'll need passion about a micro-niche that you really know something about, decent writing skills, and the commitment to keep feeding your site with fresh content. If you have the chops, there are broad-based media sites, for example, that will give you a place to hang your hat and pay you a fee based on the number of page views your blog gets each month, a set monthly fee, or a per-word payment. For example, I have been able to establish an expert online column, or blog on AARP.org, Forbes.com, and PBS NextAvenue.org to generate monthly revenue. You don't have to be a journalist to blog. You just need expertise and something to say . . . with attitude. For Forbes, which now has a plethora of bloggers, it can be in the areas of financial planning or accounting, travel savvy, even horse racing.

A successful blog is built on subject matter that's valuable to people interested in the precise topic. Computer skills are a must, and knowing how to post photos legally and YouTube clips is helpful. You have an edge if you know how to use keywords and other online links to lure people to your website via search engines such as Bing, Google, and Yahoo!.

Crafter

The nitty-gritty: It sounds divine. You carve out a workshop at home, and, inspired by your inner creativity, you churn out high-quality, handcrafted items and make some money at the same time. More people are peddling their homemade wares online, at craft shows, and at flea markets. But to really build a business beyond pocket change, you need to push out of your comfort zone of selling to friends and family, and peddle to the masses in the online marketplace.

You can set up your own shop on the website Etsy.com. Etsy charges 20 cents to list an item and lops off 3.5 percent of your sale. Other sites to market your merchandise include Pinterest.com, Madeitmyself.com, and Silkfair.com. Some sites charge a small sales fee similar to Etsy. You might also launch a blog and your own website and entice area boutiques to sell your creations, too.

Pay range: Varies widely. It's possible to net a few hundred dollars a month in profit after you pay for your materials and figure your hourly wages. You can certainly boost that with a great product, super sales, and lots of elbow grease. You're the boss, so you set the pay scale. You're probably not going to get rich, but it's a fine way to earn money and love your job at the same time.

Qualifications: It's hard to set the bar here. In general, a sense of design and artistic bent will get you noticed. But the intangible skills of self-motivation and discipline, combined with a unique product and some sales chutzpah, is what will help you succeed. You should have a handle on bookkeeping, or hire someone part time to help with recordkeeping. The IRS will want to know what you're up to, especially if you are selling online via credit cards.

Meet a Crafter

When Marilyn Arnold was 9 years old, her mother, a skilled seamstress, patiently taught her to sew on a vintage Singer treadle sewing machine in her family's farmhouse near Paris, Missouri. She was hooked.

Now 69, she is running her own small business, Marilyn Arnold Designs, in Lee's Summit, Missouri. Her initial start-up capital: $12,000. She started her home-based business when she retired from her position as a managing partner at the New York Life Insurance Company, after 29 years in the insurance business. Her specialty is custom designing and sewing 18-by-18-inch pillows, christening dresses, and blankets as mementos made from cherished wedding gowns that had been relegated to the back of a closet. She also stitches quilts big enough for a queen-size bed assembled from repurposed materials like T-shirts or scarves. And she recently added travel and handbags from recycled fabric, bridal accessories, and animal-themed pillows. To keep things rolling, she now employs three part-time contractors. Arnold has a website and an online storefront on Etsy, and she posts her designs on Pinterest and sells her goods in local boutiques.

The Home-Based Craftsman

When Mark Nelson retired in 2007 after three decades with the Postal Service, the bulk of it spent as postmaster in rural Boyceville, Wisconsin, a town of around 1,000 located about 60 miles from Minneapolis/St. Paul, he spent a year and change hunting, fishing, and fussing with his horses and mules. "But you get to the point when you've done all the playing," Nelson recalls. "You have to be productive." It might have helped that his wife, Lesley, a registered nurse, was still working part time on a nurse advice hotline at the local hospital.

A lot of things weren't possible for him to do, though. Eleven months after retiring, he broke his back falling 20 feet to the ground from a deer tree stand.

Leather-crafting had been his hobby since he got his first crafting kit the Christmas he was 13. And over the years, he had made plenty of wallets and holsters while working his day job. "I had the best job in town as the postmaster," Nelson says. "It was rewarding, but frankly government work doesn't have a lot of outlet for creativity." His duties involved sorting mail, waiting on customers, and managing the books—all structured activities. "I've always been a creative person, and leather-working as a hobby was a great outlet for that."

So when he was considering what to do next, leather-making came to mind. Then he took a step further: he turned to his old interest in saddle-making. That curiosity had been spurred back in his early 20s when he was working as a radio broadcaster and hanging out with a saddle maker in Ft. Pierre, South Dakota, during his spare time, watching him work.

"When I thought about what I would really love to do, that was it. I got the bug to make saddles, and not just any saddles," Nelson says. His love is for the old Western saddles of the 19th century, the heyday of the cowboy era from 1866 to 1899, a time when the West was really the Wild Wild West. That's his fancy.

Nelson's passion is historic reenactment of cowboy action. He even helped start a Cowboy Action Shooting club. "I wanted to know how to make saddles for my own use but realized that I had to make some money at it, too," he says.

That meant opening a tiny workshop shoehorned into a pole barn on his five-acre property, along with buying the equipment, which includes a heavy industrial sewing machine, a splitter to reduce the thickness of the hide, and other leather-cutting tools—some 100 years old—and shelling out $5,000 tuition to spend six weeks undergoing intense saddle-making tutelage at the Montana Horseman Saddle Building School in Belgrade, Montana.

During the course, he made three saddles, one for himself and two he sold to team ropers in Montana. He was hooked. When he got home, he opened Way West Saddlery. His primary clients: historic reenactors, extreme cowboy competitors, and Western stock saddles fitted for individual horses and their riders.

The drawbacks of starting his own home-based business: "There's a fine line between a hobby and an obsession," Nelson laughs. "A lot of us go over the line. One of my early challenges—keeping myself out of the workshop."

Turning a hobby into a business can pay off, but it can take a while. That's the finding of a recent study that looks at entrepreneurs who start a business based on a personal pursuit. In the study, published in the *Journal of Business Venturing*, these entrepreneurs lagged behind other founders in the first few years. But ultimately, the hobby-to-business founders were more likely than others to produce revenue and a profit.

Customer Service Representative

The nitty-gritty: You must have an up-to-date computer, a high-speed internet connection, a dedicated landline telephone during business hours, a telephone headset, and a quiet place to work. In general, you'll be answering incoming calls, taking new orders, and tracking existing orders. In some cases, you'll troubleshoot and help out with technical support. Online chat sessions and e-mail may be part of the job. You'll need to toggle seamlessly among several computer screen windows at a time. Employers often offer paid training sessions.

The solitary work demands a good dose of "get up and go" and discipline to keep from being distracted. And don't skimp on buying a comfortable, ergonomically safe chair and headset. Remember, it's tax deductible if you're an independent contractor.

Potential employers, including American Airlines, Hilton Hotels, and 1–800-Flowers.com, might hire directly. Others use third-party companies that then hire home-based workers. Virtual call center operators include Arise, Convergys, LiveOps, Sykes, and Working Solutions. Employers may require at least 20 hours a week, plus weekend slots.

Pay range: $9.42 to $188.23 an hour, according to PayScale.com. Some firms provide health, vision, and dental benefits, or access to group plan rates. Paid vacation and matching 401(k) plans may be a perk, but you'll have to clock in enough hours to be eligible.

Qualifications: Job descriptions typically call for customer care or technical support experience. Think broadly. Experience in a retail store, as a bank teller or in sales might suffice. Typically, an online test and a phone interview are required. Background, drug, and credit checks are standard. Some firms charge $30 to $45 for such screens.

Direct Sales

The nitty-gritty: Selling for a direct sales firm like Avon, Cutco, doTERRA Essential Oils, Mary Kay, Pampered Chef, and Tupperware can be lucrative, and there are plenty of opportunities to do so. It's not about going door to door ringing bells anymore. You can market the goods straight from your home office via a computer, internet access, and a telephone. But it requires plenty of legwork and some start-up costs, usually $200 or less for a "starter" kit of training materials and products. Legitimate direct-selling companies allow you to "sell back" unsold products that are in good condition if you decide this isn't your bag.

You set your work schedule, so that's a plus. You'll usually sell a company's products through home or office parties and online sales. Earnings are commission based. With some companies, you can ramp up your income by recruiting other salespeople to join your team. You then earn a commission for the products they sell, too.

Direct selling is not for slackers. You reap what you sow. You need to set monthly goals—how many new customers you will contact, how many parties you will hold, how many follow-ups with clients you will make. You can't be timid about asking existing customers for referrals, either. It's all about getting your name out there and growing your business.

An upside: Unlike starting a new business solo, where you're responsible for the whole ball of wax, your job for the most part is purely selling. The company makes the product, delivers it, and has your back if you have customer complaints and other business questions.

For a list of direct selling companies with links back to each, go to RetiredBrains.com. Contact the Direct Selling Association for information on any specific direct selling company. Be aware that direct sales also encompass other types of businesses, such as multilevel marketing companies, also referred to as MLM. Visit business.ftc.gov for guidance. Many of these companies have been scrutinized for illegal practices or pyramid schemes. Check with your local Chamber of Commerce, Better Business Bureau, or state attorney general's office to see if there have been complaints about a company.

Pay range: You can earn around $300 to $500 a month part time, up to $1,000 or more full time. Compensation systems are commission based—25 to 40 percent generally. You buy the products wholesale and sell them at retail prices. You can increase your earnings draw by recruiting, training, and mentoring new representatives at companies such as Avon.

Qualifications: The core backing you need is your own passion for the product. If you use it and understand how it works yourself, it's easy to make a sales pitch from the heart. But some expertise can come in handy. If you're selling makeup, for example, it helps to have some background in cosmetics and be capable of confidently offering beauty and skin care advice. The same holds true with cooking utensils: Knowing your way around a kitchen helps. This is a customer-centric gig, so you need smooth people skills and an ability to be at ease with one-to-one contact with your future customers. Creativity plays a role, too. Building sales stems from drumming up innovative ways to sell your product. Pull out the old soft shoe.

Financial Manager

The nitty-gritty: You're signing on for a variety of roles: part accountant, part tax expert, part cashier. Duties can run the gamut from processing payroll checks, to handling invoicing, accounts receivable, accounts paid, and other financial reporting. Even buying office supplies may be your bailiwick. Some firms may ask you to monitor checking and savings accounts and track credit card bills.

This is detail-oriented recordkeeping work and requires a focused, organized approach. Tracking down delinquent accounts can be trying on the nerves. Delivering bad financial news to a client requires a matter-of-fact, businesslike approach.

The hours will vary by business; frequently limited to one week mid-month and one week at the end of the month for invoicing or bill-paying functions. Some firms will want you on call at least once a week.

Pay range: $10.23 per hour to $24.25; $50 or more is possible depending on advanced training, degrees, and location.

Qualifications: A degree in accounting or business is generally required. The most common certification is a Certified Public Accountant (CPA). The rigorous exam is administered by the American Institute of Certified Public Accountants. CPAs are licensed to offer a range of accounting services including tax preparation. Other certifications: A Certified Internal Auditor (CIA) is someone who has passed a four-part test, administered by the Institute of Internal Auditors. Relevant experience or formal training in accounting/auditing services is a plus. Other key skills to have in your kit: data entry and being adept with financial and accounting computer software such as QuickBooks (quickbooksonline.com).

Job hunting tips: The American Institute of Professional Bookkeepers lists jobs and offers a national certification for bookkeepers, which may help you land a job if you don't have prior practical experience. You might consider posting your resume to Upwork.com and surfing the big job boards. Networking with your local business groups, industry associations, or Rotary Club for leads is often your best approach.

Grant/Proposal Writer

See Chapter 3, page 94.

Sell Your Talents

Upwork.com is an online marketplace where jobs are posted and freelancers bid on them. Upwork charges freelancers a 20 percent, 10 percent, or 5 percent service fee depending on the total amount they've billed with a client.

You can sell your hand-stitched goods online at Etsy. It's free to become an Etsy seller, but you'll pay a fee of 20 cents to list an item for four months. When it sells, you pay a 3.5 percent commission to Etsy.

At Fiverr, you can offer a service that uses your skills—voiceover for a Web ad, designing an invitation, and so on—starting at five bucks a pop. There is no subscription required or fees to list your services. You keep 80 percent of each transaction.

Graphic Designer

The nitty-gritty: The canvas is wide. You might find assignments to design letterhead, business cards, and logos for local businesses. Bigger projects: marketing brochures, snazzy websites, and e-mail marketing pieces. Most design work can be done via your home computer. You must be at ease with manipulating computer graphics and design software, and possibly know how to program animated graphics. You may, of course, find yourself sketching the old-fashioned way with pad and pen as an inspired idea takes shape. It takes more than visual communication to shine in this field.

You must be able to translate your concept into words too. An underlying ability to perceive what appeals to your clients is essential. Sometimes they themselves don't know what they want. It's your job to help them see the possibilities. Skip the artistic temper—this is a collaborative process. Tweaking and redesigns come with the territory. Be prepared for hours at the computer and last-minute crushes for deadlines.

Pay range: $11.22 to $27.43 per hour and up, according to PayScale.com.

Qualifications: Your success ultimately rests on your flair for design and ability to meet deadlines. That said, degree programs in fine arts or graphic design are offered at many colleges, universities, and private design schools. Most curricula include principles of design, computerized design, commercial graphics production, printing techniques, and website design. Associate's degrees and certificates in graphic design also are available from two- and three-year professional schools. The National Association of Schools of Art and Design accredits postsecondary institutions with programs in art and design.

Job hunting tips: A go-to resource for career information is the American Institute of Graphic Arts and the extensive job board on the Art Directors Club's site. Other job sites to scroll through include Coroflot and Krop. Let the color wheel spin.

Mediator

The nitty-gritty: Arbitration and alternative dispute resolution (ADR) have steadily gained converts from those hoping to bypass lawsuits with onerous fees and often a drawn-out legal process. From divorce proceedings to housing and medical disputes, many people prefer to settle matters privately out of court. Tense and sometimes frustrating debates can make your head throb, but mediators are the pros equipped with the calm voice of reason.

These jobs are not only for retired lawyers, mind you. An expertise in certain fields of business can be your ticket. Experience settling workplace discrimination issues, marriage counseling, and even a mental health background can land you a seat at the table to guide a sensitive negotiation.

In general, you work out of your home office, but may have to go to another location for the official meeting. You've got to be all ears. Your task: Impartially hear both sides of a dispute, cut through the sometimes emotional verbiage, and intuitively home in on the critical details. It's up to you to patiently direct and encourage both sides to keep talking in a civil fashion until a satisfactory resolution, or settlement, is struck. No taking sides. The hours vary depending on caseload. Expect to put in the hours during negotiations.

Pay range: $11.63 to $325 an hour and up, according to PayScale.com.

Qualifications: Many mediators have law degrees, but nonlegal backgrounds are acceptable. Specific training, license requirements, and certification vary by state. Mediators typically complete 60 hours of courses through independent programs or organizations, but some are trained on the job through volunteering at a community mediation center or teaming up with a practicing mediator.

Some colleges offer certificates or advanced degrees in dispute resolution. To tap into cases, network with local bar associations, insurers, realtors, and human resource departments at area businesses and hospitals. The American Bar Association Section for Dispute Resolution provides a trove of information relating to the dispute resolution field. Mediate.com is another source for international, national, and state conflict resolution organizations, and more. You must have a gift for peacemaking.

Online Juror

The nitty-gritty: Online companies such as JuryTest, OnlineVerdict, and Resolution Research will pay you to sit on mock juries to give attorneys and other jury consultants feedback on cases. Think of these as virtual focus groups. To sign up with online jury companies, you fill out an online questionnaire. When a lawyer needs an online juror that matches your demographics, you're contacted via e-mail.

An attorney posts a case on a secure website for you to log on to and review. You may listen to audio, view video presentations, or read material and answer questions. Then you submit a verdict. Once the minimum number of verdicts has been rendered (usually 50), the case concludes. A summary is posted later if you want to see the results.

The number of cases you may be asked to review will vary depending on the number of attorneys in your area who are using this service. Most companies will have only occasional work for you, so sign up for a few. Be sure to read all the disclaimers and details. The hours typically run from 20 minutes to more than an hour, depending on the details of the case.

Pay range: Employers report that payments usually start at $10 per case and can go up to $100, depending on the length of the process.

Qualifications: The qualifications are essentially the same requirements as you would have for actual jury duty. In general, you can't be a lawyer, paralegal, or legal assistant, or an insurance company representative. Nor can you be associated with liability claims adjustments. You must be a U.S. citizen, be of sound mind and good moral character, be able to read and write, never have been convicted of a felony, and not be under indictment or other legal accusation of misdemeanor theft, felony theft, or any felony charge.

Online Tutor

The nitty-gritty: Private online tutoring is a growing area in the uber-competitive march to college admissions. The subjects in demand are the core curriculum: world history, physics, science, math, and English. Foreign language specialties are also seeing an uptick. And help with preparation for standardized tests such as the SAT, GED, and GRE is always in demand.

An online employer like Tutor.com, which offers one-on-one help to students, is set up so that when a student needs assistance with homework, he or she enters a grade level and subject into the computer log-on screen. The appropriate tutor (the firm has more than 3,000 on board) connects to the student inside the secure online classroom. The student and tutor can chat using instant messaging, draw problems on an interactive whiteboard, share a file to review essays and papers, and browse resources on the Web together.

With individual accounts, sessions are saved so that students and parents can review them at any time. Course levels range from elementary school through 12th grade and the first year of college, but tutors also can help adults returning to school or searching for a job. Other online tutoring firms include Wyzant (wyzant.com), which tutors people in more than 200 subjects from accounting to Algebra to writing. Many of Wyzant's 50+ tutors are, or have been, teachers or have advanced degrees. But if you have a skill you can pass along, you may be in demand. Prospective tutors complete a proficiency exam for certain subjects, or provide written qualifications.

Kaplan and Pearson Education are two more firms to consider. For general information about tutoring, visit the American Tutoring Association or National Tutoring Association websites.

Or you might opt to tutor on your own. You'll probably forgo the bells and whistles of the interactive whiteboard, but you can easily set up chat sessions and send files back and forth with your students. And you can develop an ongoing relationship that provides steady work. Some firms ask you to plan on at least five hours a week.

Pay range: Hourly rates are between $10 and $14, based on experience, subject tutored, company, and grade level. A Wyzant spokesman recently told NextAvenue.org that some of its tutors charge as little as $15 per hour for their services, while others charge as much as $160 per hour. Part-time private tutors generally earn around $9.85 to $39.60 an hour, according to PayScale.com. Some private tutors, however, can make as much as $65 an hour.

Qualifications: Teacher certification is preferred but not required. Professional experience opens doors.

In general, with a tutoring company, you take an online exam in the subject you wish to teach. If you pass, you will be given a mock session with an online tutor. Then you must pass a third-party background check and final exam. Knowledge of more than one subject is encouraged. Your computer must have high-speed internet access and be able to run the classroom software provided.

Translator-Interpreter

The nitty-gritty: You may brag that you're fluent in two languages, but are you really? It's easy to get rusty. Having been a Spanish major back in college isn't going to be enough. Languages evolve, and being in sync with modern terms and slang is vital. Idioms matter. If you're going to be a Spanish translator or interpreter, for example, you need to know the difference between Spanish spoken in Spain, Mexico, Cuba, Puerto Rico, and other South and Central American countries. Note: Interpreters deal with spoken words, translators with written words. Interpreters are the go-betweens for two parties, such as a doctor and patient, a client and lawyer, and actors or presenters and their audience. Translatiors generally work on a computer with files they transmit electronically back and forth. Online dictionary resources can be invaluable, but they don't replace expressions gleaned from interacting with others who speak the language frequently.

Spanish is the most in-demand language, but needs for other languages are growing, such as Arabic. Specializing in a field such as the judicial system or healthcare and knowing the terminology will increase your job opportunities. This is precise work. Words have repercussions. If you don't know the vocabulary, don't take the assignment.

Pay range: $11.18 to $39.02 an hour, according to PayScale. com. Depending on assignment and expertise, pay can top $100 an hour. Translation and proofreading projects are generally billed at a rate of 15 to 30 cents per word, depending on the skill level.

Qualifications: Interpreters and translators must be fluent in at least two languages. A subject area of expertise helps. No official certifications are required, although several are offered through trade organizations, such as the American Translators Association (ATA), which provides certification in 24 language combinations involving English for its members. Federal courts have certification for Spanish, Navajo, and Haitian Creole interpreters, and many state and municipal courts offer their own forms of certification. The National Association of Judiciary Interpreters and Translators also offers certification for court interpreting. The U.S. Department of State has a three-test series for prospective interpreters. The International Association of Conference Interpreters offers certification for conference interpreters.

If you have solid language skills, you can get translation training at community colleges and universities to prepare for a translator certification. The American Translators Association has a list of programs it approves along with a job bank when you're ready. The All Language Alliance also connects job seekers and positions. Internships, apprenticeships, and volunteering via community organizations, hospitals, and sporting events that involve international competitors will build your resume. The ATA works with the Red Cross to provide volunteer interpreters in crisis situations. Working with a mentor and networking with native speakers will keep your skills fresh. The ATA also offers formal mentoring programs and has chapters in many states.

Selling point: A good ear for languages.

Virtual Assistant

The nitty-gritty: With shrinking payrolls, there's been a jump in demand—from small-business operators to executive-level professionals—for virtual personal assistants to do various administrative tasks. Duties range from making travel arrangements to sending letters and other support services that can easily be handled remotely via e-mail and phone.

The job can involve sitting for long periods, so take precautions to prevent eyestrain, stress, and repetitive motion ailments such as carpal tunnel syndrome. Look for openings and information at the International Virtual Assistants Association and Upwork.com. You can also canvas virtual assistant roles via online job boards. Search for "virtual assistant."

Pay range: $10.13 to $29.99 an hour, according to PayScale.com.

Qualifications: Employers increasingly demand knowledge of computer software applications, such as desktop publishing, project management, spreadsheets, and database management. You should be skilled in both Microsoft Word and Excel (for financial statements). Two years of work experience in an office administrative function is helpful.

Virtual assistant training programs are available at many community colleges. There is currently no national standard of certification for virtual assistants.

Writer/Editor

The nitty-gritty: You don't have to be a professional scribe to find work in this arena. You do need a clear grasp of sentence and paragraph construction, spelling, grammar, and punctuation. Jobs run the gamut from copyediting and proofreading to resume writing and technical editing. If you have expertise in a particular field or genre, that's all the better for opening doors.

Copyeditors, proofreaders, and writers can check out AARP's job search tool at aarp.org/jobs or sites like JournalismJobs.com for a range of postings for part-time writing and editing jobs. You can also set up your own shop to provide these resume- and essay-tuning services. Freelance writers can find postings on Freelancer.com or Upwork.com. If you have a LinkedIn profile, you can flag recruiters on the site to send along periodic contract or freelance openings from employer's job postings that suit your experience.

For more general writing gigs, you might reach out to local associations and organizations, community newsletters, and other regional publications. Ask if they need an extra hand on an assignment basis for online and print articles, brochures, and press releases. Freelance writers and editors typically set their own schedules based on deadlines.

Pay range: Pay for writers and editors varies widely, depending on type of writing, location, and experience. Not all jobs are billed by the hour, though; instead many freelancers are paid by project, word count, or even number of visitors to an online article. For creating a polished resume for a client, you might charge a base fee of $200. Some publishers pay freelance writers by the word or by the article, and that fluctuates widely depending on your background and experience: Anywhere from 50 cents to $3 a word is not out of the ordinary. If you write for an online publisher, you might be paid solely based on the number of times Web visitors view your article or if the content is licensed to other publishers.

Qualifications: No formal training is required. Employers often look for expertise in a variety of fields, from healthcare to taxes to resume writing. For newsier publications, a grasp of the *Associated Press Stylebook* or the *Chicago Manual of Style* might be necessary. Plus, *The Elements of Style* by Strunk and White never goes out of style.

Tips for Starting a Home-Based Business

Setting up a home-based business to make money from your natural talents requires some extra work. Here are some tips to consider:

Pay Attention to the Paperwork

If you're running a small business out of your home, you will probably need tax registrations, business and occupational licenses, and permits from federal, state and local governments to operate legally.

Check Your Insurance

It's smart to add an insurance rider on your homeowner's or renter's policy in case a delivery person or client falls on your steps. Contact your insurer about coverage for valuable work-related equipment you keep at home. Each state has rules about insurance that can be offered to home-based outfits. For more, look up the Insurance Information Institute, an industry trade group and information clearinghouse.

Don't Forget the IRS

Independent contractors pay federal and Social Security taxes on income. You will need to pay estimated taxes throughout the year instead of once a year. Go to the IRS Self-Employed Individual Tax Center for help. Depending on the location of your business, you may be required to file state and local income and business taxes, too.

Find a Mentor

Look for a mentor among your industry connections. One good way to find someone in an industry you want to learn more about is to check your LinkedIn connections to see who you know who might be a good candidate to cultivate as a mentor. Once you locate someone at a company within the industry, you can reach out and begin to build a relationship. PivotPlanet

.com, a virtual mentoring service, lets you connect with expert advisers via one-on-one video and phone conferences. The service offers access to expert advisers in hundreds of fields for people looking to change careers or add a business. It's designed to help build a concrete mentor relationship that can evolve over a series of sessions at regular intervals and on an as-needed basis. These meetings are billed hourly and can range in price from $60 to $120.

CHAPTER

3

Great Nonprofit Jobs

■ ■ ■

After being laid off from his commercial real estate job in his 50s, Steven Elson landed a job working in the nonprofit sector, overseeing the development of affordable housing projects.

For this second act of his career, Elson credits his time spent at Encore!Connecticut, a four-month workforce development program offered through the University of Connecticut's Nonprofit Leadership Program.

The program costs under $5,000, and grants are available. It consists of a crash course in nonprofit management and finance: 64 hours of classroom training held in local nonprofits and two months' full-time work, roughly 30 hours a week, at the managerial level for a Connecticut nonprofit.

The aim is to retrain professionals with at least 15 years of experience to transition their skill set to work in the nonprofit sector. While candidates as young as 40 are considered, the program's goal is to create opportunities for professionals 50+ who would like to put their experience and skill sets to work in a purposeful way.

Elson's pay is considerably less than when he was senior vice president of finance at a major regional commercial real estate developer in Connecticut.

"You know what? I don't care," he told me when I interviewed him for *The New York Times*. The other rewards make up for it. "I'm so happy and learning so much, and, thankfully, the youngest of our three children is through college now."

As baby boomers increasingly accept early retirement packages, layoffs, and mandatory retirements, a growing number are switching their corporate capability to the nonprofit world.

And the good news is that nonprofit jobs are on the rise. More than half of nonprofit groups surveyed plan to hire more workers in 2017, according to a new study by Nonprofit HR, a human resources consulting firm. A broad assortment of jobs are in demand, including finance, fundraising, management, and marketing, according to the report.

The pressing question is: How can you make a switch to a nonprofit job? A number of options are there to help you.

Encore.org, the nonprofit group based in San Francisco that promotes "advancing second acts for the greater good," is working to ramp up the encore movement through its encore network. Its goal is to help people make connections with nonprofits in their communities to help them transition to their encores. The group also offers a limited number of fellowships matching skilled, seasoned professionals with social purpose organizations.

Another resource is Pace University in New York, which offers the Encore Transition Program, aimed at helping executives and professionals explore shifts to nonprofit and public service organizations. (Pace's program, like the one at the University of Connecticut, has no ties to Encore.org.) The tuition is $795. The three-session interactive program and an online component will help you reprocess your skills and provides an overview of nonprofit and public service industries. Leaders in the arts, education, healthcare, social services, and government meet with students to share stories and make connections to tap for possible job openings or informational meetings. You also learn about resume design and the strategy of using social media for marketing yourself and researching job opportunities.

Students are also encouraged to check out corresponding programs at the university. For example, Pace offers a Master in Public Administration with a track for nonprofit management, as well as certificate courses on topics like grant writing.

In California, LA Fellows at Los Angeles Valley College offers unemployed midlevel managers a chance to find a job at a non-profit or commercial organization. Fellows receive nine weeks of training covering executive-level topics like critical thinking, advanced computer skills, and generating business leads.

Each fellow volunteers as an intern at local nonprofits, which removes gaps on resumes and delivers networking opportunities with potential employers. The program was initially financed by Los Angeles's Community Development Department and is now supported by local WorkSource Centers.

Sometimes, all that is required is a course or two to boost skills and catch a hiring manager's attention. A searchable list of nonprofit management courses offered at universities across the country is on the website of Seton Hall University (academic.shu.edu/npo/list. php) and includes undergraduate, graduate, and noncredit courses.

For example, Betsy Werley, director of network expansion with Encore.org, spent 26 years working originally as a corporate lawyer and then running projects at JPMorgan Chase.

When she decided to change to the nonprofit industry, she enrolled in courses at New York University in areas where she felt she needed some support—technology for nonprofits, for instance, and an introduction to fundraising.

That training gave her the skills to take on the role of executive director of The Transition Network, a New York–based nonprofit that helps professional women over 50 explore opportunities and make new connections, a post she left in 2013.

"You get in the door with your for-profit skills and experience," Werley says. "But those are just the starting point. You have to demonstrate that you understand nonprofit culture, by taking courses and doing volunteer work."

There is also, however, a secret ingredient. "You must truly be passionate about the organization's mission," she says.

Plenty of great nonprofit jobs are out there for you. For job-hunting help, you can start your search at websites such as Bridgestar.org, Change.org, Commongood Careers (cgcareers. org), CreateTheGood.org, and Idealist.org. LinkedIn also has a job search section dedicated to nonprofit positions.

Here are some opportunities at nonprofits.

Administrative Assistant

The nitty-gritty: Can you say jack-of-all-trades? This position calls for a mixed bag of skills and an ability to roll with the punches. You'll be working with top management as well as consultants, contractors, customers, and donors. You'll typically be responsible for the down-and-dirty clerical work from word processing to updating databases. You may be in charge of scheduling appointments, making travel arrangements for professional staff and board members, coordinating meetings and seminars, and processing registrations for workshops. Generally speaking, you'll take incoming calls; order and maintain office supplies; fulfill orders for reports, books, and other materials; and organize materials and handouts for events.

The greatest demand is from nonprofits that serve educational services, healthcare, and social assistance. At the heart of it, a versatile assistant is the point person who keeps things running smoothly with a lean staff, tight supplies, and a big agenda. Basic job description: good team player. Part- and full-time positions available; some virtual work possible.

Pay range: $11.03 to $20.74 an hour, according to PayScale.com.

Qualifications: Computer literacy. Come armed with a broad knowledge of computer software applications such as Word, Excel, PowerPoint, and Constant Contact. Core word processing, writing, proofreading, editing, and communication skills are indispensable. You should also be at ease working with software for desktop publishing, project management, spreadsheets, and database management.

Familiarity with social media, including Facebook, Instagram, LinkedIn, Snapchat, and Twitter, is a plus. Good customer service and organizational skills, and the ability to work independently, will serve you well. Employers will be on the lookout for a proven track record of getting things done, problem solving, and pumped-up energy.

Don't panic if you aren't riding the cutting-edge technology; on-the-job skills can be gleaned with the help of other employees or equipment and software vendors.

Fundraiser

The nitty-gritty: How good are you at asking for money? Fundraising is a key ingredient to a nonprofit's ultimate success and requires nurturing a rapport with donors and establishing a database of existing and potential donors. Prepare to confidently unleash your outgoing, persuasive nature.

It takes chutzpah to ask for money. You might ask for large gifts from individual donors, solicit bequests, host special events, apply for grants (see grant-writing jobs in this chapter, p. 94), or launch phone and letter appeals. In a smaller nonprofit, you very well may be asked to dig in on all of these activities. If you're hunting down a large gift, you'll be on the front line—kibitzing over long lunches and meeting with potential donors in their offices and at their homes.

But this is a job that takes more than charm and a verbal soft shoe. Good listening skills are essential, too. A successful fundraiser knows how to build relationships and patiently wait for the right time to press for a gift—especially when asking for thousands of dollars. If you revel in event planning, organizing parties with purpose, so to speak, can be a cool aspect of fundraising, too. Think black-tie dinners and charity walks. There are behind-the-scenes jobs, too—drafting form fundraising letters asking for donations, writing grant proposals, and penning those all-important "thank you for your donation" notes. Part-time consultant to full-time staff positions are available; evening and weekend hours may be required.

Pay range: $35,546 to $80,945, according to PayScale.com; $78,629 to $186,359 for a director, according to Salary.com.

Qualifications: It's not unusual for fundraisers to transfer into the position from careers in public relations, sales, or market research. One way to sharpen your fundraising skills is to enroll in classes and certification programs offered by the Association of Fundraising Professionals and the Foundation Center. The AFP's Fundamentals of Fundraising e-learning course offers introductory-level sessions—seven workshops— to introduce the novice fundraiser to the fundamental concepts and techniques of fundraising. The Foundation Center offers free and affordable classes nationwide in classrooms and online that cover grant proposal writing and fundraising skills. Many colleges and universities offer courses in fundraising.

Planned giving specialists should have a grounding in gift and tax law. There's no sweet-talking Uncle Sam when it comes to the requirements for a charitable deduction.

Exploring Nonprofits—Job Hunting Tips

Despite the do-gooder aspect of the work, nonprofit jobs have some drawbacks—starting with lower pay scales. In the nonprofit world, you work hard and often lack the resources to get it all done as fast or as successfully as you would like. Simply put, you have to do more with less.

If you're a go-getter fundraiser and can whip up creative and diverse funding streams, nonprofits want you. Administrative, communications, and accounting and finance personnel are also needed, along with technology experts.

Here are some steps to take if you're interested:

Soul-search. What issues do you care about?

Skill search. What skills do you have to help move into the sector—computer, legal, sales, financial management?

Research. The nonprofit world is broad. Understand what you can do for the specific field you're getting into by having an understanding of the organization's goals and expectations. Volunteering first can give you an insider's view and networking contacts that may lead to a job.

Add to your skill set. Consider taking a course to fill in any holes in your background. Credentials help in the nonprofit world. A number of people complete a master's or certificate program in social work in their 50s. Course work includes nonprofit marketing, fundraising, campaigns, corporate philanthropy, ethics, and law.

Salary check. Be realistic about your salary, vacation, and benefits needs. Salaries tend to be at least 20 percent lower than in the for-profit arena.

Web search. Check out nonprofit websites.

Grant/Proposal Writer

The nitty-gritty: You must have a knack for research and be detail driven. Each funder has exact guidelines that you must follow to a tee. While your proposal must be persuasive in tone, this is a form of technical writing, so save the flowery lingo. Matching a nonprofit or for-profit with a foundation or government grant requires a solid understanding of the mission of your client's organization and a grasp of the concept or program for which funding is being sought. You'll need to create a compelling pitch for why and how the requested funding can make a difference in the outfit's immediate needs and long-term goals. Former journalists often shine in this no-nonsense line of work. This is computer-based work that can hit high gear at deadline time.

Pay range: $14.31 to $51.07 per hour and up; part of compensation may be based on the value of the grant obtained.

Qualifications: A bachelor's degree in communications, journalism, or English is often the baseline. Some jobs may be geared toward those with both experience and a degree or knowledge in a specialized field—for example, engineering or medicine. A working knowledge of computer graphics is helpful because of the increased use of online technical documentation.

The Association of Fundraising Professionals offers several options to obtain certification and a grant proposal writing mini-tutorial on the site. *Grant Writing for Dummies* can help get you started. Many community colleges offer grant-writing certificate programs. Also check out the Foundation Center, which maintains a broad online database of U.S. and global grant makers.

Job hunting tips: Check online job boards like the Chronicle of Philanthropy for postings. Remember, it's not your job to get the grant, but to make the best case possible to suitable funding organizations.

Marketing/Communications Manager

The nitty-gritty: Consider yourself the "cause" messenger. You're the voice of the nonprofit in many ways. Duties can range from drafting press releases about upcoming events or capital campaigns to media outreach for coverage in print, broadcast, and social media streams. You might be writing compelling blast e-mails or mass snail-mail letters requesting donations, or producing content for quarterly newsletters.

In your public relations role, you may be asked to give speeches, set up speaking engagements, and prepare speeches for the executive director and board members. A note of caution: Nonprofits are collaborative places, and anything that reflects the face of the organization to the outside world will come under close scrutiny. Higher-ups will want to put their fingerprints on anything you write. Learn to let it go. Part-time and full-time positions are available.

Pay range: $39,562 to $94,518, according to PayScale.com.

Qualifications: In general, experience in media relations, writing, editing, and marketing are the prerequisites. A background in journalism can help. Bring a deep understanding of a nonprofit's specific field—environment, medical, social issues—plus more extensive knowledge of the core issue at the forefront of the group's mission. A bottomless basket of media contacts is vital. A working knowledge of the ways of social media—Facebook, Google+, Instagram, LinkedIn, Snapchat, Twitter, and other internet platforms— is expected.

The American Marketing Association and Public Relations Society of America both offer workshops, seminars, webinars, and boot camps on a range of topics you need to know now, such as social media, green marketing, crisis communication, and branding.

Volunteer Manager

The nitty-gritty: Your first line of duty is recruiting qualified volunteers via meetings with local interest groups and businesses. You want to drum up awareness of the nonprofit's cause and hopefully flush out helping hands. Then you interview volunteers to find out where they can best help out.

Once they're on board, you conduct direct training, coordinate schedules, supervise, and retain them. Keeping busy professionals who are willing to donate their time coming back to perform sometimes routine tasks requires some finesse. You may need to jump into the fray from time to time if volunteers don't show up or a deadline is crashing. If the volunteers are providing their support overseas, you'll be in charge of making sure all have the proper visas, passports, and shots. In the end, it's up to you to know who's on first. Part-time and full-time positions are typically available. Flexible schedules for weekends and evening work may be necessary to align with peak volunteer times.

Pay range: An hourly wage for a part-time manager may range from $20 to $25 an hour. The average full-time salary for a director of volunteer services can range from $37,598 to $64,263, according to Salary.com, but salaries vary greatly.

Qualifications: A personal history of volunteerism goes without saying. Public speaking chops are paramount. A track record of delegating and monitoring many activities at the same time will get you noticed. And those "rah, rah" motivational skills will open doors for you. It's vital to have the know-how to bring people together from all sorts of backgrounds to work together for a cause, not a paycheck.

A background in social services helps, but proven leadership and managerial skills in previous positions trumps all. Many colleges and universities offer classes in volunteer management as part of their graduate programs in public administration or nonprofit management. One credential available for volunteer managers is "Certified Volunteer Administration." The certification offered by the Council for Certification in Volunteer Administration (cvacert.org) is backed by supporters such as Idealist.org, the United Way Worldwide, and VolunteerMatch.org.

Tips on Transitioning to a Nonprofit Career

When I speak to job seekers over 50 who've spent their careers in the business world, they often say they'd love to work at a nonprofit that would let them tap their skills and truly make a difference.

Heck, I've even had unprompted conversations with my sister, brother, and best girlfriend—all in their mid-50s to age 60—about the kind of work they want to do at this stage of their life, as they prepare to transition from their corporate jobs. It all comes down to making the world a better place.

Maybe you, too, are eager to shift out of the corporate world and into the nonprofit sector so you can give back and leave a legacy. Your timing is excellent.

"The nonprofit sector is burgeoning with opportunities for career changers," says Laura Gassner Otting, author of the excellent book *Mission Driven: Moving from Profit to Purpose* and its companion guide, *The Mission Driven Handbook: A Resource for Moving from Profit to Purpose.* "In fact, it's experiencing an influx of corporate career changers. Baby boomers are looking to make their final professional chapters about meaning."

I've admired Otting for a number of years; in fact, she's become a go-to nonprofit jobs expert for many of my columns and books. I interviewed her for advice on how job seekers over 50 can find a place at nonprofits for my PBS Next Avenue/*Forbes* column. Here are the highlights:

Kerry: Lots of people in midlife want to be do-gooders, but are at a loss for where to start. What do you suggest?

Otting: One way is volunteering for a nonprofit. It not only allows a job seeker to appear credible in his or her job search, it also allows the person to determine if the nonprofit sector is a good fit.

AARP Foundation Experience Corps and the federal government's Senior Corps have been founded with the express intent of providing significant volunteer experience with demonstrable results. Programs that provide long-term, direct service or where you can volunteer in central office administrative work are a good way of testing your mettle for this type of work, your dedication to the mission, and the level at which you'd like to do it.

Where can boomers go for guidance about working at nonprofits?

The nonprofit sector is standing up and taking notice of the baby boomers. In fact, many nonprofits have been created to help ease these energetic, active, and interested professionals into a second career in the nonprofit sector. In short, these groups make the beginning of a transition easier.

Encore.org is leading the charge. Its recent research has shown that Americans in the second half of life—regardless of income, educational level, or race—want to explore options for the next stage of life; retool skills, obtain new training, or pursue educational interests; use their skills and experience in flexible work or service opportunities; and make meaningful connections with their peers and their community.

Will corporate skills transfer to the nonprofit sector?

The transition to the nonprofit sector will teach any job seeker that professional experience, education, individual skills, and personal interests all become important and relevant parts of the mix.

None of these categories is mutually exclusive of another and each brings skills that will transfer well. For example, people educated as lawyers don't necessarily need to practice law on behalf of nonprofits. Lawyers learn to negotiate, mediate, research, and apply critical thinking. Some have managed law practices with significant budgets and staff and have had to rid themselves of any shyness about asking for money. A good lawyer will have developed the ability to talk to lay audiences and patience with bureaucratic systems. Combine that with the desire to change a community, state, or country, and you have yourself a pretty powerful nonprofit leader.

That's just one example. Breaking down your entire career and the jobs that you have held will yield a fruitful dossier for your nonprofit job search.

Are there any certificates or advanced training that will help people stand out from other candidates?

Education is only one part of the equation. Your passion is what can set you apart from other candidates. However, degrees that teach skills—such as programs on nonprofit management, fundraising, accounting, and operations—are easily attainable and can make sense strategically.

This type of education provides you with a current nonprofit peer group, access to a career center, and a mind filled with the best nonprofit thinking of the day.

There are hundreds of programs ranging from certificates to full undergraduate and graduate degrees in almost every city in the country.

How should someone with a corporate career do a resume rehab to get hired by a nonprofit?

There is a whole chapter in my *Mission Driven Handbook* dedicated to just the resume rehab. But I can tell you that the biggest mistake I see from boomers is a discounting of a life of unpaid work.

A resume is an opportunity to tell potential employers what you can do by showing them what you have done. But this is more difficult with corporate transitioners who need to write a resume that details more about where they are going than where they have been.

Think about your career change to the nonprofit sector in terms of functional expertise rather than subject area expertise.

When is the right time to transition to a nonprofit? If you're nearing 60, is it too late?

Your children may have left the nest, you may have a sick relative, you may be unable to stomach one more day of corporate profiteering, or you may have benefited greatly from your career and can now write your own rules. Everyone has their reasons, and all of them are real and valid.

However, only some of them should influence your job search. The timing must have everything to do with how a particular job, including the lifestyle and financial considerations that come with it, plays into your life at this time.

Perhaps your company is downsizing, and this is a move you have always desired. Perhaps you are a board member for a nonprofit whose chief executive just announced plans for retirement. Perhaps you are just coming back to work after raising your children and because of that life-transforming experience, you realize that you cannot go back to the job you held before.

Realizing why this is the right time for you, for your family, and for your bank account is key to deciding which kind of job to seek.

But, as you can tell, there is no wrong time—only wrong amounts of preparation.

The key to the move is being able to answer three key questions:

- What is the motivating social cause or cause(s) you wish to serve?
- What skills have you gathered in your paid and unpaid work that can transition to the nonprofit sector?
- Which types of environments allow you to best thrive?

Once you know the answers to those questions, you can begin your transition and your job hunt.

4

Great Healthcare Jobs

■ ■ ■

Healthcare is hot and will be for years to come. Job seekers can find a plethora of opportunities in healthcare support, such as nursing assistants, physical and occupational therapists and assistants, skincare specialists, physician assistants, genetic counselors, and social workers.

Employment of healthcare occupations is projected to grow 19 percent from 2014 to 2024—much faster than the average for all occupations, according to the Bureau of Labor Statistics (BLS)—and to add about 2.3 million new jobs. In fact, healthcare occupations will add more jobs than any other group of occupations. This growth, as you may guess, is expected due to an aging population.

You don't have to be a surgeon or ICU nurse. There are hundreds of areas of specialization, such as paramedical examiner, school nurse, medical records administrator, medical assistant, or home care aide. Many jobs offer flexible work schedules.

According to the BLS, there is a growing need for occupations related to healthcare, such as healthcare support and personal care services like athletic trainers, audiologists, dental assistants, dieticians and nutritionists, home health aides, massage therapists, medical transcriptionists, physical therapists, skincare specialists, and more. See Chapter 8 for jobs to ride the age wave.

If you have healthcare experience in your tool kit, you'll have a leg up. Stepping into this growing and ever-changing arena, however, may require new skills to score a certification or renew a license. Many employers prefer applicants who are certified by a recognized professional association.

The soaring demand for skilled workers, though, will make the effort worth your while. Ideally you can plan ahead and add the necessary courses before you start job seeking to smooth the move. You'll find useful details about healthcare jobs in the Department of Labor's *Occupational Outlook Handbook*.

Here are some great healthcare jobs to consider.

Dietician and Nutritionist

The nitty-gritty: Employment of dietitians and nutritionists, two closely related occupations, is projected to grow 16 percent from 2014 to 2024, faster than the average for all occupations, according to the Bureau of Labor Statistics.

Factors spurring the growth: More than one-third of U.S. adults are obese. There's rising demand for special diets to address aging, allergies, and ailments such as diabetes and heart disease. And staying fit and eating healthy are mainstream life goals, particularly for those over age 50.

Duties range from meal planning to doling out expert advice on concerns such as weight loss and lowering cholesterol levels. Potential employers include operators of wellness programs, supermarkets, restaurants, hospitals, and nursing care facilities. You might opt to open your own practice as a nutrition or health coach.

Pay range: Dieticians generally make $19.79 to $35.54 per hour, according to PayScale.com. Nutritionists get $10.52 to $30.05 per hour.

Qualifications: You'll generally need a state license or certification, which requires a bachelor's degree in food and nutrition, a supervised internship, and a passing grade on an exam. You can get more information from the Academy of Nutrition and Dietetics (eatright.org). Other options include a health coach certification from the American Council on Fitness (acefitness.org) and various certifications offered by the American Fitness Professionals & Associates (afpafitness.com).

Meet a Holistic Nutritionist

A few years ago, Barbara Rodgers ventured off into a second career after over 30 years as securities industry executive. "After struggling with multiple sclerosis at the end of my corporate career, I was drawn to an education and career path in holistic nutrition because of the results I experienced personally in arresting my MS symptoms by changing my diet," she says. "My goal now is to pay it forward and help others who are dealing with chronic disease."

The focus of her business/counseling practice (NutritionLifeStrategies .com) is working with autoimmune disease, chronic stress, and infertility. "With a few older clients reaching out to me over the last year, I'm also aware that there is a significant need to address health and nutrition issues for those over 50," she says.

All appointments are held via telephone or Skype so she and her client can work together quietly without interruption. An initial 90-minute consultation is $175. Follow-up sessions are typically 30 to 45 minutes in length and are billed at $65 per half hour.

Massage Therapist

The nitty-gritty: Massage therapists are prized for their ability to ease muscle soreness and unwind stress for their clients. The employment prospects are swelling, as massage becomes an increasingly mainstream service offered by spas and clinics in recent years. Employment of massage therapists is projected to grow 22 percent from 2014 to 2024, according to the BLS.

There's a smorgasbord of treatments and techniques that massage therapists use, and you may choose to specialize in one as a targeted way to build a business as the go-to expert. You might work for a big hotel chain, which offers in-room massages to guests, or a local health club. Or your magic fingers could comfort residents of a retirement or assisted-living community or medical center. Once you get a loyal base of followers, you can attract new clients by word of mouth. Then you pack up your own table and linen and head over to their homes or offices for private sessions.

Your core work consists of evaluating the client's medical history and following that with muscle manipulation, which can be gentle or a real workout. At the end of the day, you will feel it, too. Administering massages is physically demanding, so you may need to spring for your own massage from time to time.

Pay range: The average wage is $19.30 per hour, according to PayScale.com. Annual salaries range from $22,318 to $94,367. Some therapists who make house calls charge between $55 and $125 for a 90-minute massage.

Qualifications: Most states and the District of Columbia regulate massage therapy. You must get either a license or certification after graduating from an accredited training program. You may also need to join a massage-professional organization for insurance coverage. The American Massage Therapy Association offers professional memberships, which include liability insurance, for $235 a year.

Meet a Massage Therapist

For Michele Barie-Dale, 52, who runs her own massage practice, the Personal Touch, in Pittsburgh, a typical day finds her in the homes of clients age 70 and over. She arrives with her massage table, linens, towels, aromatherapy candles, and almond oil cream. "The senior crowd is my favorite," says Barie-Dale. "It's a special relationship. It becomes a friendship."

The benefits for her clients include boosting circulation, improving flexibility, and providing stress relief, she explains. "But in many ways, it's chitchat—the social contact. They want to talk to me and to hear about my life, and I learn about their lives. It brings joy to me." But the work can be physically demanding. "I have to watch my back—sometimes I have to lift and move walkers and wheelchairs, and help my clients climb safely on and off the table."

Barie-Dale opted for private practice. But massage therapists also work in group practices, chiropractic clinics, nursing homes, airports, hospices, and hospitals.

Medical Assistant

The nitty-gritty: Administrative tasks in doctors' offices make up the bulk of the workload. Mostly you're performing routine front-office duties, such as checking in patients, verifying health insurance information, staffing the telephones, and scheduling appointments. You're on the front lines, so rev up the people-person persona. You may be in charge of maintaining supplies. Some assistants help physicians with procedures and prepare medical records. If you have the training, you may perform direct patient care such as conducting an EKG, collecting specimens, caring for wounds, administering medication, and checking vital signs. The hours vary by practitioner, but are generally on weekdays.

Pay range: $14 to $19 per hour, according to Salary.com.

Qualifications: Many medical assistants are trained on the job, but others complete programs at community colleges. Some programs offer certificates in as little as eight months and teach students to assist physicians in routine duties as well as basic office tasks. To learn more about medical assisting, visit the websites of the Accrediting Bureau of Health Education Schools and the Commission on Accreditation of Allied Health Education Programs.

Even when employers permit you to learn on the job, a certificate of training from a nationally recognized association such as the American Association of Medical Assistants helps you stand out. You can also become certified in a specialty, such as optometry or podiatry.

Medical Biller/Coder

The nitty-gritty: Skip the healing, hand me the computer. The gist of this back-office job is to convert medical terminology for everything from shingles to a torn ACL into the numerical codes that insurance companies use for reimbursement processing. You fill out electronic forms to get the claims started. Potential employers include billing companies, physician offices, hospitals, hospices, clinics, and insurers.

Pay range: Hourly pay ranges from $12.19 to $24.36, according to PayScale. Annual pay ranges from $25,684 to $52,380. The national average salary is $40,000, according to job board Glassdoor.

Qualifications: Plan on four months to one year of education, though with an online course you can go at your own pace.

In general, you'll need a high school diploma or GED, and must pass an accredited program in medical coding. Most employers require that you get certified through a nationally recognized professional organization such as the American Academy of Professional Coders or the American Health Information Management Association.

Medical Interpreter

The nitty-gritty: With the global economy running on multiple languages, the BLS projects 29 percent employment growth for interpreters and translators. Specializing in healthcare increases your opportunities, but you'll need to know quite a collection of medical terms in both languages. Spanish is the most in-demand language, but the need for Arabic, Chinese/Mandarin, German, and Russian is growing.

Interpreters help patients communicate with doctors, nurses, and other medical staff, either face-to-face or remotely by phone or video link. Translators, meanwhile, handle written material such as informational brochures, forms that patients must read and sign, and patient records.

You need to be able to nimbly translate with a calm, reassuring demeanor. An understanding of differing cultural practices concerning healthcare will help, too.

Pay range: The median annual salary for medical interpreters is $42,066, with a range usually from $37,026 to $46,108, according to Salary.com. Top earners can pull in more than $78,250, according to the BLS.

Qualifications: You don't need a college degree, but employers generally prefer to hire certified medical interpreters or certified healthcare interpreters. Some colleges and universities offer certificate programs. For example, Hunter College in New York has a 48-hour course for tuition of $1,250 and a one-time $35 registration fee.

Medical Records Administrator

The nitty-gritty: Techies with a medical bent, log on. As hospitals, nursing care facilities, outpatient care centers, and old-fashioned doctors' offices say sayonara to mounds of paperwork and rows of file drawers in favor of electronic health records, there's a soaring demand to hire workers at ease with computer-ese. The work entails transferring records of physician notes from patient visits, medical or surgical procedures, medical history, test results, and more into computerized files.

For the most part, this is a stationary desk job, so there's not a lot of running around, standing on your feet, or tending to last-minute emergencies. A hot specialty: coding. Medical coders convert the doctor's report of a disease or injury and any procedures performed into numeric and alphanumeric designations, or codes, to create a claim for insurance reimbursement. It can be tedious. If you miscode, either the patient or the doctor may be under-reimbursed by an insurer—the devil is in the details. The hours vary by medical facility.

Pay range: $11.63 to $24.40 per hour, according to PayScale.

Qualifications: A high school diploma or equivalent and previous experience in a healthcare setting are enough to qualify for some positions, but most jobs for health information technicians require postsecondary education, according to BLS. You'll probably need an associate's degree in health information technology from a technical or community college. Online courses are offered, too. Coursework covers medical terminology, anatomy and physiology, health data requirements and standards, clinical classification and coding systems, healthcare reimbursement methods, and database security.

Passing a certifying examination is not always required, but employers prefer it. This certification is awarded by the American Health Information Management Association. Visit its website for complete information, including accredited schools and certification details. The American Academy of Professional Coders offers coding credentials. The Board of Medical Specialty Coding and Professional Association of Health Care Coding Specialists both offer credentialing in specialty coding. The National Cancer Registrars Association, for instance, offers a credential as a Certified Tumor Registrar. To learn more about the credentials available and their specific requirements, contact the credentialing organization. Computer geeks, this code's for you.

Optician

The nitty-gritty: Between 2014 and 2024, the BLS projects that optician employment will grow by 24 percent. The country's aging population is driving much of that expansion.

Your job is to order, fit, and adjust new eyeglasses—and sometimes chime in with your fashion sense. You interpret the prescription written by an ophthalmologist or optometrist to help a client select the right frame and lens. Jobs are typically in stores that sell eyewear or in an ophthalmologist's private-practice office.

Pay range: The median optician salary is $43,170 a year, according to Salary.com.

Qualifications: About half of all states require a license. That usually means completing an on-the-job apprenticeship or formal education through an approved program at a community college or technical school. As of 2015, the Commission on Opticianry Accreditation had accredited 22 programs in 14 states.

Certification requires passing exams from the American Board of Opticianry/National Contact Lens Examiners. Nearly all state licensing boards use these groups' exams as the basis for licensing.

Paramedical Examiner

The nitty-gritty: Don the scrubs, grab the medical kit, and prepare to soothe nervous people.

A paramedical examiner may be hired as a contractor to perform routine medical tests that screen individuals applying for life insurance coverage. Most insurance companies require an applicant over 40 to have a medical exam before they will approve a policy. Depending on the amount of life insurance someone is buying and his or her age, these exams include visiting someone's home or office and taking a medical history, getting weight and height, drawing blood, taking blood pressure, obtaining a urine specimen, and perhaps performing an EKG.

In addition to house calls, you might be hired by corporate clients to perform random drug testing on employees or handle cholesterol screenings at health and wellness fairs. You're not expected to be Marcus Welby, M.D., but it can take some smooth talking to relax the blood- and needle-phobic. The hours are flexible. You schedule your own appointments. Expect evenings and weekends.

There are also full-time opportunities for paramedical examiners who specialize and are certified in phlebotomy. Phlebotomists work in hospitals, medical and diagnostic laboratories, blood donor centers, and doctors' offices.

And phlebotomists who collect blood donations sometimes travel to different offices and sites to set up mobile donation centers, according to BLS. So make sure you have an up-to-date GPS.

Pay range: The average pay is $36,400 per year, according to PayScale. Contractors typically are paid by the job versus the hour, and pay varies by experience and contracting firm. Firms typically cover transportation costs above a set mileage limit. You can work for more than one contractor. Hourly wages for phlebotomists range from $10.37 to $18.41, according to PayScale.

Qualifications: Paramedical examiners may have prior training as a nurse or licensed practical nurse. If not, you should pursue a phlebotomist certification, which includes practical experience drawing, collecting, and storing blood and a thorough knowledge of vein location and puncture points. Phlebotomy programs are offered through vocational and technical schools, as well as community colleges.

Several organizations offer technician certifications for phlebotomists, including the American Medical Technologists, the American Society for Clinical Pathology, the National Center for Competency Testing, and the National Healthcareer Association.

Candidates for certification typically need some classroom education, as well as some clinical experience. Certification testing usually includes a written exam and may include practical components, such as drawing blood. Requirements vary by certifying organization. California, Louisiana, Nevada, and Washington state require their phlebotomists to be certified.

Job hunting tips: An array of job listings can be found on all the major job boards from Google for Jobs to Indeed to Monster, Simply Hired to Snagajob.

Personal and Home Healthcare Aide

The nitty-gritty: If you're suited to it, there's plenty of need for paid workers at private homes, assisted-living communities, memory-care centers for dementia patients, hospice facilities, and nursing homes. It's also possible to be hired directly by the patient or their family. Your job is to assist elderly, ill, or disabled people with routine activities ranging from bathing and dressing to running errands.

Other duties might include light housekeeping, companionship, grocery shopping, meal preparation, and medication monitoring. While the work is rewarding, it can be taxing mentally and physically. Some positions require lifting patients and lots of time on your feet. Ask about the requirements of specific clients before signing on.

If you're working at someone's home, hours can vary, from three or four hours a day, two or three days a week, to live-in, which could help you save on housing expenses. These jobs are often booked through a home care agency. You might opt for a part-time position in an assisted-living facility or hospice.

Pay range: Thanks to high turnover, job openings are plentiful, especially helping the elderly in-home as well as at assisted-living and hospice facilities. Expect generally $8.56 per hour to $14.47, but pay can reach $35+ depending on experience and certification.

Qualifications: Short-term training is generally on the job by registered nurses if you're working for an agency or in-house facility. You will undergo formal training and pass a competency test to work for certified home health or hospice agencies that receive reimbursement from Medicare or Medicaid. Requirements vary from state to state. Some employers may require a Certified Nursing Assistant (CNA) certification.

A criminal background check is standard. Cardiopulmonary resuscitation (CPR) training and a driver's license are helpful, too. Contact local care facilities for job openings and training requirements. Another firm to check out is CareLinx (carelinx.com), based outside of San Francisco. It operates like an online matchmaking site for families and has over 150,000 professional caregivers ranging from certified nurse assistants all the way up to registered nurses and nurse practitioners. Launched in 2011, the network now operates in more than 3,000 cities, including Atlanta, Chicago, New York, Los Angeles, and San Francisco. For overall home care information and a nursing job board, go to the American Association of Home Care. Compassion, self-control, and a sense of humor are the nuts and bolts. Your motto: Lend a hand.

Pharmacy Technician

The nitty-gritty: Employment of pharmacy technicians is projected to grow 9 percent from 2014 to 2024, faster than the average for all occupations, according to the BLS. The main reason for the uptick is an expected increase in the demand for prescription medications, which will lead to more requests for pharmaceutical services. You'll find job openings in pharmacies, including those operating in grocery and drug stores, as well as in hospitals. Most pharmacy technicians work full time, but part-time opportunities are possible. The gist of the job is entering customer or patient information, including prescriptions, into a computer system; measuring, preparing, and packaging medications; organizing inventory; alerting pharmacists to any shortages of medications or supplies; and processing insurance claims. In most states, technicians can also compound or mix some medications. You will also use your tech skills to help maintain precise patient records. Expect to spend a chunk of the day on your feet. You should also be willing to work a variety of shifts, including weekends and holidays.

Pay range: $13 to $19 an hour, according to Salary.com. The median annual Pharmacy Technician I salary was $32,675 as of February 2017, with a range usually between $29,469 and $36,455, although this can vary widely depending on a variety of factors.

Qualifications: States typically regulate pharmacy technicians, which usually requires passing an exam or completing a training program in pharmacy technology, often offered at local or community college. These programs vary in length and subject matter and most offer clinical internships with employers to get on-the-job training. Courses cover a range of subjects, such as the math used in pharmacies, record-keeping, ways of dispensing medications, and pharmacy law and ethics, according to the BLS. Technicians also learn the names, uses, and doses of medications. A high school diploma or the equivalent is generally required. It's possible to earn a certificate in around nine months.

The American Society of Health-System Pharmacists (ASHP.org) accredits pharmacy technician programs that include at least 600 hours of instruction over a minimum of 15 weeks and provides a job listing board. The Accreditation Services Division of ASHP provides an online directory of accredited pharmacy technician training programs arranged alphabetically by state. Each state has different requirements. You should check your state boards of pharmacy for particular regulations. Links to state boards of pharmacy are found at the National Association of Boards of Pharmacy site (https://nabp.pharmacy/boards-of-pharmacy/). Requirements for pharmacy technicians in the states that regulate them typically include some or all of the following according to BLS:

- High school diploma or GED
- Formal education or training program
- Exam
- Fees
- Continuing education
- Criminal background check

Many employers will pay for their pharmacy technicians to take the certification exam.

Two organizations offer certification. The Pharmacy Technician Certification Board (PTCB.org) certification requires a high school diploma and the passing of an exam. Applicants for the National Healthcareer Association (NHAnow.com) certification must have a high school diploma and have completed a training program or have one year of work experience. Technicians must recertify every two years by completing 20 hours of continuing education courses.

School Nurse

The nitty-gritty: Got your first-aid kit ready? For registered nurses stepping away from a full-time nursing career, part-time or seasonal nursing assignments are a schoolyard away. In fact, there's a shortage of nurses in public schools around the country, according to the National Association of School Nurses. The job: Administering basic first aid to kids from elementary school- to college-age who are injured or become ill during school hours.

These "need to see a nurse" traumas can run the gamut from headaches to cuts and scrapes to stomachaches. The aim is to quickly and calmly treat and/or send them home to a parent or primary care physician for continued care. Other duties include meting out a student's medication per written physician's orders for daily prescriptions for such ongoing illnesses as attention deficit disorder, chronic asthma, or diabetes. Nurses can also conduct basic vision and hearing tests and teach classes in nutrition and first aid. Hours are flexible, from summer school stints to nine months, 20 hours a week to full time. Job sharing is possible.

Pay range: School nurse annual salaries typically range usually from $37,490 to $59,234, according to Salary.com, but vary greatly across the country. Some schools and universities offer insurance and vacation benefits.

Qualifications: A valid state registered nurse license is generally required. Each state has different rules for school nurses. You'll need to check with your state nursing board. Nurse's aides may be considered in some situations.

Clearances will include criminal and other background checks. You'll also need a current certification in CPR and first aid from a recognized provider such as the American Heart Association. You might bolster your qualifications by earning a professional school nurse certification. Contact the National Board for Certification of School Nurses for more information. Finally, add one dose of Psychology 101—a worried parent may need as much TLC as a sick child. Hidden job description: must be kid- and parent-friendly.

Extra points: If you've worked shifts in emergency care, or in pediatrics for an elementary school post, that's a plus.

Telemetry Technician

The nitty-gritty: Here's one from the heart. Telemetry technicians perform cardiac tests on patients using an electrocardiogram, or EKG. You're in charge of prepping a patient for an exam, taping electrodes to the chest, arms, and legs, and monitoring cardiac activity as it blips up and down on a computer screen. You may also perform more specific monitoring, such as stress testing, in which the patient walks rapidly on a treadmill.

Pay range: From $10.69 to $19.29 per hour, or annually from $22,366 to $41,360, according to PayScale.

Qualifications: Most of the training can be done on the job, but many employers prefer to hire a certified technician. A telemetry course usually takes about 120 hours of study and may require a high school diploma or GED and drug screening. Check out agencies such as the American Certification Agency for Healthcare Professionals or the Cardiovascular Credentialing Institute.

Travel Nurse

The nitty-gritty: Registered nurses and licensed practical nurses are in high demand at hospitals and doctors' offices in Florida and Arizona during the winter months to cater to snowbirds. The majority of travel nursing assignments run for 13 weeks—often with the option of extending the term to six months. You must have a travel-nursing license to practice in each state. These temporary licenses can cost $25 to $250 and are valid from one to six months. Plan ahead. Obtaining a temporary Florida RN license, for instance, takes an average of 30 days. Specific work responsibilities vary widely depending on specialty and facility.

Pay range: From $19.18 to $47.69 or more an hour, according to PayScale.com, plus housing stipends and health insurance are often part of the package.

Qualifications: A bachelor of science degree in nursing is a standard requirement, but an associate's degree in nursing can open doors, too. You must pass a national licensing examination, known as the National Council Licensure Examination, to obtain a nursing license. CrossCountryTravCorps.com, Nurse.com, and TravelNursing.com are a few sites to check out for openings. Other eligibility requirements vary by state. Contact the state's board of nursing for details. A background check is standard. Compassion and care count.

Veterinary Technician

The nitty-gritty: If you love animals, have an aptitude for science, and are willing to go back to school to ramp up the necessary skills, you've got a great chance of landing a job—especially if you live in a rural area. Employment of veterinary technologists and technicians is projected to grow 19 percent from 2014 to 2024, much faster than the average for all occupations, according to the BLS's *Occupational Outlook Handbook*. Employment is expected to grow as more veterinarians use technicians and technologists to do general care and lab work. Working alongside primarily small-animal vets, you might perform duties such as preparing pets for surgery, performing lab tests, administering medication and vaccines, providing emergency nursing care, collecting blood and samples, and the more mundane tasks of recording pet histories and weighing your sometimes nervous patients.

Pay range: The median annual wage of veterinary technologists and technicians was $32,490 in 2016, according to BLS. PayScale.com sets hourly wages at $9.71 to $18.56 per hour up to $30.84 per overtime hour.

Qualifications: Veterinary technicians usually have a two-year associate's degree in a veterinary technology program. There are around 231 veterinary technology programs accredited by the American Veterinary Medical Association (AVMA). Most of these programs offer a two-year associate's degree for veterinary technicians. Twenty-three colleges offer a four-year bachelor's degree in veterinary technology. Nine schools offer coursework through distance learning. Although each state regulates vet techs differently, you generally must take a credentialing exam—the Veterinary Technician National Examination. You're often the point person to explain to the owner their pet's condition, or how to manage medication prescribed by a veterinarian, so clear and calm communication skills are imperative.

CHAPTER 5

Great Tech Jobs

■ ■ ■

T ech jobs can be great for older workers with digital skills and interests.

Employment in computer and information technology is expected to grow 12 percent from 2014 to 2024, faster than the average for all occupations, predicts the Bureau of Labor Statistics's (BLS's) *Occupational Outlook Handbook.*

Helping drive the growth is a greater emphasis on cloud computing, the collection and storage of big data, more everyday items becoming connected to the internet, and the continued demand for mobile computing, the report says.

Researchers at LinkedIn create an annual ranking of the skills most in demand globally. The top skills that could get you hired in 2017 were all tied to technology from cloud computing to data mining or organizing and statistical analysis to network and information security expertise.

For an appreciation of the size and variety of this employment field, take a look at big job boards such as Glassdoor.com, Indeed.com, and Monster.com. Look too at CrunchBoard.com and Dice.com, the two big technology-specific job sites. You'll see many thousands of postings in too many categories to count.

When it comes to a sizzling job field, the computer and tech arena is hard to beat. "For someone in the second half of their career, looking for ways to transition into retirement, or to find better work-life balance, technology jobs are a good option," says Sara Sutton Fell, CEO of FlexJobs, a job board that specializes in part-time and work-from-home positions. Many of the jobs have options for telecommuting, part-time hours, and flexible schedules.

How to get in? It will of course help if you're already working in some way in a tech or related field. But you can also make the jump if you're willing to learn new skills and enjoy working with computers. Top sites to explore: Skillful (skillful.com) and TechHire (techhire.org), a program of the nonprofit Opportunity@Work. TechHire provides grants and expertise to train workers around the country and link them to jobs.

Here are well-paying tech jobs that may be for you:

Call Center Tech Representative

The nitty-gritty: If you're game to spend the entire day speaking on the telephone, this is your gig. Call centers heat up for holiday sales. You generally have your own workstation outfitted with a headset and computer. The bulk of your work is helping customers find a product, collecting payment information, and typing data in the system. Depending on your expertise, tech savvy, and employer, you might work to troubleshoot technical problems for customers. Apple, GoDaddy, and other web-based and consumer electronics companies have a need for call reps to solve customer's frustrating technology issues. Expect to answer simple questions or requests such as finding the status of an order. Be warned: Some customers are lodging complaints, so you'll need to stay cool.

Call centers can be cramped and noisy. The work is repetitious and, with brief breaks between calls, even stressful. Long periods spent sitting, typing, or looking at a computer screen can make your eyes and muscles ache. Smooth talkers should apply. Many call centers are open extended hours or staffed around the clock. Peak times may not last for a full shift, so you may be slotted for part time or work a split shift.

Pay range: Median hourly wages of customer service representatives range from less than $9.42 to $18.23, according to PayScale.com, an online salary, benefits, and compensation information company. Commissions and bonuses are extras.

Qualifications: Listening and verbal skills are key. For workers who correspond through e-mail, good typing, spelling, and grammar skills are essential. Basic to intermediate computer knowledge is vital. You'll likely be given training with background on the company and its products, the most commonly asked questions, and a review of the computer and telephone systems you'll be using. Hint: Companies favor folks who have a pleasant, neutral speaking voice.

Digital Marketing Specialist

The nitty-gritty: Do you have a mind for clickbait? Your job is to ramp up your employer's following on social media platforms like Facebook, Snapchat, and Twitter. You may also be tasked with tweaking the website's design and keeping it updated and accurate.

Pay range: $31,000 to $66,000 annually, according to Glassdoor. com. Salaries vary widely by location. In Washington, D.C., for example, a digital marketing specialist can make $67,900, which is 58 percent higher than the national median.

Qualifications: Strong writing and communications skills are essential. You'll want to be comfortable creating HTML content and working with software packages such as Adobe Creative Suite (Photoshop and Illustrator) and Microsoft Office.

IT Project Manager

The nitty-gritty: Meeting deadlines, keeping costs in check, adhering to quality standards, and motivating a team of other IT professionals, such as computer systems analysts and support specialists, are your mojo. The buck stops with you. You're responsible for developing, executing, and tracking projects related to IT, software, or web development. You work closely between the development team and different departments involved in each project, such as finance, HR, marketing, and others. You might be involved with a range of projects from running the installation and maintenance of computer hardware and software to negotiating with vendors. This job can be sliced and diced in many permutations from broad strategic responsibilities to narrow duties on one project, depending on the size of the organization.

Pay range: $80,160 annually to more than $187,200, according to BLS. The average salary is $103,085, according to the online jobs board, SimplyHired.

Qualifications: You can't pass go without at least a bachelor's degree in computer or information science, plus related work experience. Many organizations require their computer and information systems managers to have a graduate degree such as a master's of business administration (MBA) as well. The number of years of experience required varies with the organization. Generally, smaller or newer companies do not require as much experience as larger or more established ones. It helps, though, if your work experience is in the same industry you're applying to work in. For example, a medical center IT director should have experience in the healthcare field.

Quality Assurance Specialist

The nitty-gritty: No stone goes unturned here. This is a position for the detail-oriented worker with a discerning eye. You're responsible for making sure software products meet quality compliance regulations and standards through periodic reviews and testing. You may also be the conduit for customers complaining about problems.

Pay range: $36,302 to $82,233 annually for all fields of quality assurance, according to PayScale.

Qualifications: A bachelor's degree in business administration or industrial engineering can be a prerequisite, but requirements vary by company. Certification is often not required but can't hurt. The American Society for Quality offers credentials as a certified reliability engineer, certified quality engineer, and certified quality auditor.

Social Media Specialist

The nitty-gritty: This one's not for the Luddites in the crowd. Everyone from small-business owners to creative types realize they need a social media presence to increase their customer base. But not everyone has the knack or the time to smoothly navigate the sites. Managing social media is a huge time sapper, especially for neophytes. That's where you step in to build your client's professional brand by attracting followers on Twitter and fans on Facebook, then enticing them to click through to the company's website and, ultimately, become a customer. Some of the fun of managing an online brand—whether it is a person or a business—is choosing what content to feature on social media channels, including Facebook, Instagram, LinkedIn, Pinterest, Snapchat, and Twitter.

Duties may include keeping a site fresh by posting timely blogs or other news content that you ghostwrite or edit for your client. You'll chime in with online discussions and industry news as your boss's alter ego, retweet other people's posts that reflect positively on your client, and swat back spam when necessary. Most adults use social networking these days, according to research by the Pew Research Center, so little wonder that businesses of all sizes are waking up to the fact that they must attract new customers through social media. It's nonnegotiable.

Pay range: From $10.64 to $24.81 an hour, but depending on location and experience, this could jump, according to PayScale. The average per hour is $18.84, according to Indeed.com.

Qualifications: Expertise in tapping social networks and knowing how to use them is the heart of this job. This is a skill you learn by doing it day in and day out, so you can stay abreast of the ever-changing platforms. Most jobs are generated by word of mouth or referrals. But if you're a newly minted social media specialist running your own show, tap into your moxie and seek out a local small business in need of a social media presence. Initially, you might accept a few clients pro bono to get a referral list for paying customers. For an overview of the major social media sites and to learn the latest ways to use social media as a marketing tool, you might enroll in a community college social media certificate program.

Software Engineer

The nitty-gritty: Software engineers are the heart and soul of the tech world. You're the whizzes who code, design, and develop programs and applications, along with upgrades to make our tech-reliant world run effortlessly.

An uptick in the demand for computer software, and the need for new applications on mobile digital platforms such as tablets and cell phones, have spurred an increasing number of positions, according to the BLS. Cybersecurity is also a factor as security software plays a bigger role for corporations focused on protecting their computer networks.

Industries that employ software developers and engineers run the gamut from computer and electronic manufacturers to software publishers to finance and insurance firms.

Pay range: $51,630 to $180,480 annually, according to the BLS.

Qualifications: Experience in software development and engineering is a prerequisite. In general, a bachelor's degree is necessary, typically in computer science, software engineering, or mathematics. Software developers also should have a solid working knowledge of the industry in which they work. If you're shifting industries, you may need to retool to learn the essentials of another arena.

Technical Support Specialist

The nitty-gritty: Nerves of steel, a calm, reassuring voice, and tech smarts are must-haves for this troubleshooting position. Not everyone is hardwired to calm a frustrated client when a system crashes.

Employment of computer support specialists is projected to grow 12 percent from 2014 to 2024, according to the BLS. Help-desk technicians often work for support service firms that contract with clients that don't have the financial resources to afford their own IT departments. Lower-level tech support jobs can be found in call centers.

Pay range: $32,912 to $70,879 annually, according to PayScale. The highest-paid workers, however, earned more than $81,260, according to the BLS.

Qualifications: You may need certifications from a technical school or community college in specialties such as Cisco Networking and Microsoft Access. Employers often will provide on-the-job training about their specific product or service.

Something to keep in mind: For in-house positions, there may be some real-world heavy lifting—desktop computers and monitors can weigh up to 25 pounds.

Technical Writer

The nitty-gritty: Writers, get your typing fingers limbered up. If clearly explaining techie topics appeals to you, look no further. The rise of high-tech products in the home and the workplace, and the increasing complexity of medical and scientific information in daily living, arc creating many openings for technical writers. These gigs come in a variety of flavors—part time, telecommuting, and home-based projects—and run the gamut from writing how-to manuals to tutorials and frequently-asked-questions pages. You might also find yourself writing grant applications.

Pay ranges: The median technical writer annual salary is $54,027, with a range typically between $46,424 and $62,277, according to Salary.com.

Qualifications: You'll need top-drawer writing skills and a yen for technology and scientific subjects. The Society for Technical Communication and other associations offer certification for technical writers. The American Medical Writers Association offers extensive continuing education programs and certificates in medical writing. And some employers provide short-term on-the-job training.

Web Search Evaluator

The nitty-gritty: Skip the algorithms prowling beneath the cyber surface. Web-based companies and services need the human touch, too. Your job is to play the role of a typical user and rate the quality of the results of a posted internet query, helping clients improve the relevance of their search engine results and performance. This is generally an independent contract, part-time venture—plan on around

20 hours a week. Firms that hire evaluators include Appen, Leapforce, and Lionbridge.

Pay range: The average annual salary is $27,500, according to Glassdoor. Hourly pay typically runs $13.50 to $15, although you may be paid per task.

Qualifications: Before hiring, many companies will give you a basic course on their operations and then require you to pass a qualifying exam. You'll need a high-speed internet connection and a computer or mobile device such as an Android phone or iPhone.

Web Strategist

The nitty-gritty: A website is the public face of a firm and a prime marketing tool for most businesses these days. Potential customers want to be able to find a company on the internet and conduct business online—without ever picking up a phone. A savvy small-business operator will want to bring on board an expert who can pinpoint the best ways to leverage the Web and social media to grow the business.

That's where you come in. You may be hired to do one piece of a plan, but many start-ups need someone who can do it all. You may be a techie and create applications like a retail checkout tool or write software code. Your creative side may be called on to design the layout of the website and incorporate audio, graphics, and video. The job might entail monitoring website traffic, answering comments, updating content, and fixing broken links.

Pay range: Hourly pay for a web designer can range from $11.25 to $45.09, according to PayScale.com. Social media specialist might up to $36 per hour.

Qualifications: Graphic design experience and a computer degree. For design, you'll need expertise in the Adobe Creative Suite of design tools (Illustrator, InDesign, and Photoshop). For programming, experience coding in CSS, HTML, and JavaScript is important, as well as familiarity with content management systems (CMSs) such as Drupal, ExpressionEngine, and WordPress. If it's social media they're after, you must know how to use Facebook, LinkedIn, and Twitter to reach target markets, and you must be a good writer.

6

Great Jobs in Education

■ ■ ■

O pportunities for jobs in the education field cut a broad swath, from tutoring to substitute teaching to jobs a little further afield, such as conducting market research.

At the age of 10, Mary Jackson was teaching to imaginary students from the porch of her family's home in Easley, South Carolina. "I set up a chalkboard and held a yardstick, as I taught my students," she recalls. "I wanted to be a teacher."

So it was no surprise when she earned a teaching degree at the University of Virginia. For financial reasons, however, she opted to accept a job with IBM when she graduated rather than pursue a teaching career. She ultimately rose to the position of project management executive.

But things have a way of coming full circle. After three decades at IBM, she retired and returned to her love of teaching. At 53, she began teaching math and science to fifth graders at Lockheed Elementary in Marietta, Georgia.

IBM's Transition to Teaching program gave Jackson the boost she needed to make her shift to a second career as a teacher. While working full time, she spent two years studying to add courses to become recertified as a teacher. The program paid $15,000 of her expenses.

THINK is the slogan on posters scattered around her classroom, a slogan first used in 1911 by Thomas J. Watson, who eventually became chairman and CEO of IBM. "Listen, think, then speak, but think, think, think," Jackson says, is the core lesson she hopes her students carry with them.

Here are great jobs to consider for those who want to work in education.

Adult Education Teacher

The nitty-gritty: You'll rely on your communication skills and steady patience to make the most of this position. As an adult literacy or high school equivalency diploma teacher, for example, you'll work with students of all ages from different cultural, economic, and educational backgrounds as they learn English as a second language or earn their diploma. If you have a passion for teaching, it can be pure magic. The main reasons behind the rising need for this educational niche: continued immigration to the United States, and an aging population increasingly seeking out encore and second careers and turning to adult education programs to make the transition.

Pay range: The median hourly wage for an adult education teacher is $22, as of January 30, 2017, according to Salary .com, with a range usually between $18 and $29, although this can vary widely depending on a variety of factors.

Qualifications: Most states require adult literacy and high school equivalency diploma teachers to have at least a bachelor's degree. Although a bachelor's degree in any field is acceptable, some employers, such as community colleges, have a preference for hiring teachers with a master's degree or graduate coursework in adult education or English as a second language (ESL). Some states also require adult literacy and high school equivalency diploma teachers to have a teaching certificate to work in government-run programs; others require certificates specifically for adult education. For more information, contact your state's director of adult education from a list compiled by the U.S. Department of Education.

Meet an ESL Teacher

James S. Kunen, 68, teaches English as a second language at the Center for Immigrant Education and Training at LaGuardia Community College in Queens. When he was let go as the director of corporate communications at Time Warner during a round of layoffs, Kunen confronted the core question: What is it he could do?

Where did his skills translate to a job, one that made him feel some sense of purpose? And who would hire him, given his age? He enrolled in a 160-hour course to earn a certificate to teach English as a second language for adults. Today, he spends 16 hours a week in the classroom teaching two courses. "At this age and stage of my life, working with highly motivated immigrants gives me a sense of purpose and engagement with the world," he says. "Going to work is spending time with friends. I feel appreciated." The linchpin: "It also gives me an income that makes a significant difference when added to my pension and Social Security."

Adjunct Professor/Instructor/Lecturer/Visiting Professor

The nitty-gritty: Still have a hankering for a classroom? Community colleges in your area can send you back to the front of the class with a short- or long-term commitment. You'll have an opportunity to teach a range of students, from recent high school grads to career transitioning adults adding new skills or updating old ones. Part-time faculty comes in under various monikers—adjunct professor, instructor, lecturer, and visiting professor. Technical schools also may have openings.

Most community colleges have online applications. Stop by the registrar's office or go online to obtain the current course listings from the place where you'd like to teach. Do some sleuthing to discover what courses are missing in your field of expertise. Ask around to see if you know anyone in your professional network who might be teaching in the evenings and see if they can make an introduction for you. It might take some time to find the right course for you to teach.

If you're tech savvy and at ease teaching a class via a computer webcam, a growing number of community colleges now offer online courses for their students. To learn more about community colleges, go to the American Association of Community Colleges website.

The hours vary widely depending on the number of courses you teach. Summer courses are common. Night and weekend classes are standard. Figure on one to two hours of classroom time per week for each course, plus your lesson preparation and grading time, for a total of, say, five hours a week.

Pay range: $12,349 to $69,534 annually according to PayScale .com. The pay pops up, however, depending on your degree level, teaching experience, the department, and number of credits the course offers.

Qualifications: A master's degree within your discipline is usually preferred, but depending on your experience and the course, it's possible to land a post with a bachelor's degree. Of course, you'll need to be an expert in the subject area. You'll need to provide teaching references and probably perform a tryout session to demonstrate your teaching skills. Generally speaking, technical schools hire with only a bachelor's degree. As with most teaching gigs, expertise, passion for the subject, and experience trump all else.

Job hunting tips: Stop by the college where you might like to teach and meet the head of the department where your expertise falls. Find out what might be missing from their offerings and if there might be any openings. Look for job listings on HigherEdJobs.com. The professor is in.

Career Center Counselor

The nitty-gritty: This one's for your inner mentor. Career centers tend to need staff during the busy fall and spring semesters. Think of yourself as a matchmaker: You put students and employers together with something they love through networking, suggestions, employer interviews, internships, and more.

You'll probably find yourself the interpreter of a battery of vocational assessment tests. You hone resume and cover letters with smooth wordsmithing. You dole out dress-for-success and etiquette advice for interviews. You rehearse your charges with mock interviews. And chances are you'll be called to develop and present career education workshops for small groups and help run career fairs. In recent years, boomer alumni have been reaching out to their alma maters' centers for career transition assistance as well, so your pool of clients can cover a wider range of ages, challenges, and needs.

Pay range: $33,789—$75,025 per year, according to PayScale. com; $14.67—$49.07 per hour.

Qualifications: Familiarity with national career trends and labor markets. Experience in general counseling, career counseling, human resources, and education or career development.

The International Coach Federation (coachfederation. org) has a list of certification programs and offers its own certification. Recognition as a National Certified Counselor or licensing as a professional counselor is sometimes preferred. Some employers might require a master's degree in counseling or higher education.

Need more information on counseling? The Bureau of Labor Statistics *Occupational Outlook Handbook* suggests the American Counseling Association, the National Board for Certified Counselors (nbcc.org), and the National Career Development Association (ncda.org).

Librarian Assistant/Aide

The nitty-gritty: Duties might include fielding questions, shelving books, helping patrons check out, tracking overdue material, and sending notices, as well as cataloging and keeping an eye out for lost and damaged items.

Schedules vary widely. Big libraries, or those on university campuses, tend to keep the doors open 24 hours a day, while small, local libraries might offer limited day and evening hours.

Pay range: Small libraries can be cash-strapped and rely on volunteers, but at colleges, large city locations, and specialty niche libraries, pay generally ranges from $9.04 to $18.21 per hour, according to PayScale.com. Those figures can more than double, depending on experience and where you live.

Qualifications: Experience working in libraries is desirable, as is an undergraduate or master's degree in library science. Larger libraries favor research skills using library resources, databases, and other tools, along with the ability to get along with the various denizens of the library. Some skills that will help: knowledge of word processing, data entry, and online searching; ability to keep accurate records; understanding of library operations; and general secretarial skills. Love of books is a given.

Market and Survey Researchers

The nitty-gritty: Combining research and people skills makes these jobs appealing to those who have mastered academic life. In general, if you're a newcomer, you're often on the front lines conducting surveys of customers—either on the phone, online, through questionnaires via mail, or door to door. You might even find yourself working a shopping mall booth to help get the "man or woman on the street" snapshot of consumer preferences. Typically, you'll be asked to write a detailed report and provide an analysis of your findings. In some instances, you're sizing up potential sales of a product or service. Other times you're pulling together statistical data on competitors, prices, and more.

The list of potential employers runs the gamut from consumer products firms to university research centers to financial services organizations, government agencies, healthcare institutions, and advertising firms. You'll need to be a stickler for details, since this kind of work tends to rely on precise data reviews. For information about careers and salaries in market and survey research, contact the Council of American Survey Research Organizations and the Marketing Research Association. The hours: Flexible, project-based, full time for short assignments.

Pay range: Market research analysts in the United States take home approximately $51,000 annually on average, according to PayScale.com. Overall cash earnings for market research analysts stretch from $36,000 on the lower end to $75,000 near the top, and the heftiest packages can encompass around $8,000 from bonuses and $10,000 from profit sharing.

Qualifications: A bachelor's degree is the baseline. A background in liberal arts and social science courses—including economics, psychology, and sociology—is helpful. A master's or doctoral degree may be required, especially for more analytical positions. Quantitative skills are important for some survey research positions, so courses in mathematics, statistics, sampling theory and survey design, and computer science are helpful. An advanced degree in business administration, marketing, statistics, and communications may give you an edge. Having some training in survey research methodology can help you get a foot in the door. Curiosity doesn't kill the cat—it gets it work.

Job hunting tips: Check out the human resources section at university and college websites for job postings.

Substitute Teacher

The nitty-gritty: Stepping out of full-time teaching but keeping a toe dipped in has long been a way for retired teachers to stay engaged and supplement income. Subbing can take on a fairly regular schedule, but it's your prerogative to just say no when the request comes in. The life of a sub can have its challenges. Picking up a course midstream takes some fancy footwork, memorizing two dozen students' names in a blink of an eye can be daunting, and quickly gaining the respect of students trying to test you takes some special mojo. Some teachers will leave a prepared class plan. But if you are filling in at the last minute, you may be in improve-mode to keep the class on track.

Depending on your background, you may be tapped to teach a range of subjects in grade levels from kindergarten through 12th grade. If you have a proclivity for special-needs kids, you may find your services in demand. Never forget that flexibility is your calling card. School districts typically keep an active roster of substitutes on call who are willing to drop everything and step into a classroom with little advance notice. The hours: Flexible half-days to several-week stints for the entire school day.

Pay range: Each school district sets its own pay scale for substitute teachers. Currently, the pay rate for per diem (day-to-day) substitutes is $20 to $190 per full day with half days being half the rate of a full day, according to the National Substitute Teachers Alliance. Generally, the pay will match the length of the assignment and the area's cost of living. Some subs may get benefits.

Qualifications: A minimum of a high school diploma is needed, but a person substituting for more than 19 days needs a teaching certificate. Most substitute teaching jobs require a bachelor's degree from an accredited college or university. The National Education Association's State-by-State Summary provides the minimum requirements. Your state's department of education has the details. Learn about the full requirements for substitute teachers in each state at NEA.org. There are often fewer requirements at private schools. You should expect a background check.

Teacher's Aide

The nitty-gritty: Kid central. This position can take nerves of steel and patience, but the rewards are plentiful. It can be frustrating for some aides to have to defer to the guidance of the teacher in charge, so you need to have a good rapport and working relationship. The teacher needs to respect and value what you bring to the classroom. If not, it's a bust. Be prepared for some grunt work—clerical duties such as grading papers, recording grades, setting up equipment, and entering computer data.

One of the best aspects is one-on-one tutoring for a student who needs special help, or has a disability that requires individual attention. These are bonding moments of giving back that are worth more than a paycheck. While some of the school day is spent standing, walking, or kneeling, the lion's share is sitting while working with students. Teacher's assistants also supervise students in the cafeteria, schoolyard, and hallways, or on field trips. About 37 percent work part time.

The hours are generally three to five days a week, six to seven hours per day during the traditional school year (eight to nine months). Summer school hours may be available in some districts.

Pay range: $8.46 to $15.38 per hour, according to PayScale.com.

Qualifications: You'll need a high school diploma, and some states or school districts may require additional education beyond high school. A college degree, related coursework in child development, and previous experience helping special education students can open up job opportunities. Self-starters who can multitask and work independently are highly valued.

Fluency in a second language, especially Spanish, is in demand. Many schools require previous experience in working with children and a valid driver's license. Most require you to pass a background check. For more information, go to American Federation of Teachers, National Education Association, and National Resource Center for Paraprofessionals. The promise: Gold stars.

Tutor/Counselor

The nitty-gritty: If teaching experience is in your bag of tricks, then you'll find plenty of opportunities in working as a private tutor throughout the year, although opportunities ramp up at the fall opening of school and before major tests. Some prep firms hire tutors to help teens and adults with standardized tests and professional certification exams. The firms provide tools and training materials. Fall and spring are the top seasons for college-bound kids to take the SAT and ACT aptitude tests. A demand also exists for ongoing private tutoring in a range of subjects to boost student grades.

Tutoring sessions can last anywhere from an hour after school to three hours on weekends. Private sessions can take place at your place, theirs, the library, or online. Plan to work at least four hours a week.

A variation of this tutoring role is someone who works as an independent college counselor or consultant for students preparing for college admissions. An increasing number of families are looking for consultants to help their children navigate through the college choice and application process. You work with high school students starting in their junior year to prepare essays and correct grammar, keep them on track for deadlines, help with choosing where to apply and perhaps delving into financial aid options. This role can be critical in helping applicants get a handle on what kind of college or university will be a good fit for them and also help them hone in on an area of study they want to pursue. Educating about the college process is an essential role for students and parents on this path and an outsider can often provide the perspective necessary to make good choices.

Pay range: $10.27 to $24.21 generally, but landing rates higher than $65 and up an hour isn't unusual, if you have expertise. Some consultants offer comprehensive packages, for a multiyear bundle of services, of about $4,500, according to the Independent Educational Consultants Association; others bill at rates of around $150 an hour.

Qualifications: A background in education and working with students in a classroom is generally a prerequisite. A certified teacher is preferred. That said, professional experience can open doors. There is no certification to be a private tutor. Experts in a range of fields from nursing to finance to law and business may find opportunities, as can those with foreign language skills. If you're interested in becoming a college admissions counselor, you can learn more about how to prepare from the Independent Educational Consultants Association (IECAonline.com) and Higher Educational Consultants Association (HECAonline.com).

Job hunting tips: You might get your foot in the door by volunteering at a local library. Create a "Tutor" business card and drop it off at nearby school counseling offices to let them know you are available. You might want to post a classified ad in a community newspaper, supermarket jobs board, or online news board. No chalkboard needed.

Meet a College Admission Counselor

Doretta Massardo McGinnis, 53, is a sought-after private admissions counselor in Gladwyne, Pennsylvania. In 2015, after 18 years as a law professor at Widener University Delaware Law School, she became an independent educational consultant, providing private college and pre-law counseling in the Philadelphia area when she cofounded a company called Admission Logic, LLC (admission-logic.com).

A faculty buyout program offered to all law faculty spurred her exit from academia. McGinnis decided to use it as a time to redirect to something new. "I was looking for something that would build on my skills and the things I enjoyed about my teaching job," she says.

"My work today has the counseling component, as I had with my law students," she says. "And the feedback and guidance on the essays is very close to what I did teaching legal writing in terms of improvement in organization, clarity, and style—elements of writing as critical to college essays as to legal memoranda."

With an in-demand private practice, she also carves out time for the nonprofit organization Strive for College (striveforcollege.org), a free online community where aspiring college students from low-income families can connect with mentors. "I'm strongly committed to working with college applicants who may be the first generation in their family to go to college," says McGinnis. "It's personal for me. My mother did not attend college. My father was a first-gen student. The son of Italian immigrants who dreamed of becoming an engineer, he went to school at night for his BS and MS in mechanical engineering."

McGinnis spends about an hour a week mentoring each of her five mentees, depending on their needs. "They may be unaware of the range of colleges and the availability of financial aid," she says. "I also provide feedback on their essays, assisting them in finding their voice, choosing a good topic, and telling the most compelling story they can."

Her reward: "I love seeing students take another step toward their dream and exposing them to options they might not have been aware of," says McGinnis.

In other words, it feels good.

University Bookstore Retail Specialist

The nitty-gritty: Bookworms, take note. This job requires more than a passion for reading. You've got to be a cool and organized person to take charge in this venue. The campus bookstore is a central hub of campus life. There are all those textbooks to sell. And visitors stop in to purchase a T-shirt or pair of socks with the school's logo; on home game football weekends in the fall, homecoming weekend, or alumni reunions, the store can be a madhouse. You'll be directing shoppers and stocking the sales floor. Some lifting is involved. It's likely you'll be ordering merchandise, too, and at peak hours putting in time at the cash register. Be prepared to be on your feet for long periods.

Pay range: $9 to $19 per hour, according to PayScale.com. It is possible to find positions over $20 an hour.

Qualifications: Basic computer skills and retail experience. Customer service skills, knowledge of merchandising, and ability to multitask.

7

Great Skilled Trade Jobs

■ ■ ■

It took six years, but Charlene DeWindt of Newport News, Virginia, became an electrician at the age of 58. She's also a production planner and scheduler at Huntington Ingalls Industries (the largest military shipbuilding company in the United States), earning more than $50,000 a year. DeWindt honed her trade at the firm's Newport News Shipbuilding Apprentice School and, in August 2016, graduated with an associate's degree in business. That's when she completed the school's Production Planning Program. Even better, throughout her coursework, she continued working for the company.

DeWindt calls the apprentice program a life-changer for her. "I had been out of school for 40 years and suddenly there's algebra, calculus, physics I and II," DeWindt told me when I interviewed her for my column that runs on PBS NextAvenue.org and in *Forbes*. "But I was persistent, and now I have a great job, benefits, and a chance to excel." And, she adds, "This program has allowed me the opportunity to learn so much, keep my brain and body active, and save more for retirement."

You might be thinking: Aren't apprentice programs just for recent high school grads and people in their 20s? As Nobel laureate Bob Dylan would say: "The times they are a changin'."

I learned about that age-friendly apprentice program in the new report from AARP Public Policy Institute, "Disrupting Aging in the Workplace: Profiles in Intergenerational Diversity Leadership." The report looked at five employers that are wisely approaching the issue of age diversity in the workplace: DeWindt's employer Huntington Ingalls Industries as well as AT&T; Centrica PLC, parent company of British Gas, an energy and services corporation; PNC Financial Services; and UnitedHealth Group.

Let's start with DeWindt's apprentice program. Of Newport News Shipbuilding's 21,000 employees, about 2,900 are Apprentice School alumni. Many of them are now in leadership positions at the company.

Sixty years ago, the program's age limit was 21. "I actually applied when I was 28, but I was too old," says DeWindt.

Over time, the age ceiling was raised, and in 1996, ultimately eliminated as a result of the Equal Employment Opportunity Commission's determination that apprenticeship programs should be subject to the requirements of the Age Discrimination Employment Act.

The Bureau of Labor projects considerable job growth in skilled labor professions, including brick masons, block masons, stonemasons, tile and marble setters (and their helpers), and electricians. Employers are currently having the most trouble filling openings in these and other skilled trades.

Find Your Niche

It's possible to hang out your own shingle and redeploy, as I like to say, your talents into work you are passionate about.

Consider this second-act motorcycle mechanic. Joe Anania, now 59, laughs at his favorite childhood memories: being a teenager and ripping through an open field on his dirt bike.

"Motorcycles have always been part of who I am," he says. "I grew up racing motorcycles, competing in motocross, and, as I kid, when something broke, I taught myself how to fix it," he says. "If you have a passion for it, you'll learn it."

He gets that same thrill all these years later—both riding and fixing the two-wheelers, but the bikes are a little bigger and classier. His current favorite: a 1985 Kawasaki 125.

Best of all, Anania owns and operates his own business, Joe's V Cycle, repairing and restoring vintage motorcycles in South St. Paul, Minnesota. "I can complete any job from a minor motorcycle tune-up to a complete restoration," he says.

This is a second career for Anania and a coming home at the same time. In the mid-70s, while he lived and breathed motorcycles, working seasonally at a Kawasaki dealership in his hometown of Pittsburgh, Pennsylvania, he needed to earn a steady income. "One day, a guy I knew asked me if I ever thought of aviation tech and working on aircraft," Anania recalls. "Never, I said, you have to be a smart person to do that. I'm just a motorcycle mechanic. But bing, bang, bong, I enrolled in aviation school."

He earned an associate's degree in aviation technology, along with both airframe and power plant certificates, and shifted his talent for mechanics to a different arena. After graduation, he spent the next three years with Pratt & Whitney's Aircraft Research & Development Center in Palm Beach, Florida, building prototype fighter engines. Afterward, he moved over to working for the airlines.

For decades, Anania was a mechanic for several airlines. But for the bulk of those years, 21 in fact, he was employed by Northwest Airlines as a lead aircraft technician maintaining Airbus, Boeing, and McDonnell Douglas commercial jets, working out of the hangar at Minneapolis–Saint Paul International Airport.

That was until his Northwest Airlines mechanic colleagues went on strike in 2005, and he joined them. To bring in some money while waiting out the strike, he looked to his motorcycle hobby and started repairing motorcycles in the garage of his home. "I bought some equipment, and I met a guy in the antique motorcycle club, who sent some repairs my way," says Anania. "I thought maybe I can do this again. I can fix old bikes regular shops can't handle. I even make my own tools."

When the strike ended several months later, Anania decided he didn't want to go back to the airline. "I loved fixing airplanes and was proud of working for Northwest, but the strike took the fun out of it," he says. He was given the choice of going back or taking early retirement. "I had enough years in, so I decided to stick with the motorcycles."

The bikes kept rolling in. Although he has advertised on Craigslist, most of his customers heard about him by word of mouth. "It has taken a few years, but it has worked out well," he says. "I usually have more work than I can handle—around 20 to 30 vintage bikes at a time. I have a loyal clientele. And customers come in from hundreds of miles away."

Start-up capital: An estimated $1,000, but Anania has spent roughly $15,000 over 10 years to buy new equipment a little at a time. "Every year,

I make sure to invest some money to buy a piece of equipment. I never had to borrow or dig into savings," he says. "I'm quite frugal, and I don't throw money around. Three-quarters of the equipment that other repair shops buy, I've made myself for pennies on the dollar. I see that I can use this, this, and that, and I weld the part."

Lesson learned: Test it out first. "I was in limbo after the strike," says Anania. "I could go one way or the other, but I had a safety net there. I was able to do it for long enough to realize that I really enjoyed it, and I could make it work financially. I probably wouldn't have started this business if I had to jump right into it to make ends meet."

Biggest challenge: Pay attention to the numbers. "For me, the biggest challenge is all the bookkeeping," he says. "There's always paperwork to do, the billing, paying invoices, banking, taxes. I've had different accountants, but I'm always confused. It's amazing how much time it consumes."

The second hurdle—loneliness. "I began to miss my colleagues and having people around," says Anania. "I was working by myself all day long. I could hear the clock ticking. The work became isolating. I had to learn to deal with that and accept it."

Biggest reward: Sole responsibility. "It motivates me to work when I know it's up to me to make or break it," he says. "It's satisfying that you can survive on your own talents."

Advice for others: You can't cut corners. "If you aren't good at what you do, you're not going to survive," says Anania. "There are too many other people out there in the repair business. And you can't rip people off. With all the social media out there, word gets around. And remember, there is [a] difference between passion and a business. With a business, you can't get away for a weekend the way you can if it's your passion as a hobby."

Employees: "Just myself," he says. "My dog, Ginger, is my assistant. She likes to move the parts to places I can't find them, and when I take a break, she rides along with me on the motorcycle."

Commitment and payoff: "I make a living off of it, but it's not quite as much as I made as an aviation mechanic," Anania says. "This is life in the fourth quarter. I want to enjoy what I have, so I back off sometimes now. I'm able to take as much work as I want. I used to work seven days a week, 10 to 12 hours a day. I loved it. But I realized that money is not everything.

"I do add to my 401(k) every year, and I buy vintage motorcycles for myself that I restore. I have a collection of about 25 at the moment, including a 1953 BSA 500 custom café racer; each are worth thousands of dollars. I figure they're another piece of my retirement savings and far more fun than my 401(k)."

Here are some great jobs to consider.

Auto Mechanic

The nitty-gritty: This job is best for problem solvers with a persistent nature. Service technicians and mechanics typically identify problems, often by using computerized diagnostic equipment. They test parts and systems to confirm that they work properly, and perform basic care and maintenance, including changing oil, checking fluid levels, and rotating tires. And of course, there's the responsibility for repairing or replacing worn parts, such as brake pads, wheel bearings, and sensors. A tricky part of the job is actually explaining the problems and repairs to clients in language they can understand.

"The number of vehicles in use continues to rise, and more entry-level service technicians will be needed to perform basic maintenance and repair, such as replacing brake pads and changing oil," according to the Bureau of Labor Statistics. Many job openings will be in automobile dealerships and independent repair shops, where most service technicians currently work.

Pay Range: The median annual automotive mechanic salary is $37,335, as of August 03, 2017, with a range usually between $32,792–$43,040, however this can vary widely depending on a variety of factors, according to Salary.com. The median hourly wage is $18, with a range usually between $16 and $21.

Qualifications: Job opportunities for qualified applicants should be very good, whether you obtained your knowledge through education or experience. That said, those who complete formal postsecondary training programs or achieved Automotive Service Excellence (ASE) certification should enjoy the best job prospects. Programs usually last six months to a year and provide intensive career preparation through classroom instruction and hands-on practice. Short-term certificate programs in a particular subject, such as brake maintenance or engine performance, are also available.

Some service technicians get an associate's degree. Courses usually include mathematics, electronics, and automotive repair. It's also possible to land a job with a dealer that offers programs where you can earn an associate's degree. Students in these programs typically spend alternating periods attending classes full time and working full time in service shops under the guidance of an experienced technician.

Certification from the National Institute for Automotive Service Excellence (ASE.com) is the standard credential for service technicians. Certification demonstrates competence and usually brings higher pay, according to the BLS. Many employers require their service technicians to become certified.

ASE certification is available in nine different automobile specialty areas: automatic transmission/transaxle, brakes, light vehicle diesel engines, electrical/electronic systems, engine performance, engine repair, heating and air conditioning, manual drive train and axles, and suspension and steering.

Baker

The nitty-gritty: There's nothing quite like the wafting aroma of bread baking or the sweet pleasures of whipping up a batch of chewy chocolate chip cookies. If you can take the heat, get in the kitchen. Look for bakery jobs at local bakeries, schools, cafeterias, hotel restaurants, and in the bakery sections at grocery stores and chains such as Dunkin' Donuts and Panera Bread.

Baking chores are typically done at night or in the predawn hours so the goods are fresh at the start of the business day. Tasks can be routine. You measure, mix, mold, shape, and bake ingredients adhering strictly to recipes. The bigger the facility and larger the quantities needed, the more standardized the work will be. Kitchens can be hot and noisy. Plan on bending, stooping to grasp goods, and climbing ladders, as well as lifting or pushing and pulling carts with 75- to 150-pound loads of ingredients. You also have to be good with the old kitchen timer—no burned bagels, please. The hours: generally after midnight to early morning. Full shifts may run from 10 pm to 6 am for a bakery with a morning clientele.

Pay range: $8.75 to $15.41 per hour. Full-time bakers employed by large grocery store or restaurant and hotel chains generally receive benefits, such as paid vacation days and health and dental insurance.

Qualifications: The hop from home baker to professional takes practice. Your best bet is to find an apprenticeship or trainee position at an established bakery, or even offer to moonlight for free. You'll learn how to run a range of equipment used in the production process, and be sure your basic math skills—for calculating ingredient quantities—are up to snuff. If you have time to plan your path into late-night baking, consider scoring a certification through the Retail Bakers of America (retailbakersofamerica.com). RBA offers certification for four levels of competence from $50 to $750 for members. The American Institute of Baking (AIBonline.org) offers online seminars covering baking fundamentals from cake baking to muffin making and more.

Community colleges near you may offer one-year baking and pastry arts degrees or certificate programs that can be completed part time for around $5,000 and are great launching pads for job placement. Grab your spatulas!

Casino Worker

The nitty-gritty: Given the 24-hour, nonstop action at venues spanning the spectrum from flashy big-name mega-casinos like Harrah's and MGM Grand to riverboats and "racinos" at racetracks, the need for workers who like the night life is unending. Typical positions include card dealer, ticket writer, pit boss, security guard, and valet. The upside: an energizing workplace with nonstop action.

It's not all bright lights, though. Jobs that require you to work the casino floor front and center can be high pressure and fast paced. You've got to turn on the megawatt charm and stay calm when the clientele get unruly. The work can be demanding physically, too, particularly if you're standing for long stretches or pacing the spread-out gaming floor. The noise from clanging slot machines and keyed-up patrons can be rough on the nerves. There's also the silent stress of being watched by supervisors and security cameras to make sure you're doing the job right. Big Brother or Sister really is watching. One more potential drawback: Many casino floors still allow smoking, including at table games. The hours are flexible, from part time to full time to seasonal. Eight-hour shifts are the norm, but partial weeks or weekend evenings and nights are often available.

Pay range: Wages range from $7.25 an hour to $30.30 for dealers, according to Indeed.com. The average casino dealer salary in the United States is approximately $38,879, but can top $60,000 at some casinos. Slot positions that require verifying and paying off jackpots and resetting slot machines after payoffs range from $11.87 to $21.78 per hour, according to PayScale.com; total annual pay can hit around $50,000. Security positions range from $38,781 to $112,783. Many jobs, such as valet and wait staff, are lower wage, and income is dependent on tips.

Qualifications: All gaming service workers must obtain a license from a regulatory agency, such as a state casino control board or commission. Applicants for a license must provide photo identification and pay a fee. Some states may require gaming service workers to be residents of that state. The licensing application process includes a background investigation and drug test.

Some of the major casinos and slot machine manufacturers run their own training schools, which last anywhere from four to 12 weeks. Almost all provide some form of in-house, on-the-job training. Most casinos also require prospective dealers to audition for open positions. Prior work experience in a hospitality-related field and strong customer service skills can help. The American Gaming Association is a good resource to learn more about the industry.

Job hunting tips: Your best approach may be to go straight to the source and log on to the career or employment pages of casino websites, including headliners like Caesars Entertainment or a local establishment in your town, and browse the latest job postings. If you thrive on never having a dull moment, roll the dice.

Electrician

The nitty-gritty: From discerning the nuances to blueprints to installing wiring, and inspecting transformers and circuit breakers, this is another puzzle-solving position with plenty of specialty niches within the profession. You're typically called on to diagnose electrical problems, then repair or replace wiring, equipment, or fixtures using hand and power tools. But new construction or remodeling projects demand new circuits and wiring to be installed. There are plenty of state and local building regulations that must be adhered to. Many electricians work solo, but there are positions with contractors, and construction/manufacturing companies that can place you on a crew.

Pay range: An average of $20.57 per hour, according to PayScale. The range is $13.43 to $34.34 with overtime pay easily topping $52 per hour. Electricians can earn annual income ranging from $29,000 to $81,000, depending on bonuses, profit sharing, and commissions. The most important factor affecting compensation for this group is the specific employer, followed by geography and tenure.

Qualifications: Electricians often attend a technical school or learn their trade in an apprenticeship program. For each year of the program, apprentices must complete at least 144 hours of technical training and 2,000 hours of paid on-the-job training, according to the *Occupational Outlook Handbook*. In the classroom, apprentices learn electrical theory, blueprint reading, mathematics, electrical code requirements, and safety and first-aid practices. They also may receive specific training related to soldering, communications, fire alarm systems, and elevators.

Unions and contractor associations typically sponsor apprenticeship programs. Many apprenticeship programs also have preferred entry for veterans. The Home Builders Institute offers a pre-apprenticeship certificate training (PACT) program for eight construction trades, including electricians.

Most states require electricians to pass a test and be licensed. Requirements, however, vary by state. For more information, contact your local or state electrical licensing board.

Many of the requirements can be found on the National Electrical Contractors Association's website (necanet.org).

Flooring Installer and Tile and Marble Setter

The nitty-gritty: This can be physically demanding work, and takes a real craftsperson who can work with precision and patience. Overall job prospects in these trades can rise and fall with the well-being of the economy. As boomers prepare homes for aging in place, or give homes a facelift to ready for a sale as they downsize, demand can be robust. Any uptick in new building construction also ramps up demand. Jobs can take place in homes, offices, restaurants, and retail stores, among other locales. Basic duties involve removing existing flooring or wall covering and tiles. You might replace countertops, backsplashes, and shower tiles. If you're working in flooring, expect to sand, clean, and level the surface to be covered. These jobs require accurate measuring and fitting the new materials, applying stains and finishes to floors. In commercial settings, installers may work evenings and weekends, often for higher wages, to avoid disturbing regular business operations, according to BLS's *Occupational Outlook Handbook.*

Pay range: The median annual wage for flooring installers and tile and marble setters is around $40,000, according to the most recent BLS data. The lowest 10 percent earned less than $22,310, and the highest 10 percent earned more than $72,530.

Qualifications: Most contractors have their own training programs for flooring installers and tile and marble setters. New workers typically learn by working with experienced installers. Although workers may enter training directly, many start out as helpers.

Unions and contractor associations often sponsor apprenticeship programs. Some flooring manufacturers offer product-specific training for their products.

The Ceramic Tile Education Foundation (CTEF) offers the Certified Tile Installer (CTI) certification for workers with two or more years of experience. Applicants are required to complete a written test and a hands-on performance evaluation.

The International Masonry Institute (IMI), the International Union of Bricklayers & Allied Craftworkers (IUBAC), the National Tile Contractors Association (NTCA), the Tile Contractors' Association of America (TCAA), and the Tile Council of North America (TCNA) offer Advanced Certifications for Tile Installers (ACT) programs. Certification requirements include passing both an exam and a field test. The National Wood Flooring Association (NWFA) has a voluntary certification for floor sanders and finishers. Sanders and finishers must have two years of experience and must have completed NWFA-approved training. Applicants are also required to complete written and performance tests.

CHAPTER

8

Great Jobs to Ride the Age Wave

■ ■ ■

As the 50+ population explodes, so does the number of jobs that serve those in that demographic, from fitness experts and retirement coaches to home health aides and geriatric nurses.

By 2060, according to U.S. Census Bureau projections, about one in four Americans will be over age 65, up from 14.5 percent of the U.S. population in 2014. And the number of those 85 and older is expected to more than double.

This demographic shift is already creating a wave of new fields and opportunities for workers of all ages. It's just a tease of what's to come. To get in, though, you might need to bolster your resume with new skills, preferably added while continuing to work full time in your first career.

True, some of the positions do require a degree, say, an associate of applied sciences degree in gerontology. Employers and clients in many arenas, however, are increasingly accepting professional certifications, which are faster and cheaper.

Where are these jobs? There's high demand for healthcare workers across a wide gamut, despite the tight job market. The number of health-related jobs in hospitals, clinics, nursing and residential care facilities, and home-centered services is growing. Projections from the U.S. Bureau of Labor Statistics (BLS) *Occupational Outlook Handbook* forecast employment of healthcare occupations to grow 19 percent from 2014 to 2024, much faster than the average for all occupations, adding about 2.3 million new jobs. This growth is expected largely due to an aging population. The handbook lists a variety of home and personal care jobs in healthcare as fast-growing occupations.

There are hundreds of areas of specialization, such as music therapists for Alzheimer's patients and occupational therapists for the elderly. (When my friend Carol visited her Uncle Bob in a New Jersey assisted-living home, an instructor was leading a tap dance class to the tune of "Stayin' Alive.") Other positions include registered nurses, mental health counselors, social workers, physical therapists, physician assistants, dental hygienists, fitness trainers, and nutritionists. A helpful website is the Health Professions Network (hpnonline.org), which features different allied health professions.

But healthcare isn't the only area. "As tens of millions of people live into their 80s and 90s, we'll need millions of others in their 50s and 60s and 70s to help care for them—not just within families, but through second careers," says Marc Freedman of Encore.org and author of *The Big Shift: Navigating the New Stage Beyond Midlife.* "They'll be able to fill millions of positions—as nurses, home health aides, health navigators, and roles we've yet to even define."

Open your mind and consider the possibilities.

Here are some jobs that benefit from an aging population. Some of these jobs were also discussed in earlier chapters, but I've pulled them all together here. Many of these do require additional schooling or certification; some require physical strength. Look through to see what best suits you.

Aging-in-Place/Home-Modification Pro

The nitty-gritty: Your specialty is to create or rehab a home that will serve long term for people who want to age in place. A variety of experts can get into the act, from contractors to architects and interior designers. The key is to figure ways to creatively convert or adapt homes with lighting, ramps, grab bars in the shower, and more to stave off accidents.

Pay range: $40 per hour and up.

Qualifications: The National Association of Home Builders offers a course that teaches design and building techniques for making a home accessible to all ages.

Audiologist

The nitty-gritty: Hearing loss and aging can go hand in hand. You'll examine, diagnose, and treat individuals for symptoms of hearing loss and other auditory, balance, and neural problems. Most of these positions (about 64%), are in healthcare facilities. The hours can be flexible and part to full time.

Pay range: $65,694 to $91,032, according to Salary.com.

Qualifications: You will need a doctor of audiology degree. Career information and information on state licensure is available from the American Speech-Language-Hearing Association (asha.org) and the Audiology Foundation of America (audfound.org).

Driver

The nitty-gritty: Think of the movie *Driving Miss Daisy*. There is a growing need for drivers to transport elderly clients who can no longer safely drive to appointments, airports, activities, and longer road trips. College campuses, too, need people to drive shuttle buses and vans (see Chapter 1, page 59).

Pay range: From $8 per hour to more than $20, plus car expenses if you use your own wheels. Those figures vary widely depending on experience, where you live, the number of hours worked, and customer tips.

Qualifications: A safe driving record is a prerequisite. Background checks are standard. You might be asked to undergo a drug screening as well. You'll need sharp eyes and ears, too.

Financial Planner

The nitty-gritty: Are you good with numbers and sharp when it comes to money matters?

There is a huge demand for experts who can help older people manage their money. It's not unusual for people as they age to start struggling with managing investments and even paying bills in a timely fashion.

A good planner can devise an overall financial plan that will recommend how to allocate assets and determine if someone has the right blend to meet his or her specific goals.

What's more, a planner advises on how to draw down funds from accounts when needed and handle estate-planning and tax matters. It's a trust relationship, so it can take some building and slow steps. There are also money management jobs that aren't as full blown as a planner. Consider starting a job-paying or budgeting service that helps folks track their monthly inflow and outflow and make sure payments are met on time.

Pay range: $120 to $300 per hour, or a percentage of assets under management, generally 1 percent to 3 percent. $10 to $50 an hour for daily and monthly bill and budget aides.

Qualifications: There are myriad designations, from certified financial planner to fee-only planner. As a rule, an adviser should have the Certified Financial Planner (CFP) designation awarded by the nonprofit Certified Financial Planner Board of Standards, Inc. Anyone can call themselves a financial planner or adviser. No minimum experience or education is required by law.

But don't fall into that trap. This job is too important. Nearly half of all investor complaints submitted to state securities agencies came from seniors, according to a recent survey by the North American Securities Administrators Association. As a result, the association is aggressively cracking down on unscrupulous brokers and others using titles like "certified senior specialist."

To learn more about the training necessary, visit the Certified Financial Planner Board of Standards at cfp.net. The CFP designation is a professional certification mark for financial planners conferred by the Certified Financial Planner Board of Standards, Inc. Substantial coursework and a comprehensive, 10-hour exam are required to attain this title. In general, you'll need a bachelor's degree or its equivalent in any discipline, from an accredited college or university. If you already have an Association of Chartered Certified

Accountants (ACCA) or Certified Public Accountants (CPA) credential, for example, you can register for and take the exam without having to complete the education requirements. You must keep current with the annual certification fee and complete the continuing education (CE) requirement every two years.

You can also do a search on the websites of the Financial Planning Association (onefpa.org), the Garrett Planning Network (garrettplanningnetwork.com), and the National Association of Personal Financial Advisors (napfa.org). Another excellent source is the Association for Financial Counseling and Education (AFCPE.org) website.

Bonus points: Bone up on Psychology 101. Where money matters, emotions must be handled with care.

Meet a Financial Planner

Kathy Frakes grew up in Cocoa Beach, Florida, and earned a bachelor's of business administration in accounting from the College of William & Mary in 1986. After college she worked as an auditor for Price Waterhouse.

During the next 23 years moving around as an Army wife, she had a variety of paid and volunteer jobs—advisor with the IRS's Volunteer Income Tax Advisor program; bank teller; media aide responsible for a computer lab in the local elementary school; volunteer treasurer for a variety of Cub Scout packs; and worship leader at her church, among others.

Once her husband retired and her three kids were launched, she returned to school and earned the Certified Financial Planner Certification from Northwestern University. After passing the exam in 2014, her first financial planning job was with the Family Firm, a fee-only personal financial advisory firm in Bethesda, Maryland, as a paraplanner. After fulfilling the experience requirements, she became a Certified Financial Planner professional in June of 2016. Three months later, she landed a position at Omega Wealth Management, based in Arlington, Virginia.

In her spare time, Kathy serves as a trained member of her church's Early Response Team (ERT). The ERT, a program through UMCOR (United Methodist Committee on Relief), assists survivors in the early days after a natural disaster. Meantime, she and her husband travel and spend time with their three adult sons, and she decompresses by playing piano and bridge.

Fitness Trainer

The nitty-gritty: If you're a natural athlete, working out is in your blood. That's why teaching active-adult exercise classes might just be your dream job. More fitness clubs and gyms across the country are offering classes catering to the silver-hair set, according to fitness industry experts. Employment of fitness trainers and instructors is projected to grow 8 percent from 2014 to 2024. As businesses, government, and insurance organizations continue to recognize the benefits of health and fitness programs for their employees, incentives to join gyms or other types of health clubs are expected to increase the need for fitness trainers and instructors, according to the BLS.

Trainers lead group classes and one-on-one sessions that usually run 45 minutes to an hour. Knowledge of human physiology, proper exercise practices, and an ability to judge a client's fitness level are crucial. And you might even take a dive into the pool. Low-impact aqua aerobics are popular, as is "accessible" yoga, which adjusts techniques for people with chronic illness and physical disabilities. Hours are generally flexible, but plan on evening workouts, and it's not unusual to have a class load of two dozen sessions a week.

Pay range: $9.92 to $48.40 an hour, according to PayScale.com, but in larger cities, hourly rates may be $60 to $100 or more for private sessions. Most health clubs collect the cost for the session from their members and dole out a percentage to you.

Qualifications: Certification is not required by law, but most fitness clubs insist. Several national groups offer some type of credential. These include the Aerobics and Fitness Association of America, the American Council on Exercise, the Arthritis Association, the International Sports Sciences Association, the National Exercise Trainers Association, the National Strength and Conditioning Association, SilverSneakers, and YMCA. For credentials, you must be certified in cardiopulmonary resuscitation (CPR) and pass an exam that consists of both a written test and practical demonstration. You'll need to be up to speed on human physiology, understand correct exercise techniques, be able to assess a client's fitness level, and know the ins and outs of proper exercise programs. You may also need liability insurance. Programs cost around $200 to $400 and generally consist of a written test and a practical exam.

Meet a Fitness Instructor

At 63, instructor Roseann Brown has seen attendance double in active-adult exercise classes since she became a senior fitness instructor eight years ago. Little wonder that the number of fitness clubs and gyms across the country offering these special classes is rapidly multiplying.

Brown has tapped into a growing field. As the population ages, jobs like senior fitness trainer and others in health-related arenas that serve their needs are on the rise.

And they don't require you to head back for an intensive and expensive course of study. Employers and clients are increasingly accepting professional certifications as proof of your expertise.

Brown's repertoire, for example, ranges from certifications in aqua-aerobics and chair aerobics (where chairs are used for seated or standing support) and SilverSneakers classes to workouts that strengthen the body via techniques that emphasize balance, abdominal strength, and muscle control using techniques from yoga and dance. She has also studied low-intensity workouts designed for older adults with arthritis or other joint challenges, using light weights and Dyna-Bands, which are nationally certified by the Arthritis Foundation.

Brown earned a certificate via a written and performance exam with the Aerobics and Fitness Association of America (AFAA) to teach as group fitness instructor, as well as the AFFA-accredited Personal Trainer Certification, so her total out-of-pocket education cost to date is less than $1,000. It's a dream job for Brown, who spent 35 years working in the garment industry selling wholesale age-appropriate teenage clothing. "The basic fitness instructors are 20-year-old kids," recalls Brown. "So I asked myself, how can I stand out? How can I be different?"

She leads 17 classes a week to groups ranging in size from 15 to 40 seniors at a variety of locations and earns $40 to $50 an hour. "I have always loved to exercise, and I love being able to set my schedule. It doesn't feel like work. I need to move. I can't sit on a couch." She now works four hours in the morning, takes her afternoons off, and gets back to the paid workouts in the evening hours.

Healthcare/Patient Advocate

The nitty-gritty: You're in change of helping patients navigate the complex medical system. You can get to the bottom of billing mistakes and contest insurance-coverage rejections. At times, you might lend advice in making medical decisions, help find a specialist or hospital, go with patients to doctor appointments, coordinate multiple-doctor care, and pick up prescriptions. Knowing how to fill out insurance forms and even negotiate with doctors for better rates might fall under your jurisdiction. Job opportunities range from working privately for one person or a couple to working on staff as an advocate at a local hospital, nursing home, rehab center, or insurance company.

Pay range: $11.81 to $21.73 an hour, but pay can rise with experience.

Qualifications: Community colleges and nonprofit organizations are developing training and certification programs to help more people tackle this post. Nurses, social workers, medical professionals, and insurance experts are in high demand for these positions. But if you've steered your own exasperating path through the medical system, you might be the perfect person to take on this role. Do take the time to add the necessary skills to get certified. No licenses are required to practice, but there are several credentialing programs. Contact the National Association of Healthcare Advocacy Consultants (nahac.memberlodge.com/), a professional group in Berkeley, California, and the nonprofit Patient Advocate Foundation (patientadvocate.org) for more information.

Massage Therapist

See Chapter 4, page 103.

Medical Equipment Maintenance and Repair

The nitty-gritty: Were you the kid who always took things apart in the garage for the sheer fun of putting them back together? From wheelchairs to gurneys, if you've got the fix-it gene, this is a fast-growing job that plays right into your innate mechanical ability. Medical equipment repairers maintain and fix a variety of equipment, from electric wheelchairs to EKG machines. For the most part, the tasks call for steadiness and good hand-eye coordination. But it's the inner awareness of how things work and fit together that allows you to not only enjoy this work, but also succeed in it. It can be physically demanding, as bending, crouching, and standing go with the territory.

Employment of medical equipment repairers is projected to grow 6 percent from 2014 to 2024, according to the BLS. Greater demand for healthcare services from an aging population and the use of increasingly complex medical equipment will drive employment growth. Those who have an associate's degree in biomedical equipment technology or engineering should have the best job opportunities. As you might expect, jobs can be found at hospitals, assisted care communities, medical centers, physicians' offices, health and personal care stores, and medical equipment wholesalers. You might be called in for emergency repairs, so fast work under pressure must be in your wheelhouse.

Pay range: $10.39 to $20.80 an hour, according to PayScale.com.

Qualifications: Education requirements for medical equipment repairers depend on what kinds of equipment you're in charge of. If you stick to hospital beds, gurneys, and electric wheelchairs, you may learn entirely through on-the-job training. Medical device manufacturers, too, often provide technical training. If you work on high-tech equipment, such as CAT scanners and defibrillators, however, you may need a bachelor's degree in engineering or biomedical equipment technology. Even so, medical equipment technology is swiftly advancing, and new devices are coming online all the time. As a result, repairers must constantly update skills and knowledge of equipment. Employers, particularly in hospitals, often pay for their in-house medical repairers to become certified.

Move Manager

The nitty-gritty: Making it fit. Downsizing is your bailiwick. You are in charge of coordinating a move and configuring a new home setup. Your typical clients are relocating to smaller quarters, usually an apartment or retirement community. They need advice on choosing what furniture, artwork, china, collectibles, and household goods make the cut to head over to the new digs. And you tally up what can be sold, donated, or given to friends and family. You might even be in charge of shopping for new furniture that suits the new pad, or organizing and running an estate or yard sale. This job calls for configuring and cajoling. Must be handy with a tape measure.

Pay range: Fees range from $30 per hour to $75+.

Qualifications: Knowledge of interior design is essential. An "in" with a local realtor can jumpstart your business, as well as provide a steady clientele down the road. A calm but take-charge demeanor is a desirable personality trait—no drama queens or kings here. This type of move is fraught with emotion. For more information on courses and certification, contact the National Association of Senior Move Managers (nasmm.org). You must be compassionate, but ruthless.

Job hunting tips: For leads on jobs, stop by local realtors' offices and visit retirement and assisted living communities in your area to ask about their future residents' needs. Find out who is handling this type of work for them. The community's management office usually provides soon-to-be residents with suggestions for moving specialists to lend a hand with what can be a daunting endeavor for downsizers of any age. Hiring an unbiased expert can be invaluable. What do you need to do to be featured on their list of recommended helpers?

Personal and Home Healthcare Aide

See Chapter 4, page 110.

Retirement Coach

The nitty-gritty: Are you a good listener? A problem-solver? With this job, you're the one in charge of counseling soon-to-be retirees on what to do with the rest of their lives. No surprise that retirement is one of the fastest-growing segments of the coaching industry.

Retirees are often looking for their "what's next" direction. They need a guiding hand to help them identify their passions, their skills, and the best kind of work at this stage of life. Should they invest in education? Should they start their own business—one they've always dreamed of? What about moving to a new locale or retirement community?

It can be life coaching and job coaching all mixed into one. This is a process and takes someone who is patient, intuitive, and good at coming up with creative solutions and action steps. This can be an awkward stage. We are living longer and healthier lives, so most of us want to stay active. The question is, doing what and where?

Pay range: $50 to more than $250 per hour.

Qualifications: Career and life coaching is a self-regulated industry and emerging profession. Many coaches have been doing it for years without adding professional designations. If you have a corporate background in human resources, counseling, or even teaching, this might be a natural next step for you.

To learn more about certification, go to the nonprofit International Coach Federation (ICF). The ICF is the only organization that awards a global credential, which is currently held by over 4,800 coaches worldwide. ICF-credentialed coaches have met certain stringent educational requirements, received specific coach training, and achieved a designated number of experience hours, among other requirements.

For coursework, you can search the ICF's database for a program. Some coaching courses are offered online. Others consist of a few workshop sessions. More intensive programs run over the course of a few semesters combining online and in-person study. As I mentioned earlier in this book, you might check into programs such as the Coaches Training Institute (thecoaches.com), New Ventures West (newventureswest.com), or the Rockport Institute (rockportinstitute.com). Check your local colleges for course listings, too. Universities such as Duquesne University and Georgetown University, for example, offer coach training programs. Tuition is all over the map, from under $1,000 to more than $10,000. The tuition for the Professional Coaching course at New Ventures West, for example, is currently $12,400.

Retirement Coaches in Action

When Guy Johnson retired from his tax-management position at Unilever, one of the world's biggest consumer products companies, he was sure that he was ready. Not so.

"I lost myself when my wife, Barbara, and I moved to Sarasota, Florida, from Bergen County, New Jersey," Johnson says. "I planned my retirement financially, but I didn't plan it otherwise."

Through weekly sessions with a retirement coach, Debbie Drinkard Grovum, he worked hard to accomplish the goals in life that he had been putting off. She motivated him to get back on track, he says.

Retirement coaches like Grovum are trendy these days. The specialty has surfaced in the teeming coaching field to serve a growing number of boomers who are wrestling with what's next.

"Retirement is clearly no longer the destination that it used to be," says Dorian Mintzer, a retirement coach and co-author of *The Couple's Retirement Puzzle: 10 Must-Have Conversations for Creating an Amazing New Life Together.* "Now, the likelihood is, you have 20, 30, maybe 40 more years ahead of you, and that's a long time to not know what you want to do."

Retirees need to rebuild their lifestyle, which may mean embracing a range of activities from part-time work to volunteering to entrepreneurial adventures and artistic endeavors, and it can help to have a sherpa to guide the way.

The retirement coaching process typically starts with a self-assessment that scrutinizes values and strengths and refines goals, hopes, and visions for the years ahead.

Retirees answer difficult questions, Mintzer says, such as, "Do you need to have work be part of it? If you're in a couple, are you in sync in terms of retiring, or not working?" It's not unusual for women, who may be younger than their spouses or have stepped out of the workforce for a time, to be at career peak while the partner is winding down, she says.

A big segment of people who seek a retirement coach retired without much of a plan and after a year, or two, or 10, have determined that the situation is not working for them, Grovum says. "They want to rethink their life."

Wendy Fox, who lives in Milton, Massachusetts, retired after more than 35 years as a journalist and media liaison. "The retirement thing sounded great before I did it," she says. Her husband, Al Larkin, was already retired. "The first year was wonderful. Then I realized that I missed the newsroom community. I'm an extrovert."

She hired Mintzer. "I was basically acknowledging that I was incapable of figuring out the rest of my life," Fox says. "One of the first things she told me is 'you are not alone.'"

For Fox, her goals were "to have some purpose in life and not just take up space for the next 20 years," she says. "I didn't need a therapist, I just wanted to talk to someone about what to do."

Mintzer has encouraged her to find new undertakings—in addition to expanding her existing volunteer duties—like joining or starting an activity group, taking regular hiking treks, and asking fellow dog lovers for dates to walk with her and Lucy, her chocolate Labrador retriever.

Johnson's challenge also was primarily a social one. When he was working at Unilever, he had a schedule and a very active life. But when he relocated to Florida, it disappeared. "I was in trouble," says Johnson. "I was spending too much time in the house watching the stock market and not getting out and meeting people."

One change he made: getting back involved with bowling, one of his passions. "I was an avid bowler up North," he says. "And I made a lot of friends as a member of Unilever's company bowling team." He joined a league near his home.

And he dipped into work-related activities. After he retired, he took a course to earn the certification of an enrolled agent for the IRS and began working part time at H&R Block to prepare individual tax returns and volunteering for AARP Foundation's free Tax-Aide service.

For someone working with a retirement coach, it's critical to have an open mind. This is a new adventure and asking for help can make it a great one.

Seniors' Real Estate Specialist

The nitty-gritty: This sales job takes a bit of finesse. You'll need to gently smooth the emotions of selling the family home first and help locate a suitable downsized abode.

Pay range: 2.5 to 3 percent of the purchase price.

Qualifications: The SRS Designation or Seniors Real Estate Specialist Certification (seniorsrealestate.com) are via the National Association of Realtors. Hone your soft-sell side. Tea and empathy may rule the day. These moves can be wrenching, so you need to stay positive and keep the client focused on the upside of a downsize.

PART

THE GREAT JOBS WORKSHOP

■ ■ ■

Landing a job is not a matter of luck. It's that oft repeated phrase—it's when preparation meets opportunity.

I've written this Great Jobs Workshop for people who want to think and plan ahead to find a great job. In these next chapters, you'll find tips on writing a resume, revving up your web job-hunting skills, interviewing, and finding a mentor to guide you, among other job-seeking strategies.

My hope is that you will use my specific suggestions to learn new ways to job-hunt with confidence—with an appropriate dollop of swagger—and to make thoughtful long-range decisions about the kind of work you choose to do.

In my book *What's Next? Finding Your Passion and Your Dream Job in Your Forties, Fifties, and Beyond*, I profiled people who radically and successfully changed their working lives in their 50s and beyond. I wrote about what they did to make the turn a winning one. Career change is an underlying theme for many people who are contemplating what they want to do in their next act.

So I decided to kick off this workshop with my advice on starting a second act rather than just landing a job to stay busy. My reasoning? Simple. I think dreaming big is a great launching place for any job-hunting journey. Whether you want to work part time or a full schedule, trying something new might just be the ticket. This is precisely the time in our lives when we all start yearning for something that brings more meaning to life.

And it's not just the dreamers who are doing this. Even those with their feet on the ground have eyes on the sky. It intrigues me how that quest to do work we love inspires and pushes so many of us to keep at it long after what might have been a time to take it easy.

As great American jazz pianist and composer Dave Brubeck explained to Pulitzer Prize–winning journalist Hedrick Smith in the PBS documentary *Rediscovering Dave Brubeck*: "There's a way of playing safe, there's a way of using tricks, and there's the way I like to play, which is dangerously—where you're going to take a chance on making mistakes in order to create something you haven't created before."

So let's get started.

CHAPTER 9

How to Plan for Your Second Act

■ ■ ■

There are loads of reasons to pursue work in a new field. You've retired, but still want to stay in the workforce. You're returning to the work world after some time away. You've been laid off. Or you are simply burned out in your current job. For many workers, switching careers has become a necessity thanks to a topsy-turvy job market.

Then too, a life crisis may remind you of how quickly life can be snatched away—a health scare of your own, perhaps, or the death of a close friend, colleague, or family member. You pause and think twice about what really matters, and how you can find meaning in your day job.

Forty percent of professals between ages 55 and 64, and 19 percent of professionals 65 or older are interested in changing careers, suggesting many older adults are seeking a new gig, rather than retirement, according to a 2017 national University of Phoenix survey conducted by Harris Poll.

But changing careers and redeploying is not new. It's deeply rooted in the American spirit. Benjamin Franklin got his start making candles before turning to the printing trade, then writing, and then becoming a statesman, inventor, and scientist. The Wright brothers were in the newspaper business, followed by bike repair, before turning to aviation and the great blue yonder. Ronald Reagan was an actor before he became a politician.

Martha Stewart was a stockbroker. And the list goes on, from generation to generation.

Childhood dreams, for instance, can inspire second careers. When Sandra Colony was a child, she was mesmerized by the sleek photographs of mysterious places in the pages of *National Geographic*. Those tantalizing images inspired her to explore the world as she grew older. To date, she has visited 100 countries. "I knew I loved to travel as a little girl, but I certainly never knew at 68 I would start a career out of it," Colony says. The New York City resident has done just that with her venture, Personalized Odysseys (personalized-odysseys.com), a travel agency.

Prior to that, for more than 25 years, Colony worked in the cable industry, managing corporate communications. Her job responsibilities often made it tough to take off for two or more consecutive weeks, but she often coaxed her bosses into giving her the time to globe trot.

Predictably, her friends who were seeking an interesting vacation and were well aware of her travel expertise regularly turned to Colony for help with trip planning.

So when her job as a senior adviser for employee communications at Time Warner Cable ended in April 2012, she opted to tap into her thirst for travel and make it her full-time job.

The majority of the trips she plans are for groups of 10 or fewer women, 50 or older, whose spouse, partner, or friends don't want to travel with them, but who don't want to go solo. Destinations include Easter Island, Namibia, Nepal, Papua New Guinea, and Zimbabwe.

"Namibia has proven to be one of my most popular destinations as more and more Americans learn about this amazing destination," says Colony. "And I've added Uzbekistan and Vietnam to my trips for next year."

Another bonus: "A huge unexpected benefit from my five years of organizing travel is that I continually meet women from around the country and form new, lasting friendships."

Colony didn't plan to make money the first few years. "If my income from the business can pay for two international trips a year for myself, that's fine for now," she says.

But not everyone is fortunate enough to know instantly the second act they want to pursue. For these people, it might not be a full-blown childhood dream that turns into a job; it might simply be an activity one was good at as a child.

How do find your second act? If you don't have a passion that began in childhood, try soul searching with people who know you well. Ask your friends and family what skills seem to come naturally to you. It may well be it's something you like and something you're too modest to admit is something you do really well.

Don't limit yourself to one passion, either. Go for a few of them. You never know which one will have the legs to morph into a job that provides a paycheck or meaning for you.

Take time to review experiences in your career that you relished. What times were you most happy? What would you happily do gratis even if you weren't getting paid? Write it all down. With these lists, look for connections. My guess is something will bubble up that will help you start to identify a place to launch a second act.

Another approach to finding a passion to pursue as a job is to cultivate side interests. Learn something new. Your interest may not be sparked straightaway, but as you delve deeper into something, you become captivated, and a passion often develops. Being open to a new path is essential.

If a second act is calling to you, go for it, but please take your time. Change is a process, and it takes confidence that comes from laying the groundwork. The most successful 50+ career switchers take a few years to learn new skills, network, and prepare financially.

When people considering a midlife switch ask for advice on how to succeed, I always begin by saying, "Get a fitness program." You need to be fit all around:

- **Physically fit.** Physical fitness provides the strength and mental sharpness to deal with stress, especially when changing jobs or making big decisions. It sounds superficial, but an in-shape and energetic appearance is a bonus in the work world. You give off a positive, can-do vibe that you're up for the job.
- **Spiritually fit.** Mind–body balance helps you calmly roll with the punches and teaches you to quietly listen to the inner voice that can guide your decisions. A meditation practice, yoga, tai chi, or just long walks with your dog can help here.
- **Financially fit.** Economic stability gives you freedom of choice. It provides the nimbleness you need to start a new career, whether that means opening your own business,

paying the tuition to go back to school, or making it easier to work in a job that you love—even if it pays less than your old one. Financial fitness gives you choice.

To be honest, this three-step fitness regime is good for most things in life. That said, here are the essential steps to planning for a second career that I recommend.

Go slowly. No one dives into a second career on a whim. You've got to have a plan and have saved money, added skills, and done some moonlighting. Start working at age 50 on a career you might kick off in another five years. If you have lots of time, you can sample some ideas and possibilities.

Search inside. Look at your skill set and past experience as transferable to lots of different challenges and fields. Answer some important questions: What am I best at? What do I love to do? What don't I like to do? Ask friends and colleagues, too. They might see things that you take for granted.

Think of it not as *reinventing* yourself, but rather as redirecting or *redeploying* many of the skills you already have in place. Retired Navy captain Don Covington, who became the company manager for the Big Apple Circus in his mid-50s, told me: "When you think about it, the military and the circus are not that different." What he meant is that the leadership and management skills honed in his naval career translated to moving a circus troupe of 100-plus from town to town.

Research. Look for jobs and opportunities that leverage experience. Check out websites like aarp.org/jobs, Encore.org, RetiredBrains.com, RetirementJobs.com, and Workforce50.com to get a flavor for what others are doing and what jobs are out there now. AARP Foundation's Back to Work 50+ (aarp.org/aarp-foundation/our-work/income/back-to-work-50-plus/), for example, connects 50+ workers with career counseling and training opportunities through a network of community colleges, work experience, and access to employers.

Review the companies who have signed AARP's Employer Pledge program (aarp.org/work/job-search/employer-pledge-companies/). Participating organizations, such as Ace Hardware,

Aetna, Charles Schwab, and UnitedHealth Group, have signed a pledge that they:

- Believe in equal opportunity for all workers, regardless of age
- Believe that 50+ workers should have a level playing field in their ability to compete for and obtain jobs
- Recognize the value of experienced workers

Investigate growing fields like healthcare, elder care, skilled trades, sustainability or "green" arenas, and education, which have a rising demand for workers. The Bureau of Labor Statistics *Occupational Outlook Handbook* (https://www.bls.gov/ooh/) is a good reference for researching the fastest-growing occupations.

Shape up your financial life. Starting over can mean a pay cut, the cost of a startup, tuition for training, and out-of-pocket health insurance costs. Start by charting a budget. It's smart to have a cushion of six months or more of living expenses set aside for transition costs, as well as unexpected emergencies.

Pay off outstanding high-interest credit card debts, education loans, and auto loans. This can take some time, but starting a new venture with as clean a balance sheet as you can makes a difference. Pare back your discretionary living expenses to reflect a more realistic view of what you'll earn. What things can you give up?

Depending on your situation, you might consider downsizing to a smaller home, townhouse, or condo. Refinancing your mortgage to a lower rate might be an option. Or perhaps you're able to move to an area that has a lower cost of living. You might even be able to write off moving expenses.

If you're opening your own business, keep in mind that startup costs can easily top $10,000 for the average small business owner, if you need a brick-and-mortar office. Luckily, today it's increasingly common to start a virtual online business with a website, which is far more affordable. Nonetheless, if you do need office space, your monthly nut—electric, rent, payroll, and other ongoing outlays—starts rolling in immediately, often before your revenues do. You will need operating funds to meet these expenses.

Keep your hand out of the cookie jar. It's tempting to dip into retirement accounts and tap home equity and other savings, but that has obvious implications for retirement security.

Invest in additional education and training. Research the skills or certifications required for your new career. Add the essential expertise and degrees before you make the leap. Check out offerings at community colleges for retraining.

Consider taking one class at a time. A host of certificate programs in a specialized field of study are aimed at adult students looking to retool their careers. Some of these programs offer graduate-level courses in the subject area that you can use as a start toward a master's degree if you have the time, desire, and funds to do so. Certain fields, say healthcare, counseling, and technology, require a certificate for specific jobs. A certificate can also show that you have a specialty in the area—sustainable landscape design, or grant proposal writing, for instance.

Community colleges also offer courses to train people over 50. An increasing number of these programs are available online. Then too, many colleges are starting to offer second career workshops at reunions. Moreover, four-year colleges and graduate schools—from Harvard's Advanced Leadership Initiative to Stanford's Distinguished Careers Institute—have programs for folks looking to prepare for second act opportunities.

If you have some advance time to get ready, you might start to take classes while your current employer offers tuition reimbursement. Under federal law, employers may offer up to $5,250 a year in tax-free education-assistance benefits for undergraduate or graduate courses. You may not need to be working toward a degree. But gradually gearing up new skills and adding to your kit, while you're gainfully employed, will prepare you for your transition when the time comes.

For those of you who dream of opening your own business, AARP's small business resources and webinars (aarp.org/work/small-business/), SBA.gov, and Score.org, a nonprofit group that provides small business assistance, are top resources for seminars, webinars, and other help to ease you off the ground.

Use tax breaks for your education. As for the expense, yes, budget for it, but look into what financial aid offerings and tax breaks might be available to you. Depending on your income, you might qualify for various tax credits, such as the lifetime learning credit, worth up to $2,000 each year for an unlimited number of years. That credit can be used for tuition and required fees.

- **Shop for a student loan or grant.** Check out low-interest Stafford loans, the main federal loan for students. Go to FastWeb.com and FinAid.org for details and a list of education lenders. Look for scholarships and grants available specifically for older students that are offered by different associations and foundations.

Apprentice, volunteer, or moonlight. Do yourself a favor—do the job first. It's a great way to get in the door and see what goes on behind the scenes. It's also a networking opportunity.

If you're job hunting in a new field, apprenticing, volunteering, or moonlighting can catch a potential employer's eye. LinkedIn members can add a "Volunteer Experience & Causes" field to their profile. If you've spent some time helping out organizations such as the American Red Cross, Big Brothers Big Sisters, or the Humane Society of the United States, then put it on your profile.

Professionals often have the misunderstanding that volunteer work doesn't qualify as "real" work experience. You may be a salesperson by trade, but if you planned your nonprofit's fundraising event, you can add skills like event planning or event marketing to your profile. Having those additional skills can potentially make you a more attractive employee and business partner.

One of my favorite examples of how this can work out is Anne Nolan, who was president of Crossroads Rhode Island, the state's largest homeless service organization. She started as a volunteer board member. She didn't know what she wanted to do when she lost her executive-level job. She had a year's salary and time to think her options through. She decided to look into volunteering at the shelter—not because she dreamed it would turn into a full-time job, but because it was an activity to get her out of her rut and do something besides worrying about what was next. She was asked to join the board and then was hired on as the president.

Check out sites like CreateTheGood.org, Handsonnetwork. org, Idealist.org, and VolunteerMatch.org, as well as Catchafire. org (for professionals) and Serve.gov and TaprootPlus.org (for pro bono work). Encore.org has a searchable map that shows encore programs around the country. Look around you. Where might you lend a hand? Opportunity often comes from places where you least expect it.

Set up a retirement plan. If you're starting a freelance business, or moving to a nonprofit or small firm without an employee retirement plan, this is key. One of the biggest mistakes you can make is not planning sufficiently for your retirement.

Shop for health insurance. If you're heading off on your own, check out any industry or alumni associations you belong to for group policies. Don't drop your current job insurance (you can continue it for a time under a law known as COBRA) until you have a new policy in place.

The Affordable Care Act has been important in providing coverage for so many who were not able to find insurance. For more, check out HealthCare.gov, the government's site hosting the public insurance exchange for most states.

"What do you do about health insurance?" is always one of the first questions I'm asked when I tell someone I run my own business. If you work for yourself, finding health insurance can be a big pain. While there's no holy grail, there are ways to navigate the maze and find good coverage at manageable prices. What you'll pay for that coverage depends on a myriad of factors—where you live, your gender, the age, and the health of who is being covered, your deductible, plus the type of policy you need, among other things.

About 35 percent of U.S. workers are technically their own boss. We're self-employed freelancers and independent contractors. Some workers who fall into this cadre are temps or part-timers. Others have already officially retired and are continuing to work a reduced schedule, or have accepted an early retirement package, then launched an entrepreneurial enterprise.

Regardless of the job description, the problem is the same: finding health insurance until you reach age 65 when Medicare kicks in for most, but not all, of your coverage. You might be covered by a spouse's employer policy or be able to join a group policy from a membership you have in an association. Check your state insurance department website, to see if it provides a listing of health insurance choices for residents.

Options to consider: premiums, deductibles, copays, coinsurance, and the annual limit you have to pay out of pocket before insurance covers the remainder. Premiums vary broadly based on your age and physical condition.

Other online sources to check for availability and get an idea of costs by comparing dozens of health insurance plans that are available in your area include eHealthInsurance.com, GoHealthinsurance.com, Insure.com, and Netquote.com. You can also go directly to the insurer sites for quotes. Keep in mind that these quotes can be all over the map and are just there to give you a notion of what it might cost. It will ultimately depend mostly on your individual medical situation and age.

Focus on smaller companies, start-ups, and nonprofits. They're more likely to value your overall work experience. You can provide the depth of practical knowledge and versatility that's worth two junior hires. For nonprofit job-hunting help, go to Chapter 13.

Network. In this era of online resumes, it's all about who you know that can get you in the chair for a face-to-face meeting. People want to hire someone who comes with the blessing of an existing employee or colleague. Networking is about building relationships. One way you can do that is to join a networking group.

I'm a member of The Transition Network (thetransitionnetwork.org), a nonprofit networking group for women over 50. It's based in New York, but the group has chapters in cities like Atlanta, Chicago, Houston, San Francisco, Santa Fe, and Washington, D.C.

You might also consider joining a peer group associated with your profession or your alma mater. For instance, my alma mater, Duke University, has Women's Forums in Atlanta, Charlotte, Chicago, Dallas, Denver, Houston, Los Angeles, New York, San Francisco, Seattle, Washington D.C., and even London.

There are also a growing number of online networking organizations. Join Facebook, LinkedIn, and Twitter. They are a great way to pull together your professional network. But don't ignore networking in unlikely places. You might find the mother of your son's friend can help. That's what happened to author James S. Kunen, and it led to his job teaching English as a second language.

Ask for help. Find a mentor or two working in your new field. Seek out mentees you have worked with in the past. Over time, things shift, and now they may be in a position to help you make your next move. Many corporations also offer career coaches and counseling on a limited basis to help employees who have retired or lost their jobs. Check out career centers at your alma mater and those operated by area colleges or local government agencies offering workshops on resume writing, career counseling, job fairs, and retraining programs. If you're interested in a particular industry, join an association affiliated with it and attend conferences. (These are also great places to connect with potential mentors).

Get up to speed on the latest technology. Social media platforms such as Facebook, Google+, Instagram, LinkedIn, Pinterest, Snapchat, and Twitter have changed how you job hunt. To get into today's job market, you must be at ease with computers, basic software programs, the internet, e-mail, and mobile technology. Chapter 15 has more on web job-hunting strategies.

Prepare to be a beginner. When you leave one career or job, you lose your identity. And it can be unnerving, unsettling. Some people even grieve for their old job. Then when you start again, you find you're the new kid, and the rules of the game are alien. You might long for your old job, where you were the expert. This can take some mindset tweaking. All of a sudden, your paycheck is slimmer, and you might even be making some mistakes. Give yourself time—at least a year—to get comfortable.

Don't mess with your hobby. Be aware of the difference between a hobby, which is a breather from your working world, and an interest that brings in an income. I'm passionate about horses, for example, but a career training horses would never suit me. It's my escape and relaxation. If the barn became my office, I would lose that magic.

Career guru Nicholas Lore, who founded the Rockport Institute (rockportinstitute.com) and developed a pioneer program in the career-coaching field, explained it to me this way: "Your passion is a clue," he says. "To find a job you love to do, you need to become a career detective looking for the clues about the fit between yourself and the working world."

It's not too hard to find those clues. They are what turns you on and what excites you, what matters, and what you do well. It's something you would do for free.

Lore, for instance, is passionate about plenty of things, like sailing. "But I wouldn't want to be a charter-boat skipper," he told me. As a clue, what he learned is that when you're sailing, you're making hundreds of little decisions all the time. He likes constantly problem solving. "You need to put together a clues list that becomes a definite components list and then turns to career ideas."

Be prepared for setbacks. If you've spent the time laying the proper groundwork, you'll push through the bumpy patches. Having a supportive family, partner, or friends is key, though. We all need a fan base to remind us of why we took this path and why we're going to make it work.

Keep in good shape. When you're eating healthy and have a normal workout regime, you have more physical vigor and mental sharpness. You'll need that get-up-and-go to face the challenges ahead. And the truth is, change *is* stressful, and exercise can counter that beautifully.

Do something every day to work toward your goal. Changing careers can be nerve-racking. Begin with a mental picture of where you want to go, tape a photograph on your office wall of what it might look like, journal about your goals. Get things moving by taking small steps. That might mean making a phone call to ask for advice, or reaching out with an e-mail a day to make a lunch date to knock around possibilities. People like to do small favors. And it helps build a relationship that may lead to your next job.

Be realistic. Nothing lasts forever. You might have several new "careers" from here on out. Accept that thesis, and it makes a next move more manageable. And who knows, you might do a couple of things at the same time and be a Jack or Jacqueline of many trades. One 50-something woman I know is self-employed as an SAT tutor, a community college associate professor, a personal fitness trainer, and a caterer. Bon appétit.

Strategies for 50+ Job Hunters

■ ■ ■

A good friend of mine started looking for full-time work when he was laid off from his job at the age of 60. A digital media strategist, he was senior vice president at a firm where he had worked for 14 years, and the abrupt wave out the door caught him by surprise.

He stayed busy, working part time in media relations for an environmental nonprofit, writing a blog for an online magazine, and sharing wisdom for money, which "crasser types refer to as consulting," he told me with a laugh. But his search for a full-time gig left him feeling that while the interviews go well, he had the sense that "the person across the desk was looking at his 'expiration date.'"

His frustration was palpable.

But there's a happy coda. It took nearly three years, but he did it. He landed a full-time position as digital editorial director for a media company specializing in healthcare coverage. "I was hired by the same woman who hired me for my previous job who had moved to the new firm a year earlier," he told me with a tinge of gratitude. "She really didn't care about age because she knew what I could do."

If you're over 50 and pounding the pavement these days, you can face certain challenges. On average, it takes someone age 55 or older three months longer to find a job than a younger person.

The Benefits of Experienced Workers

Whether you want to work in an office job or teach a senior fitness class, there is evidence that more companies are starting to realize that hiring workers age 50 and older is good for business. Grasping that employers need you can give you the fire and confidence to set out on your job hunt.

The old worries that hiring someone our age would probably be too costly are being debunked. Contrary to common perception, workers age 50-plus don't cost appreciably more than younger workers, according to the report "A Business Case for Workers Age 50+: A Look at the Value of Experience," commissioned by AARP and conducted by Aon Hewitt.

Shifting trends in reward and benefit programs mean that adding more age 50+ talent to a workforce results in only minimal increases in hard-dollar total labor costs. These trends include a broad move by large employers to performance-based versus tenure-based compensation, and the decline in traditional benefit pension plans.

Meanwhile, in today's global and fast-paced workplace, employers often don't have the time to waste while a younger worker ramps up skills and knowledge. Companies are gradually realizing that to stay competitive, it's smarter to seek out and hire experienced workers. Trust me, you're on the cutting edge of a widespread change in the demographics of the workplace. And it's being guided by the boomer generation. When organizations need someone to step in and do the job right now and solve an existing problem, it's the experienced worker they're eager to hire.

Why? Employers find that workers age 50 and older are more loyal and aren't as liable as younger workers to job jump. And that lower staff turnover boosts the bottom line. The costs of high turnover are real. Finding, hiring, and training a new employee is a pricey venture, and it becomes even more so when that well-trained employee elects to leave and work for a competitor.

Finally, the Aon Hewitt data show that older workers typically love their jobs more than younger workers do. Yes, we're more engaged than our younger counterparts. Perhaps we're grateful for the jobs in a way that someone new to the workforce has yet to learn to value and appreciate.

In addition to all those qualities I've already mentioned, older workers naturally have the following:

- An ability to make quick decisions and solve problems
- Greater maturity and professionalism
- Superior communication skills, both written and oral
- The ability to serve as mentors
- The critical qualities of reliability and dependability
- More knowledge, wisdom, and overall life experience

One way to sell a product is to take away every reason a potential customer has for saying "No," and that's the approach for overcoming ageism. If you do everything else right in terms of overhauling your resume, marketing yourself online, networking, and so forth, you've already given employers plenty of reasons to say yes. I will review all of those steps in the chapters that follow to be certain. Now, you just have to take away their reasons for saying no. Here are some of my top recommendations.

Turn Everything into a Positive

As an older worker, you have a lot to offer. Here's how you can make the most of it. I will explain each in more depth in later chapters.

Stay on top of your game. Make sure you have done everything you can to keep up with technology and changes in your field. Add the essential expertise and degrees before you apply for a new job. If you've recently updated any software certifications, or you are proficient in social media, let the recruiter or hiring manager know, even if that's a brief mention in your discussion.

Look your best. Be physically fit and look and dress with an eye toward a vibrant, youthful appearance. Interviewers do judge a book by its cover. Invest in some new duds, update your hairstyle, and find fashion-forward specs if needed.

At the very least, you should freshen up your hairstyle with a good cut and shaping. But don't do anything too radical the day before, of course.

I'm a stickler for good grooming. Pay attention to your entire look—head to toe. I recommend a manicure for both sexes. Men, you can forgo the polish.

Always overdress. If you know someone who works at the company, ask them about office attire, providing that doesn't make you feel awkward. Alternatively, you might surf for a Google image on your computer of someone in management there, even the CEO. That can give you a sense of what dress for success might be appropriate at the firm. Importantly, even if you're told the office is casual work attire, don't go there.

Prepare for age-related questions. Your potential employer might use being overqualified as a reason not to hire you. Have a good answer for that. You need to show why you are sincerely interested in the job and aren't taking it as a placeholder to continue looking for new one.

Stress that you have the ability to work well with co-workers of any age. You look forward to learning from younger workers and vice versa. Focus on your ability to learn and adapt. Speak up about your flexibility in terms of management style, your openness to report to a younger boss, your technological aptitude, your energy, and your knack for picking up new skills. For many employers, it's not only about the candidate with the best credentials; it's about who's the best fit overall for the team. You have to make the case that you're the person who is going to both play your position like a pro and lend a hand to the team.

Don't hide your age. Never lie. Don't leave the age question blank on an application. That makes it too easy to toss out the incomplete file. Online applications might not even be accepted if you skip it. If you're in an interview, preface your response by saying you don't see why it is relevant for the position, if it isn't.

Be flexible when it comes to pay and title. These can be deal breakers on both sides. If it's a job you really want, look at the whole compensation package and remember a title's prestige is wallpaper. It's the job itself that matters.

Ask for help and advice. *Networking* is just one letter off from *not working* is a phrase I like to say. In this era of online resumes, it's all about who you know that can get you in the chair for a face-to-face meeting. When businesses are looking for candidates, they rely on employee referrals more than job boards or any other source.

Simply put, people want to hire someone who comes with the approval of an existing employee or colleague. It makes their job easier. That's a card younger workers can't play as often. LinkedIn, for instance, is a great way to pull together your professional network.

You have got to pick up the phone and make connections with people who work at the company you have targeted. That's the way to get an interview. If you don't establish any personal connection to the company, you're probably wasting your time.

Brainstorm. Sit down with your partner and friends and ask for help. Write down the names of previous employers and former colleagues, immediate and extended family. Don't be embarrassed to call family members when you're out of work. Get over it. Call friends of friends; people in your place of worship, athletic club, and volunteer organizations; and parents of children's friends.

If there's a particular industry you're gunning for, join an association affiliated with it and seek out volunteer opportunities. Attend industry and professional meetings and conferences.

You never know who will know someone who is hiring. College and university placement offices are there to help no matter how long ago you graduated. Seek out career centers operated by area colleges or local government agencies offering career counseling, workshops on resume writing, job fairs, and retraining programs.

Canvass local lawyers, accountants, and bank officers in town and see if they know if any clients are hiring. Leave no stone unturned.

Don't be bashful. No matter how good your resume might be, unless it helps you get face-to-face interviews with hiring managers, your efforts are squandered.

Getting interviews is hard work. It requires tenacity, persistence, determination, and courage to thrust yourself upon people, even if that doesn't come naturally to you. No one likes being rejected. The sooner you face this reality and prepare for rejection, the sooner you will be able to find a job.

Market your age as a plus. Think brand management. You are responsible for your own image. Workers 50+ tend to be self-starters, know how to get the job done, and don't need as much hand-holding as those with less experience. A great benefit to being older is that you have a good deal of knowledge and leadership ability. And whether you realize it or not, you have a network. You have a lot more resources to draw on than people in their 20s and 30s. So pitch your age as a plus. You need to be able to articulate your value. Strut your stuff.

Change it up. Look at your skill set and past experience as transferable to lots of different challenges and fields. Don't get stuck in a moment trying to replicate your old job. If you're switching industries, you're *redeploying* skills you already have in place, not reinventing or retraining for entirely new ones.

Reframe your experience. You're selling how your deep knowledge base and skills can solve business problems right now and in the future regardless of the employer.

Look for openings at small businesses, start-ups, small associations, or local nonprofits. They're more likely to value your experience as someone who can help them. You can provide the depth of practical knowledge and versatility that's worth two less experienced hires, and the learning curve is not as steep.

Keep your resume alive. If you're unemployed now, do something. Try volunteering for a nonprofit organization or do pro bono work in a job that uses your skills. Get out of your head and into the world.

You might also check with an employer that you're interested in working for, or one in a field that you would like to move into, to see if they offer unpaid internships for more experienced workers. It never hurts to ask. They might even refer to you as a "visiting professional." In the past few years, these internships for workers of all ages have broadened beyond just college students and new graduates.

As I see it, the rewards of volunteering are fourfold: It gives you an opportunity to network and get your foot in the door with future employers, it explains gaps in your resume, it feels good, and it helps someone else. You never know where you might meet someone who will lead you to a job opportunity. It bears repeating: Landing a job these days is all about *who you know.*

Use your skills to create your own business at home. Be open to consulting or short-term projects. You might find that creating multiple income streams is just what you are looking for and gives you the income, variety of work, and flexible control of your time that makes sense after decades of reporting into an office.

It's easy to get sucked into the mindset that a full-time employer is the only money-making option that's safe and worth your time. If you can work freelance or as a consultant for several employers and not have all your eggs in one basket, that gives you flexibility.

You might even make more money, if you know how to package and sell your skills. A good career coach might be able to help you focus your pitch. Of course, not everyone has the temperament or self-motivation to work for himself or herself.

Add some classes to boost your expertise in a new arena, say, nonprofit fundraising, if that's an area that appeals to you. Travel experiences, too, show that you've been actively learning and growing. You'll probably bump up your list of personal or professional references at the same time.

This is where a well-crafted resume is key. Achievements trump titles and responsibilities. Kick off your resume with specific examples of what you have accomplished in various positions, not a list of job duties. Hiring managers want resumes that put into words concrete examples of how you've helped the companies you've worked for make money, grow, and be more efficient.

Fine-tune your interview skills. It may have been a while since you have been on the other side of the table. Don't be nervous. It helps if you psychologically approach the interview as if you're a highly paid consultant called in to troubleshoot. Think like an expert. If you're desperate and thinking, "I just need a job and want to make money for the next 10 years," employers are on to you. They are going to pick the best, most interested, most innovative candidate.

You need to be able to articulate your value. State clearly what you think needs to be done and why, based on your experience, you're the one to do it. By taking a genuine interest in the firm you're interviewing with, learning about the company's history and goals, and talking to people who work there, you can demonstrate that. In a nutshell: Focus on the company's needs, not yours.

If you have done your homework on the firm, and Google alerts have kept you up to date on the latest developments with the company and its competitors, you'll have lots to pull from in your conversation.

- **Stay present.** Don't chatter on in interviews about successes you had 10 years ago. Focus on what you've done lately.
- **Don't name drop.** Refrain from throwing out names of powerful people you worked with two decades ago—that makes you seem ancient. And who really cares?
- **Practice positivity.** In truth, one of the biggest stumbling blocks to landing a job is negativity. You probably don't need a Botox treatment. What works better is a faith lift. You've got to believe in yourself. When you do, it shows from the inside out. People dwell on the negative—"I've been unemployed for too long. I'm too old." Have faith in yourself. After you've been out of work for a while, you forget your value. You take your accomplishments and contributions for granted.
- **Don't be a know-it-all with a chip on your shoulder.** Inevitably, the talk will turn to you. The interviewer needs to learn as much about you as possible, but steer clear of lengthy resume regurgitation. Answer questions with crisp, dignified responses. Take time beforehand to internally focus on your best moments and what situations you shine in. Be clear in interviews that if an employer put you in those situations, you will perform.
- **Don't badmouth past employers**. Keep it positive, even if you are bitter from being ushered out the door in a downsizing move. Zip your lip. No good will come from this, and it will only reflect back on your character.
- **Overqualified?** Deal with it, if you want the gig. Repeat after me: What matters to me at this stage is having the opportunity to work with exceptional people in a company whose values and products I believe in and where my skills and knowledge can be used in a meaningful way.

Chapter 18 includes even more interviewing tips.

Shoot for the sky. This is a little out there, but think about what the coolest job in the world would be, or who would be your dream person to work for. This is your time to do something fabulous, right?

"I tell my clients to play longshots," career coach Beverly Jones of Clearways Consulting says. Great jobs often come from unlikely sources. Once you have done the obvious networking with people who already know you, or those within your industry peer group, "you have to pursue the off-the-wall possibilities, jobs, in theory, you have never done, but have the skills to do. I have found these are often the ones that pay off," she says.

You will need to be fearless about doing this, says Jones. "What's the worst that can happen? They don't call you back?"

Sometimes it's hard to toot your own horn. Self-promotion is uncomfortable, especially if you've always thought of yourself as a team player. If this is an issue for you, ask people who know you well, whose opinions you value and trust, to evaluate you in writing: your best skills and talents, your personality, the roles you have been really good at.

What you will receive back is a solid list of your best selling points. Then when you're in the interview, networking, or doing informational conversations, you can say, "Well, people have said about me that…" It's easier to talk about your attributes because you're using someone else's tribute.

Overcoming Biases

When I was the featured expert at AARP's Virtual Career Fair, attendees peppered me with questions on how to fight back against ageism. They worried that the gray hair in their LinkedIn picture was why recruiters ignored them and employers didn't call for interviews. They surmised that the years of work experience on their resumes worked against them because employers quickly did the age math.

These concerns, of course, are legitimate (and I will give you ways to fight back in this book). Yes, ageism exists. Some employers figure that your salary demands are out of their ballpark, and if they hire you for less, you'll resent it and probably jump ship if you get a better offer. They often perceive, true or not, that you're set in your ways, or that you lack the cutting-edge skills or even the energy to do the job.

Then too, some hiring managers might surmise that you have age-related health problems, or are likely to, and you will take too much time off for periodic sick leave. And, of course, as my friend so aptly put it, there's the nagging issue that you've got an "expiration date," and you're not in it for the long haul, even if that's far from the truth. Finally, there's reverse ageism—the employer thinks you won't want to take orders from a younger boss who is probably making more than you.

But these are broad stereotypes. There are ways to prove them wrong, and many workers are doing just that.

It's up to you to lay their worries to rest. "The vital first step in fighting ageism is to be physically fit, energetic, and positive in attitude," executive career coach and author Beverly Jones counsels.

That's just the topcoat. You need to speak up about your flexibility in terms of management style, your openness to report to a younger boss, your technological aptitude, your energy, and your knack of picking up new skills.

Job search is difficult for everybody. And everyone seems to have a different take on what it takes to break through. It's not automatically your age that's holding you back. People want to employ people they know, or someone they trust.

And your experience does matter, but maybe not as much as you think it does. For many employers, it's not about the candidate with the best credentials. It's about fitting in with a crowd, its culture, so you've got to make it *personal* on some level.

"You have to make the case why you are the person who is going to both do the job brilliantly and fit in," says career pro Nicholas Lore of the Rockport Institute.

AARP studies repeatedly have shown that a large percentage of those surveyed say they have either personally faced or observed age discrimination in the workplace. And my 50+ friends who have been laid off and are out looking for work right now tell me about their roadblocks all the time.

"I bet there's a lawsuit here," my job hunting pals complain. Inevitably, that's when for the 10th time, the job beauty contest is whittled down to the final round of candidates, and they lose out. The dismissal goes something like: "Since we last spoke, we've changed our direction with this position," "We're reevaluating our needs," or some such excuse that somehow smacks of a soft brush-off.

It's illegal for employers to discriminate based on age if you're 40 or older, but many older job seekers know it's a fact of life. Confirming that it's your age that's holding you back from getting hired is darn near impossible. It's a gut feeling that you have. It's hard to really provide facts that you didn't get a job because of your age.

The truth is many employers do prefer to hire younger workers who will presumably work for less and with potentially more enthusiasm. "Some employers think older workers are less productive, less healthy, and more resistant to change," says my friend and go-to guy on these issues, Mark Miller, an expert on aging and retirement who operates the website RetirementRevised (retirementrevised.com). "Human resources experts and recruiters say older workers do often bring a false sense of entitlement to the workplace and resist adapting to changing business conditions."

The real issue, in many ways, is not age but oomph, inquisitiveness, self-confidence, and a yearning to keep learning. If you show those qualities, you'll be attractive to employers.

The fact is that compared to their younger colleagues, workers with a few decades of experience under their belt are typically better problem-solvers and people-managers and have honed leadership skills over time. I know I'm preaching to the choir, but you need to show that to potential employers.

You can do it. In truth, the message I want you to take away from this chapter is that to find a job today requires serious effort on your part. Accept that and get on with it. Job hunting isn't a piece of cake. No excuses.

Frankly, in my experience, rejection is often a form of protection. What you thought was the perfect job may have been a disaster for you. It might take time, but when you look back at it, trust me, you will know what I mean and be grateful you did *not* get hired.

Second, being unemployed, or seeking something new that will make you fall in love with work again, is not something to be ashamed of at all. You can hide away and isolate. That leads to depression, and it's a true game changer. Reach out. Get out.

Finally, your best strategy for circumventing age bias—and a job market that's rapidly changing from the way jobs are posted, resumes are delivered, how you are interviewed, and more—is believing with all your heart in your own talent to get the job done and shine. No one can take that away from you.

The ninth anniversary of my dad's passing happened recently. He pops into my mind almost every day. I want to share my favorite career advice he gave me.

The most important tip about work that Dad shared, which I follow daily, is to believe in myself and to take charge of my career. "No one else is going to do it for you," he liked to say.

I've continued to adopt Dad's can-do philosophy throughout my career. Whenever I sought his counsel about a goal I had or a job I wanted, he would always ask, "How can you?" even when others were telling me I couldn't, or I shouldn't. He never once doubted that I could.

And then he and I would break the goal down into steps for making it happen. Dad always said that "you have to dream" to get somewhere. And sometimes that meant dreaming of a better job and work life.

11

Adding New Skills

■ ■ ■

Career moves often require a skill refresh, or in some cases, even a serious hitting of the books. Once you decide what job you are aiming for, check to see the credentials required for the position. To get hired, you may first need to expand your skill set.

Adding the right skills can take some planning. For Cornwall-on-Hudson resident Alan Zollner, an IBM mechanical engineer for more than two decades, it took three years to move into teaching high school physics. He was able to take advantage of his employer's Transition to Teaching program. The company paid for around $15,000 of education, and his manager at IBM's plant in East Fishkill, New York, agreed to give him flexibility with his schedule. As a result, he was able to complete a student teaching internship, complete a master's of science degree in adolescent education, and become certified to teach in New York State.

While Zollner's education was intense, he didn't just leap in. He prudently started by enrolling in one education course to be certain it was something that he would enjoy.

Helen White also needed to add new skills to switch fields. Shortly before turning 60, she received her master's degree in sport management at George Washington University. Formerly a manager of information services at AARP, she attained her goal: to teach basketball and pickleball and organize recreational programs and tournaments for older adults throughout the Washington, D.C., area.

"I wanted to change the stereotype of older adults by getting them to move and enjoy the power of play," White told me. "The degree opened opportunities for me to do that."

White, who played basketball and tennis competitively throughout her high school and college years, had a previous degree in physical education and recreation, so she knew sports was her thing. Nonetheless, it was still a gamble on her future after leaving AARP. White, who lives in Arlington, Virginia, spent about $24,000 as a part-time student for four years to prepare for her new chapter.

Not everyone wants or needs to devote the kind of time Zollner and White did to changing gears. That said, a Merrill Lynch study conducted in partnership with Age Wave, a research firm that focuses on aging, found that nearly three of every five working retirees said retirement was an opportunity to shift to a different line of work. And it might take some added skills to do that.

If you still have a job and are eyeing what's next, get those wheels in motion a few years in advance. Planning ahead makes good sense. This gives you the time to add the skills you will need to make a transition to a job you love or work you've always wanted to do.

My advice is if you're changing fields and need to add a certification, talk to graduates and the director of the course of study you're pondering. Get a list of employers who have hired graduates, too. If possible, ask those employers whether the credential affects their hiring decisions.

Learn before you quit. If possible, keep your current job while you add the education you need for your new pursuit. Many employers offer tax-free tuition assistance programs—up to $5,250, not counted as taxable income—and the contribution doesn't have to be tagged to a full-degree program.

Fifty-four percent of employers offer tuition assistance to employees, reports the Society for Human Resource Management. Be careful, however, because employers can levy a variety of restrictions such as taking courses that relate to the employee's duties, taking courses as part of a degree program, and requiring you to work a certain length of time after taking the course—or requiring repayment of tuition if you leave early.

Seek financial aid. You don't need to be college age to get a subsidized loan—there's no age limit and you're eligible as a part-time student, too. The federal aid formulas don't take into account your home equity or retirement accounts, and because you are an adult, a certain amount of your savings is protected—usually from $20,000 to $60,000, depending on your age and marital status. To apply for aid, complete the Free Application for Federal Student Aid (FAFSA) form.

Take advantage of educational tax breaks. Depending on your income, you might qualify for the Lifetime Learning Credit, worth up to $2,000 each year. There's no limit to the number of years you can claim the credit. The credit can cover up to 20 percent of tuition and expenses for college and graduate courses, or for any class you take to obtain or increase job skills. (The benefit phases out completely for married couples earning $131,000 and singles earning $65,000.)

If you make too much, the income ceiling is higher for claiming a deduction associated with tuition and fees, up to $4,000. There's also a maximum student loan interest deduction of $2,500. For details, see the IRS website (irs.gov) or the tax benefits guide available from the National Association of Student Financial Aid Administrators (nasfaa.org).

If you're studying more than half time at participating schools, you can also take out a federal Direct Unsubsidized Loan (see studentaid.ed.gov); the current professional-school interest rate is 6.21 percent. Go to Edvisors.com, Fastweb.org, and FinAid.org for information on scholarships and grants for older students. Some state schools offer free or discounted tuition for older students. If you must borrow, look first at federal student loans, which offer lower interest rates than private student loans.

Consider applying for a Stafford loan. Although it might be tempting to borrow from your home equity, you're better off with a low-interest Stafford loan (staffordloan.com). If you meet a financial needs test, the government will pay the interest as long as you're enrolled in school. Rates are fixed for the life of the loan, but the rate for new loans will change annually. Many private lenders also offer loans, though rates will be higher.

Tap into Online Courses

Here are some resources that can help:

AARP Learn @50+ (aarptek.aarp.org) offers workshops, events, webinars, and online resources that can boost your career and improve your technical skills.

Coursera (coursera.org) courses are taught by professors from leading universities. Putting those university brand names on your LinkedIn profile or resume can be an added bonus.

CreativeLive (creativelive.com) features video classes on a variety of topics from photo editing to art and design. While classes normally charge a fee, the site also airs many courses live for free.

Khan Academy (khanacademy.org) is a nonprofit that offers free classes in math, science, computer programming, economics, and more.

Lynda.com, owned by LinkedIn, offers a wide range of courses for honing workplace skills. There is a monthly fee. Plans start at $25 per month.

Udemy (udemy.com) has more than 45,000 courses on topics ranging from web design to public speaking. Classes start at $12 each.

Of course, a return to school usually carries financial risk. There's no promise that a degree will increase earning power enough to warrant the expense.

Paying for your career education doesn't have to cut too deeply into your wallet. Community college courses are typically a few hundred dollars per credit, and certificate programs are mostly cheaper and more focused on the professional skills you want to add now than a degree program. Online webinars and workshops offered by industry associations are other avenues to consider.

Be practical. Get a grip on the precise degrees or certifications required for your new endeavor. Certain fields—such as healthcare, counseling, and technology—often require advanced training for certain jobs. If you'd like to go to graduate school, like Zollner did, perhaps start by taking a night course. You don't have to register for a full course load. You can add classes as your route and enthusiasm become sharper. And beware of spending big bucks on advanced degrees, when a couple of courses or a certificate program will do. Countless community colleges, trade groups, and associations offer certificate programs for adults in concentrated fields of study.

Do your due diligence. You can earn a certificate in art appraisal, bookkeeping, chocolate making, eco-landscaping, fitness training, financial planning, fundraising, home modification, and restaurant operations, to name a few. And employers and clients are increasingly accepting professional certifications as proof of someone's understanding of a subject area.

That said, study these programs with the eye of a possible employer, talk to students who are presently enrolled, and ask the program's director for details of where past grads are now working. Talk to employers about the value of the programs. Track a few down certificate holders, if possible, and find out how the credential has helped them in their job search and new career path. You want that certificate to have value in the workplace.

Keep in mind, though, that the quicker the training, the less value it may have for you. A quickie career coaching certificate that you can earn in seven or eight days of classwork for under $2,000 probably won't give you the depth of knowledge and gravitas you really need to succeed in your new career.

When career coach and author Beverly Jones decided to become an executive coach after a career as a lawyer, she opted for the seven-month Georgetown University Leadership coaching program, which consists of 142.5 hours of class time and now costs nearly $12,000. "The cachet of that certificate and the rigorous training required has made it worth my investment many times over," says Jones.

Research scholarships and grants. These, too, are available for older students, usually offered by associations, colleges, religious groups, and foundations. Try sites such as Fastweb.com to find what's available.

Take an educational trip. This can be a great way to study with a master chef, for instance, and get a taste of a potential new line of work. Typically a week or two long, these intense training sessions with professionals allow you to accumulate experience while you are still working at your current job. They can be a great way to build the expertise and proficiency needed for a new career.

They can be pricey, but far less than you might spend if you enrolled in a full-time degree program at a local college. The sheer variety of offerings worldwide is mind numbing. Serious cooks, for instance, might want to thumb through the *Guide to Culinary Arts Programs & Career Cooking Schools* published by ShawGuides (shawguides.com). It contains detailed descriptions of more than a thousand schools, colleges, culinary apprenticeships, cooking vacations, and wine programs worldwide. The comprehensive ShawGuide has more learning vacations. It's divided into two sections: one for career programs and one for recreational programs. Not-for-profit Road Scholar (roadscholar.org) is another source for learning opportunities. Given the demand for software engineers, CodingNomads (codingnomads.co) teaches coding boot camps around the world from Europe to Mexico to Thailand that combine travel and on-site coursework. The courses generally consist of accelerated 12-week Amazon Web Services (AWS), Java, and SQL courses: eight weeks on-site followed by four weeks online. The founders' theory is that by getting out of your daily regimen, you're able to focus on learning. I like that. Universities and colleges also offer learning-oriented trips, so you might check in with alumni office or local colleges for possible opportunities.

Review What You Have Already in Your Kit

Before you head back to campus, take stock of your existing skills.

Jot down any licenses or certifications you currently hold or held in the past.

Record any proficiencies you have in any subject areas. Perhaps you picked up a foreign language on your own, taught yourself how to build websites or blogs, or developed public speaking skills as a member of a local Toastmasters group.

List all office software you're proficient with, such as spreadsheet applications, presentation programs, database management software, desktop publishing or graphics programs, and blogging platforms.

Write down any hobbies that have taught you new skills or helped sharpen existing skills.

List your soft skills. For example, maybe you're good at solving problems, planning and overseeing projects, or resolving conflict.

Ask friends, relatives, and former coworkers and supervisors to list your best qualities. You may not realize skills you possess until others call attention to them.

Don't restrict yourself to skills you developed on the job. If you volunteered as treasurer for your local parent-teacher organization, for example, you have experience with financial management and budgeting. If you raised children, you have experience in childcare, scheduling, and training. How you developed your skills is less important than the fact that you have the skills and how you can present those skills in a way that meets an employer's needs.

Seek out local apprenticeships and fellowships. If you want to become a chocolatier, for instance, volunteer at a local gourmet grocery or restaurant that makes its own confections. If you're interested in learning the ropes of the restaurant industry, offer to help out on weekends, perhaps sautéing for the chef, filling in as a greeter, or even keeping the restaurant's books, if that's your forte. These are all ways people I know have made transitions to new lines of work.

Look into Encore fellowships. If you're looking for a career with a social purpose, consider applying for an Encore fellowship at Encore.org/fellowships. These are one-year paid fellowships at nonprofits, typically in a professional capacity, to help mature workers reenter the job market.

Explore internship, fellowships, and returnship opportunities. Internships, fellowships, and returnships (jobs for people who've taken a career break, often to raise a family) can fill a gap in your resume, and employers like them because they can test out prospective employees before committing.

If you sense a hiring manager is interested in giving you a job but wavering because you've been out of work or are making a career shift, consider asking whether you could have an internship, so the employer can appraise you after several weeks.

Check out websites featuring midlife internships and fellowships. For leads on internship programs for 50+ workers, visit these two sites:

1. **iRelaunch** (irelaunch.com). This company helps connect individuals who want to return to work after career breaks with employers interested in hiring them.
2. **OnRamp Fellowship** (onrampfellowship.com). OnRamp is a program whose goal is to replenish the talent pipeline in law firms, legal departments, and financial services firms with

experienced women. The law firm and legal department fellowship positions are for one year and the financial services fellowships last six months.

Do some sleuthing. A growing number of employers—Michelin North America, the National Institutes of Health, and Stanley Consultants, among others—have programs designed to attract and keep workers past 50. Companies with internship programs for older workers include Harvard Business School, McKinsey, MetLife, PwC, and Regeneron.

Take on a part-time job in the field of your dreams. To get a feel for what a new career will really be like, get a part-time job or moonlight in the field that interests you.

If you're interested in teaching, you could offer to guest-lecture at a nearby college. Even if you have to do the job for free, it's probably still worth your time so you can make sure this is what you really want.

Get started as a volunteer at a nonprofit. This unpaid work can help you build the skills you need. Search for prospects through sites like AARP's Giving Back, Create the Good, HandsOnNetwork, and VolunteerMatch.org.

If you're good with numbers, look into the AARP Foundation Tax-Aide program, where volunteers help lower-income seniors do their taxes. It's a great way to develop your tech skills, since the tax prep is done on a computer.

Seek out nonprofits that need your particular professional expertise through the Executive Service Corps and Taproot Foundation. Also, Idealist has a searchable database of both volunteer and paid positions. See Chapter 12 for much more information on volunteering.

Gain experience through contract gigs. Consider taking a contract job that can lead to a full-time post or that gives you the ability to weave together a patchwork of jobs in the Me Inc. mode. After you get in the door, you can make the job your own and grow the position to fit your talents. See Chapter 21 for more detail.

Volunteer Your Way to a Job

■ ■ ■

*G*o volunteer has become my mantra when doling out advice on career transitions for job seekers of all ages. If you don't know what you want to do or should be doing, or your stomach is in knots because *NO ONE* is calling you back for a job interview, or you think you might be interested in a specific field or company but aren't sure, then get up, get out, and *do* something for someone else. Get out of your head and into the world, I like to say.

The payback is plain when you volunteer for the charity that's near and dear to your heart. And chances are, you've already been devoting your time to one or two for some of your working years already. You can also volunteer for for-profits.

Baby boomers today have the highest volunteer rate of any age group. They also volunteer at higher rates than past generations did when they were the same age, according to a report by the Corporation for National and Community Service. Based on U.S. Census data, the number of volunteers age 65 and older will top 13 million in 2020, up from fewer than 9 million in 2007. Volunteering offers chances to advise, teach, arrange events and activities, do bookkeeping, and charm potential donors, among other options. Whether it is working with clients directly, say, serving meals at a homeless shelter, or helping out in the office, you're touching peoples' lives, and making a difference.

Moreover, volunteering may increase your life span. In a study of U.S. retirees, researchers from the VA Medical Center and The University of California, San Francisco found that volunteering may improve health outcomes by expanding retirees' social networks, increasing their access to resources, and improving their sense of self-worth. Another often overlooked benefit to lending a hand gratis is that you can gain actual work experience that can train you for your new line of work. For example, if you're in Washington, D.C., and you're interested in moving into work as a nutritionist, or even opening a restaurant, you might volunteer at DC Central Kitchen (dccentralkitchen.org) to help prepare healthy meals cooked from scratch.

Volunteering can shape the next chapter of your life and lead to a specific job. It might spur an idea for a job to pursue, or open a door to meet someone who can help you in your hunt.

Simply put, doing good makes you, well, feel good—even if you're just singing songs with patients in an Alzheimer's unit at an assisted-care home on Sunday afternoons. It's a warm glow of giving back to others, and for a brief time you get out of your own brain that's perhaps riddled with anxiety if the job market has you down. It gives you a perspective on the world outside your private worries. It's a confidence booster. You're needed. You make a difference. You're engaged.

You also make new acquaintances. I'll say it again: You make contacts, get fresh ideas, and perhaps get a spark of inspiration from these unexpected and sometimes unlikely connections. Sorry, it's worth repeating. Get out of your TV weatherman Phil Connors's *Groundhog Day* routine. It may also be a test run for a potential job. If you choose a volunteer post with an eye to your future, you may be able to take advantage of the chance to do a job before you actually "do" a job, if you get my drift. Volunteering is a way to get inside and see what goes on behind the scenes. It's not unusual for this kind of undercover detective work to lead to a paying job with the organization, or one involved with a similar cause.

The underlying job-seeking strategy: If you pick a volunteer opening that's in line with the type of job you want, you might run into people with the same interests or someone currently working in areas similar to the one you're seeking.

Volunteer Checklist

When you're hunting for a volunteer job, there are some important things you should think about. Here's a checklist:

- For starters, are you ready to go after a volunteer job with as much determination as you would a paying job? To apply for volunteer work, you don't just call up and show up. You need to apply, send a resume, and go in for an interview.
- What type of business or nonprofit is in line with your job interests?
- Would you choose a small organization with a clear mission or assignment where you can really play a big role? Or would the lure of potential skill-building and training at a bigger organization be better for you in the long run?
- Are you an out-in-the-field kind of person, or would you rather be back in the office working on strategy?
- How much time do you practically have to offer? Don't overcommit; you may not be able to bring your best effort. Volunteering more hours than you can rationally afford can also be a losing proposition if it takes away from time you need to spend job hunting.
- How long of an obligation do you want to make? Don't get roped into a year-long project if you really have only a few free weeks to focus on the project.

Finding the Right Spot

Where can you find a project that actually puts your skills and talents to good use? Skill-based volunteering is what you're looking for. A growing number of websites try to match your skills with a volunteer project.

ReServe (reserveinc.org) is a nonprofit that matches skilled professionals workers age 55+ with organizations in the nonprofit and public sector that need their expertise and pays a small stipend. I talk more about ReServe in Chapter 13. I also recommend you check out HandsOn Network (Handsonnetwork.org). This is the volunteer action arm of Points of Light, a network of 250 volunteer action centers that extend to 30 countries around the world.

Another free site is Catchafire.org, which is based in New York City. The site sets you up with a nonprofit or social enterprise, where you can volunteer a handful of hours a week over a period of a few months. You can also dedicate just one hour via a phone call for a specific subject question, for which you dole out expertise to solve a problem.

After you file your professional profile and check your expertise, the site pops you a personalized list of potential projects, so you can pick a volunteer opportunity and organization.

If you're having trouble seeing how donating your time is a good use of your day, try viewing it as a skill-building exercise. Believe me, if you've been in charge of the silent auction at a nonprofit's fundraising event, you can surely add event planning or event marketing to your resume and online professional profile. Tackling a fundraising job or chipping in to organize an entire event for a nonprofit shows off your sales, marketing, and management skills. Managing a team of volunteers is sometimes a paying job at a nonprofit (see Chapter 13 on nonprofit work), so being able to show that you have done this type of work is valuable information for a hiring manager.

Moreover, volunteer experience can pique a potential employer's interest. Many corporations have a soft spot when it comes to social responsibility. Do-gooders are valued. Volunteering also draws attention to your willingness to learn new things, contribute creative ideas, and provide hands-on help in situations where organizations are understaffed and lacking resources.

In fact, professionals that LinkedIn surveyed stated that when they evaluate candidates, they consider volunteer work equally as valuable as paid work experience. If you already have a history of volunteering, list on your resume and LinkedIn profile the specific charity or business and the dates you worked. Don't, however, use the word "volunteer" in the title. List it as "fundraiser" or "project manager." Highlight the bottom-line results, returns, special awards, or accolades you received for your efforts. Of course, in the actual job description, you can mention that it was a pro bono project. This highlights your altruism, but by defining it as a professional job, you give it the cachet and respect it deserves.

In the final tally, volunteering builds out your resume with a new dimension and shows you in a positive light.

There can be a downside: Many organizations do a pretty lousy job of managing their volunteer pool, so it may be up to you to find ways to donate your time productively. Importantly, though, don't present yourself as a great resource who has condescended to land in their laps and silently wait on the sidelines for someone to recognize that. Be willing to respectfully do what's requested, but don't be shy about speaking up about other talent you might be able to bring to the party.

If you have volunteered in the past, you probably know that it can be maddening. It's hard to believe they don't tap all the skills you have to offer. You feel as if you're wasting your time. So take action.

My insider tip: Give 100 percent to your volunteer effort. Show up when you're asked to and do what you promise you'll do. Be proactive. Anything less has the potential to reflect badly on your work ethic and level of commitment.

Not Just for Charities

It doesn't always have to be volunteering for a good cause. To figure out if a certain type of business is going to be a good fit for you, give it a test run by working as an unpaid helper. And yes, volunteering at any type of business is a viable path to a full-time engagement. Here's why: An employer gets a chance to size you up with few consequences and vice versa.

If that employer doesn't suit you, you're still able to get the essence of that type of work, or a general idea of the industry. If you want open a restaurant or start a chocolate-making business, or even get hired to work in one, for instance, you might start out by volunteering in the kitchen behind the scenes. You'll chop carrots and turnips, dip strawberries in gooey chocolate. You'll discover pretty fast how glamorous those tedious and long hours can really be.

You may love it. Hopefully so. And while you're doing the job for free, you have the pleasure of working alongside some pros, who may very well turn out to be super mentors for you. They can be great sounding boards, introduce you to others in the field, and offer advice that can smooth your way into that line of business.

Why Volunteer?

- It feels good.
- It offers a peek at whether a certain career field is right for you.
- It keeps your professional skills current.
- It broadens your resume.
- It adds networking contacts.

If you want to be invited to volunteer at a company, make an appointment with the hiring manager or owner and meet face-to-face to present your offer of free labor. If it's a small business, say, a gourmet chocolate shop or neighborhood restaurant, introduce yourself to the owner and explain what you're looking for and what hours you're available to work. Offer a trial work schedule, perhaps a few hours a day for several days, so they don't feel that they need to get tied down with a commitment to you. Be willing to do the grunt work. Then stay loose and see where it leads.

Some Places to Look for Volunteer Projects

- All Hands Volunteers (hands.org) is a volunteer-powered disaster relief organization dedicated to projects associated with areas impacted by natural disasters all over the world. Over the last 12 years, the group has enabled over 39,000 volunteers to donate 200,000 days impacting 500,000 people worldwide.
- Ashoka.org supports the work of social entrepreneurs. Volunteers are needed to translate documents and do a range of other work. Ashoka and Ashoka Fellows are sometimes in need of experienced translators to be "virtual volunteers" and translate documents such as articles, newsletters, surveys, brochures, reports, and proposals. Volunteers are also needed to assist with fundraising, marketing, website design, research, writing, graphic design, and technical support. You fill in the Ashoka Volunteer Form, attach a resume if possible, and send it directly to the contact person listed on any posted opportunity to which you would like to respond. When volunteering abroad, you should be prepared to cover your own travel, housing, and living expenses, and feel at ease in "rustic" environments.
- BoardnetUSA.org helps individuals interested in board service or a nonprofit looking for a new board member. Over 12,000 candidates and nonprofit boards are currently using boardnetUSA. You fill out a profile of your interests and professional skills; nonprofits then choose whether to interview you for their board positions. There is no fee for an individual to register as a candidate.

- Board Member Connect (Boardmemberconnect.com) matches individuals to nonprofit boards. To be considered for a nonprofit board, you complete the candidate profile. A member of the Board Member Connect staff contacts you if there is a potential fit.
- Create The Good (createthegood.org) is AARP's site that posts volunteer opportunities and lets you find good works to do in your community. You can also learn from how-to videos how to start your own volunteer project.
- Doctors Without Borders (doctorswithoutborders.org) provides aid in nearly 60 countries to people whose survival is threatened by violence, neglect, or catastrophe, primarily due to armed conflict, epidemics, malnutrition, exclusion from healthcare, or natural disasters. Volunteers are doctors, nurses, logistics experts, administrators, epidemiologists, laboratory technicians, mental health professionals, and others.
- HandsOn Network (handsonnetwork.org) features skills-based volunteer opportunities. This is the volunteer-activation arm of Points of Light. HandsOn Network includes 250 community action centers that deliver 30 million hours of volunteer service each year and extend to 30 countries around the world. These centers focus on helping people plug into volunteer opportunities in their local communities, partnering with more 250,000 service projects per year.
- Idealist.org offers leads to thousands of volunteer opportunities nationwide, plus internships and jobs in the nonprofit sector. Go to the volunteer resource center on the site for more.
- Lawyers Without Borders (lawyerswithoutborders.org) and Judges Without Borders direct pro bono legal services and resources to human rights initiatives, legal capacity-building projects, and rule-of-law projects around the world. It seeks volunteers with a legal background—practicing or retired lawyers, judges, law students, and others who have worked as legal support staff—to manage projects and sustain home and branch office operations.
- Onlinevolunteering.org is a database to find online volunteering opportunities with organizations that serve communities in developing countries. There are opportunities in

educational institutions, grassroots organizations, international NGOs, local governments, and United Nations agencies.

- Operation Hope (operationhope.org) seeks volunteers with a background in the financial industry (mortgage brokers, bankers, tax consultants, etc.) to work as virtual volunteers. For instance, in one program, volunteers provide free financial literacy empowerment programs for students; this program has reached over 896,000 students in more than 3,250 schools and community-based organizations in the United States and South Africa. The Mortgage HOPE Crisis Hotline (MHCH) provides toll-free services to assist homeowners needing answers and guidance for mortgages and credit. The Small Business Empowerment Program is an outreach for entrepreneurs in low-wealth neighborhoods.

- Senior Corps (seniorcorps.org) is an arm of the Corporation for National and Community Service and offers the RSVP (Retired and Senior Volunteer Program) service for those 55 or older to match them with volunteer opportunities. These programs are typically sponsored locally by area nonprofits. Some offer compensation or a small stipend, too. For most of the programs, health insurance is available for the volunteers, according to their site.

- Serve.gov is a national online resource for finding volunteer opportunities in your community and also creating your own. It's managed by the Corporation for National and Community Service.

- Taproot Foundation (taprootfoundation.org) places teams of business professionals who are doing pro bono consulting to help a local nonprofit increase its impact via marketing, design, technology, management, or strategic planning on issues like the environment, health, and education. Connect to nonprofits through the online platform for short-term virtual volunteering, four- to six-week projects that can be done remotely. Work with a team of skilled volunteers to deliver on a large scope of work over six to nine months with the Service Grant program. Join at an event that pairs you with one or more nonprofits to solve specific challenges in one day. It operates in five U.S. cities—Chicago, Los Angeles, New York City, the San Francisco Bay Area, and Washington, D.C.—in a variety of fields, including finance, marketing, and information technology.

- Volunteer.gov is a one-stop shop for public-service volunteer projects sponsored by the U.S. government. It's searchable by agency, city, and state.
- VolunteerMatch.org allows you to search more than 100,000 listings nationwide.

Finding the best place and assignment to match your interests and skills—that's the hard part.

Personally, I think my Labrador retriever, Zena, would make a tremendous therapy dog based on the feedback I get when I visit my mother's assisted-living community with her. "She made my day," is a comment I frequently hear from petters. Seeing the smiles Zena puts on the faces there makes me feel good, too. So I have put that on my list of volunteer projects to pursue and find out what training she may need to be credentialed to do this kind of work with me.

Everyone's different. So how can you find your volunteering joy?

As Richard Eisenberg, my Next Avenue editor, noted: "There's a growing body of scientific research proving that aging with purpose is really, really good for your health. But to receive the potential health benefits, it helps to volunteer for the right reason."

Nine Tips to Find an Ideal Volunteering Gig at a Nonprofit

Here are my nine tips for finding a volunteer gig that works for you:

1. **Know what you have to offer.** Nonprofits are often seeking people who can help them in precise areas, like fundraising, PR and marketing, event planning, and finances. Specific skills run the gamut from coaching and mentoring to web design, writing, and accounting.
2. **Consider your true purpose.** Volunteering can be something you want to do "to add a dimension to your life," explained Betsy Werley, a director of network expansion at Encore.org, who successfully pivoted from the corporate to the nonprofit arena. "A number of people who are looking to volunteer are searching for community, being with other people, and are not as specific about the mission of the nonprofit," says Werley. "If you've never previously volunteered, this is a way to meet new people and get engaged," she says. Or perhaps reengage

in an activity that you had to set aside at one point in your life. Say you always loved horses and riding, but for financial and other reasons, you were never able to pursue that passion. You might be able to volunteer at a therapeutic riding program.

3. **Be realistic about your availability.** If it's going to be too time consuming or too much of a schlep to get there, your burnout factor will ratchet up. Trust me.

4. **Decide where and how you want to make a difference.** Do you want to devote your energy to a local nonprofit, where you can quickly see the fruits of your efforts and work alongside people in your community? Or spend your time on a larger national effort, perhaps a virtual one, where you're working on your own via your computer with no face-to-face social interaction?

5. **Reach out to alumni associations and faith-based networks.** I've been a member of two alumni boards: one at my high school, Shady Side Academy in Pittsburgh, and the other at Duke University. The board work has offered me intellectual engagement, makes me feel my expertise is valued, and has an impact on the organization at some level. It has also allowed me to make new friends.

Recently, I reached out to Duke's D.C. Women's Forum to find out if there were more ways I could be involved close to home. I quickly received an e-mail from the one of the forum leaders with a list of five suggestions that could be useful for you in volunteering with an alumni group locally, too. They were: (1) serve on one of the local group's committees; (2) obtain speakers or create a program; (3) manage the group's presence on the umbrella organization's website; (4) volunteer at the group's community service events; and (5) speak one on one to young alums looking for career guidance.

6. **Check out websites geared to skill-based volunteering.** A few excellent ones, all mentioned earlier in the chapter, where you can find appropriate nonprofit opportunities include Catchafire.org (for professionals), Handsonnetwork.org,

Idealist.org, Serve.gov, TaprootPlus.org (for pro bono work), and VolunteerMatch.org. Encore.org has a searchable map that shows encore programs around the country.

Typically, you can filter through prospective volunteering assignments based on a cause, what you're good at, and time commitment. For example, at Catchafire.org, which is mostly virtual volunteering, you can choose from a one-hour phone consultation with a nonprofit needing advice to a two-month project.

7. **Look for places that let you interview before committing.** A conversation with a nonprofit honcho can give you a sense of the group's agenda and needs so you can see if you think it's a good fit. Conversely, the talk lets the group decide if it thinks you'll be right for them.

   The federal government's RSVP (Retired and Senior Volunteer Program)—one of the largest volunteer networks in the nation for people 55 and over that focuses on using your skills—has a well-established interview vetting process to help make the volunteer effort a success for both parties.

8. **Investigate local nonprofit matchmakers.** "The local lens is a good one for people who aren't quite sure but kind of want to get their feet wet," says Werley. "Every big city has some sort of a connector for volunteer opportunities." For example, there's Metro Volunteers in Denver and NYC Service in New York City.

9. **Start with baby steps.** "Each nonprofit has its own culture, and it might not work out the first time," counseled Werley. "Treat it as a learning experience, and you will find out what you like and don't like." Commit to a short-term project and then, if you're not finding the volunteering fulfilling, politely move on.

"If you are new to volunteering, look at it as dating," says Werley. "You're not getting married to the organization."

CHAPTER

How to Prepare for Nonprofit Work

■ ■ ■

Workers who end their for-profit jobs often eye the nonprofit sector as their next stomping grounds, either for full-time or part-time jobs.

This may be the time in your life when it feels right to give back to society. And getting paid for lending your expertise makes it even better. According to a 2014 survey from Encore.org, more than 4.5 million Americans aged 50 to 70 identify themselves as working in encore careers—jobs or volunteer work with a social impact, particularly in education, healthcare, human services, and the environment. Another 21 million are contemplating doing so.

"Those who aren't ready to wind down have a new option: Gear up for the greater good," says Marc Freedman, founder of Encore.org.

This chapter offers advice for those wanting to segue to non-profit work available in different parts of the country. I realize you have read about some of these organizations in other parts of this book, but I have gathered the resources together in this chapter for a handy go-to reference.

Tap Available Resources

Any number of resources available can help you find your way. You'll also want to do some exploring in your own town to see what organizations might have a program.

Encore.org has a network of fellowships aimed at helping workers making the transition to nonprofit work. To learn more about the Encore Fellowships, go to Encore Careers' website (encore.org/fellowships).

By 2017, over 1,500 Encore Fellows have been matched with host organizations across the United States. The programs have been supported by a wide range of corporate, foundation and individual supporters and the participating nonprofits. At the site, you'll find an application to fill out with basic information. Once you have submitted the form, your information will be added to Encore's database and routed to appropriate Encore Fellowships programs for their consideration.

A note of warning, though. With a limited number of fellowships available and a large number of applicants, the application and selection process is competitive. For more information, you can e-mail info@encorefellowships.net.

Seek out your local options. Here are a few examples. As I mentioned in the last chapter, one resource is ReServe (reserveinc.org), a nonprofit agency that connects professionals over 50 who have experience in marketing, accounting, and other areas with government agencies and nonprofit groups. ReServe works locally and is available in the Greater Boston area, Maine, New York City and Long Island, and New Hampshire, as well as the Mid-Atlantic region of Delaware, Maryland, Pennsylvania, Virginia, and Washington, D.C. And most recently ReServe partnered with Community Living Campaign in San Francisco. Jobs are usually part time that pay a modest stipend, say, $10 an hour. You might work 10 or 20 hours a week. ReServists come from all backgrounds, from marketing managers to social workers, HR professionals to financial analysts, and many use their experience to launch new careers in the nonprofit sector.

Here are some other examples, of local efforts. If you're interested in using technology for social change, you might apply for a five-month paid fellowship focused on the challenges faced by seniors and their caregivers being offered by Blue Ridge Labs @ Robin Hood (labs.robinhood.org/fellowship), a Brooklyn-based social impact incubator and a program of the Robin Hood Foundation. Acting as issue area experts, previous fellows have helped to build things such as a mobile app that makes applying for food stamps simple and a platform that helps renters get things fixed in their apartments. No design or technical experience is necessary to apply as an issue area expert. Fellows joining for the entire program receive a stipend of $22,000. Fellows joining for only the Research Phase receive $10,000. In addition to their individual stipends, each team of fellows will receive a small budget to develop their products, including funding for direct user research.

Leadership Pittsburgh Inc. (lpinc.org) offers a nine-month educational program that bolsters civic engagement. You spend roughly 10 to 12 hours each month learning and exploring ways to make a difference in the Pittsburgh region's economic development, education, human needs and human services, arts and culture, criminal justice, and quality of life issues in the community. Afterward, graduates gain firsthand experience with nonprofit boards for 10-month stints. They're matched based on their interests and skill sets with the needs of local nonprofit organizations, including United Way agencies and state commissions that serve the region.

To establish some contacts in the nonprofit world, volunteer for a mission whose cause you are passionate about. Search for volunteering prospects at AARP's Create the Good, HandsOnNetwork, and VolunteerMatch. Seek out nonprofits that need your particular expertise through Taproot Foundation and the Executive Service Corps–United States. Bridgespan runs an online job board for nonprofit positions. Idealist has a searchable database of both volunteer and paid positions. Chapter 12 covers opportunities surrounding volunteer work in more detail.

Preparation Is the Key to Success

Here are some ways to prepare.

Follow your passion. Your passion for and commitment to the organization and cause are what set you apart from other candidates.

Narrow your search. What causes are you serious about? Can you genuinely show that you have a passionate interest in a certain nonprofit's mission and care deeply about the challenges and pressing issues on its agenda?

Volunteer. Join community boards, offer your services pro bono, and get involved by volunteering for the organization or other, similar nonprofits serving the same community. If you have an interest in making a switch to nonprofit work, getting active now in the causes that interest you will show your commitment to making the transition. It also builds your network in the sector, increases your knowledge about trends, and helps you get a feel for the culture of the sector. You'll find more on volunteering in Chapter 12.

Wear your heart on your sleeve. Do so, and the nonprofit sector will applaud your fashion sense. A desire to give back in general is good, but it won't cut it alone. And a proclamation that you have deigned to lend your business thinking to save the nonprofit sector is a deadly sin. Nonprofit hiring managers want to hear why you want this specific job for this specific cause. The work is going to be harder; pay is probably going to be less. Your story matters and makes credible your intended major life shift.

Look at other factors, too. What size organization suits you? Do you favor a small group with a tight focus and a smaller amount of resources, but a greater chance to make a difference? Does a start-up appeal to you? Or are you drawn to a bigger organization, which might offer training to help you get started in the nonprofit arena but less hands-on work? Do you want to be out in the field working directly with people, or would you rather strategize in an office? Are you willing to travel?

Know what you have to offer. Consider your expertise. This can run the gamut from legal to financial management/bookkeeping (can you say shoestring?) to computers, to writing skills that can shore up grant writing efforts.

A financial background, for example, is in demand these days. Nonprofit boards are increasingly focused on bottom-line results for money spent and invested. Agencies need someone to help make decisions about benefits, insurance, grants, purchasing, and staff salaries. And the best people for these jobs are those who have done this kind of work in the private sector.

As a result, nonprofit organizations are more willing to hire people from the for-profit world who get the bean counter bottom-line approach. Donors often see themselves as investors these days, too, so they want to see that the organization is run like a business and hitting its financial goals.

Cash flow is a huge issue for many nonprofits. It's the people who have fiscal and operation management skills who are in demand. If you have a background as a chief financial officer, controller, or accountant, they're looking for you. One caveat: You'll need to have your internet-based accounting skills up to date.

Add credentials. You might think about taking a course to fill in any gaps in your background. There are master's degree and certificate programs in public administration, philanthropic studies, and social work—some can even be earned completely online. Coursework includes nonprofit marketing, fundraising, campaigns, corporate philanthropy, ethics, and law.

Institutions that offer training include Case Western Reserve University, Columbia University, Indiana University, New York University, the University of San Francisco, and Seton Hall.

A number of organizations and community college programs are designed to help experienced professionals transition into nonprofit jobs via training programs, fellowships, and part-time assignments. ReServe, of course, is one. So is Encore!Connecticut (dpp.uconn.edu/academic-programs/nonprofit-leadership/encore-hartford/program-overview/), if you live in Connecticut. Experience Matters in Phoenix is another organization that works with private sector workers who want to find work with community-based nonprofit groups.

For the most part, the shift from a corporate arena to a nonprofit is a do-it-yourself initiative. But programs like Encore Fellowships, Encore!Connecticut, Experience Matters, and Social Venture Partners (socialventurepartners.org) offer educational and matching services for those interested in a second-act career.

Research jobs and job-hunting resources online. Check out nonprofit-oriented websites to help you make the transition. These sites offer employment resources; volunteer opportunities, which can lead to paying jobs; board opportunities; and full- and part-time openings.

Read the job descriptions carefully. You will need to translate your skills in the corporate world *literally* to their lingo.

If you've worked in marketing, advertising, or even journalism and know how to be an advocate in prose, that's extremely important. Anyone really comfy sitting down in front of their computer and blogging, tweeting, and pulling articles that relate to the organization to highlight on a nonprofit's website will get a hiring manager's attention. That's because web content marketing is the primary vehicle for communication to potential donors for many nonprofits these days. So don't call it public relations or marketing; call it, say, blogging.

It's all about figuring out how you can advance the mission of the organization, whether it is tweeting, writing grants, or managing its financial affairs. LinkedIn (see Chapter 15) also has a job search section dedicated to nonprofit positions.

Work as a consultant. If you aren't in a position to work for free, you might be able to land a position part time on a reduced consultant-fee basis. Most nonprofits would jump at that. Plus, it's a great way to prove yourself in the nonprofit world and get the credentials that you have done it. If you've been a controller in a small manufacturing company, for example, and have been let go, you should be willing to take on a position in the nonprofit sector at a reduced rate, even working two or three days a week. Then, after a year, you can say, "I was a controller at the Evergreen Childcare Agency and managed a budget of $15 million."

Don't be the first one in. Just because nonprofits say they want to bring in best practices from businesses, it doesn't mean they necessarily know how to or are sold on it. Nonprofits might think they want someone from the business world, but that might be because they are getting pressure from a funder or board member and haven't really bought into the idea. So do your homework to find out if there are others like you in staff and leadership positions.

Be realistic about your salary, vacation, and benefits requirements. Nonprofit work usually comes with a lower salary. But can you put a price on the potential reward? Only you will know.

Use nonprofit work as a springboard. Working for a nonprofit might not be your ultimate goal. By offering your services for a period of time, though, you can get the flavor of that type of work, or an overview of the industry. If you yearn to be a landscape designer, for example, volunteer at your city's botanical gardens or lend your hand to a grounds committee for a historical home known for its manicured gardens.

Once you land a position, here's some advice to keep in mind: You might not be welcomed with open arms just because you were a star in the for-profit world. It can be a culture clash. Hello, humility. Your confidence and experience will win them over, so be patient.

In the meantime, decisions are generally made by group accord. If you're a take-charge type who gets turned on by making things come to pass fast, this can be exasperating. Your ability to be a team player will serve you well.

Then too, in the nonprofit world, you go all out, often lacking resources to get things done as swiftly or professionally as you'd wish for. All in due time, so take a breath. You will make a difference.

Tips for a Great Resume and Cover Letter

■ ■ ■

"Can you take a look at my resume and see what you think?" If I had a dollar for every time I've been asked this, I wouldn't be rich, but I would have some extra dough.

It's true. Since I write, speak, and consult with individual job seekers about jobs and careers, it's not surprising that I frequently field calls from friends and colleagues who want me to take a look at their resume to see what's missing, and give some pointers. I try to help. They agonize over the details. They're frustrated beyond belief. They shoot their resume off in a flick of a button when they hear about a job opening, and then radio silence—no response.

Sound familiar? I offer my two cents to them. Your resume is your calling card and needs to capture the essence of who you are and what you have to offer an employer. A great resume is at the core of a fruitful job hunt. But the more experience you have, the slipperier it can be to create one that's concise and truly conveys your expertise.

Every resume and cover letter is distinctive, or at least it should be, so there's not one foolproof formula. That said, there are some basic rules to consider. Essentially the trick is to boil all of your experience down into a clear, sharp, and engaging one-dimensional presentation. Challenging, I know, but doable.

This is your highlight sizzle reel. It's your advertisement, not your obituary. Typically a resume is reviewed in less than five minutes before it's decided whether a job candidate advances to the next step in the hiring process, according to a Society for Human Resource Management (SHRM) Resumes, Cover Letters, and Interviews Survey. I would be surprised if even that much time is spent, to be honest. Several studies indicate that often a resume has only about six seconds to make the first cut. Among human resource managers, who are typically the gatekeepers of which applicants get in front of the actual hiring managers, more than two in five (43 percent) said they spend less than a minute looking at a resume, according to a CareerBuilder survey. Nearly one in four (24 percent) spend less than 30 seconds.

Here are the best ways your resume can pique a hiring manager's attention.

Use a Simple Format

Simple is always best. Here are my best tips:

- Keep it to two pages. In certain situations, it can be three pages, but only make your resume as long as you need to underscore your credentials.
- Get rid of the objectives and summary. Employers don't care about your objective. They care about theirs.
- Skip personal information such as "married with three kids." Sounds steady to you, but to a hiring authority looking for someone to travel, it may keep you from being interviewed.
- No photos on your resume. You're looking for a job, not a date.
- Select a font that's modern and easy on the eyes. I recommend Arial or Helvetica, Calibri, Garamond, or Times. Stick to a 10- to 14-point size, and use black type against white paper for the body of the resume. Your name, however, might be in 15-point size, all caps; your contact information and section heads might be in 12.
- Be consistent in formatting. Use boldface type, italics, and underlining sparingly. Avoid using any of them together.
- Prepare the document in a plain Microsoft Word document format that can easily be viewed on most computers. You will also use this version to print out as a hard copy or to upload into

an online job application form. Most job postings will state what type of format is preferred. You will typically use a .doc or .txt format when uploading your resume for sending electronically.

- Put your contact information at the top of the resume: your first and last name, e-mail address, phone number (just one), a customized LinkedIn URL, and website, if you have one. Including your LinkedIn URL and blog or website address makes it easy for recruiters and hiring managers to find out more about you online. Refrain from using a middle initial or middle name unless it's part of your professional identity. List the city and state in which you live. Recruiters want to know what town you live in so they can estimate your commute time. Omit your street address for privacy reasons.

- You might need a new e-mail address. Using an AOL, Hotmail, or Yahoo! e-mail address on a resume can hold people back from landing an interview. There's discrimination relating to the domain name of your e-mail provider if it dates you. Trust me, AOL does just that. Ideally, use an e-mail address that includes your full name, such as johnsmith@ gmail.com, or one that includes your own domain name, such as kerry@kerryhannon.com. You can get a free Gmail address by going to Google's site.

- Below your contact information, list the precise title of the job for which you are applying.

- Use a reverse chronological order. Start with your most recent job. State the name of the company you work for, or have worked for, and what the firm does, how long you were there—month and year. Then list in bullets the position or positions you held. Each position ideally should include a snippet of a story.

Be a Storyteller

Numbers, statistics, and percentages get attention if you put them in bold type. These are quantifiable results that no one can quibble with when you're touting why you're a good person to hire. You want to say, for instance, that you grew sales by 25 percent, or you completed a job three months ahead of schedule. Resume writing pros refer to this as telling your CAR story. This stands for "challenge, action, and result."

Don't use full sentences. Begin with verbs. "Managed company tax reporting, finance, invoicing, purchasing," for example.

In your CAR story, write about a problem you faced, what you did to solve it, and the specific tangible result of your efforts. Don't be too formal in your writing. This is where you can show a little character and let reviewers hear your voice and pride in your achievements.

Importantly, make sure the CAR stories are relevant to the job for which you are applying.

Cherry-Pick Your Professional Experience

What employers want to see is your most recent 10 to 15 years of experience. No one wants, or needs, to read every one of your job entries over a four- to five-decade career.

Bundle your earlier experiences into one tidy paragraph at the end of your resume's "experience" section, and skip dates. Only use the work history that's germane to the job you're applying for now.

Here's an example suggested by Susan Whitcomb, author of *Résumé Magic: Trade Secrets of a Professional Résumé Writer.*

> *Prior Experience (Commercial Development, Business Development and Technology): During tenure with Ecolabs, promoted through positions in Food Business Development, Industrial Commercial Development; Applied Research and Commercial Development for Performance Materials; and Applied R&D. Initially recruited from UCLA as Research Chemist for Shell Oil.*

You have a few options for organizing your resume. Most job seekers use the traditional chronological or reverse-chronological resume format. You can also highlight your particular skills first, focusing on those that are most transferable to the job you're looking for.

In a skills-based resume, you do, of course, incorporate your employment history—but that goes at the end of your resume. This type of approach can be valuable if there are gaps in your work history of a year or more, or if you're switching careers or industries and your prior job titles don't correspond.

The top three or four key broad skill categories mandatory for the job you're targeting will help you to pick what to include in this

Skills Summary section. In your bullets, you magnify with detailed achievements or experiences. You will mention companies here, but you don't have to be too precise about the exact position.

Following the skills section, you'll have a concise work chronicle section. Include the company name, your job title, employment dates, and the city and state of the organization. Include volunteer positions or internships in this section—related experience doesn't just have to be paid positions. I advise including any volunteer work that suggests you have management skills. Being in charge of a gala fundraising event, for instance, converts to sales and marketing chops. Holding a board position shows leadership capability. Also, if you work for a family business, you don't need to mention that it's a family business on your resume.

Then, present your professional experience in reverse chronological order, starting with your most recent position. Include the following details for each organization you served:

- Start and end dates (month and year)
- Organization's name and what the organization does or did
- Position(s) you held and major accomplishments at each position

If you've had any specialized education and training over the years that is relevant to the job you're applying for, include a section for it on your resume. By adding recent training, education, and certifications, you emphasize your commitment to professional development, show that you're up to date with industry and management trends, and display an eagerness to learn new things.

Every resume you submit should be tailored to the specific organization and position you're applying to. Open your generic resume and use the "Save As" feature in your word processing program to save the resume under another name so you can make changes without affecting the original. After you research the organization and read the job description for the position that interests you, create your custom resume. It's essential that when you're applying for a specific position, you pay close attention to the qualifications and responsibilities described in the job ad, and fine-tune your resume to match.

Mind the Gaps

Extended unemployment, coupled with age discrimination and other barriers, can add to the challenges older workers face in finding a job, as the AARP Public Policy Institute report "The Long Road Back: Struggling to Find Work after Unemployment" found.

That's why it's important to fill holes in your employment history on your resume. It's best to have a good experience to sub for it, say, during a period between jobs—you traveled, performed community service, added a degree, or pursued other education.

Include a one-line explanation, such as "Volunteered for Habitat for Humanity," to fill in for any extended periods of unemployment. Otherwise, the gap is a major red flag that something is wrong with you even if that's far from reality.

If you were out of the workforce for caregiving duties, you can sell that, too. You were skill-building. No doubt you were a "project manager," managing a team of other caregivers—from nurses to doctors and physical therapists. You were a "researcher" tracking down the best doctors and medical care. You may have been a "financial manager" in charge of bill-paying and insurance claims.

Use solid action verbs to portray your caregiving experience and skills: directed, enabled, facilitated, hired, supervised, controlled, coordinated, executed, organized, planned, implemented, spearheaded, navigated, negotiated, secured, and resolved.

Add Some Zing

Interests, hobbies, activities, and professional memberships can also help you get noticed or even show that you're physically and intellectually dynamic. That can be a great way to subtly deflect an employer's opinion that older workers don't have the stamina for the job. It might even provide a personal connection to someone who is reading your resume, if he or she shares a similar passion.

Be Aware of Automated Screening Systems

If you're submitting your resume to an online portal, don't embed charts or images that the screening system can't read. Save your resume as a .doc or .txt file. These programs are the most universal and are easy to upload. Use .pdf files when it's listed as preferred or when you want to keep your formatting intact.

List the names of your employers first, then the dates you worked there. When tracking systems screen a date before the employer, they can reject resumes.

Scatter throughout your resume words and unique key phrases that appear in the descriptions of the jobs for which you're applying. If an employer's computer scans your resume and doesn't see the words or phrases it's programmed to look for, you'll end up in the black hole of cast-off applications. For example, if the job requires someone who has "managed" a team, use "managed," not "directed" or "operated," or any other synonym.

Be sure to include hyperlinks or addresses to sites where additional information can be found, such as to your LinkedIn profile or your website, if you have one.

One website to consider for help is Jobscan (jobscan.co). Upload your resume to the site, then copy and paste the company's job description. Jobscan then scans the two documents to evaluate how well your resume tracks the words used in the posting.

Consider Hiring a Pro to Help

It's hard to brag about yourself, and the sheer mechanics of composing the details can be exasperating and time-consuming. There is help.

If you're a college graduate, check with your college career center to see whether it offers free resume services. Another option is to seek the assistance of a career counselor, coach, or consultant to help you write your resume as well as hone your job search skills and strategies. You can also check out www.aarp.org/work for resume examples and best practices. LinkedIn has a "Profinder" feature that suggests resume writers who can help you. You can receive free quotes from potential writers via the site's matchmaking service after you fill in a short form that describes your needs—say, that you are looking for help with a traditional resume or your LinkedIn profile. Here are a few professional resume services you might explore:

- AvidCareerist (avidcareerist.com)
- Career Trend (careertrend.net)
- Chameleon Resumes (chameleonresumes.com)
- Executive Career Brand (executivecareerbrand.com)
- Great Resumes Fast (greatresumesfast.com)

You can also find certified resume writers through Career Directors International (careerdirectors.com) or the National Resume Writers Association (www.thenrwa.com). Fees range from $300 to $1,500 or more. You can probably deduct the cost of preparing and mailing your resume from your federal taxes.

At the very minimum, proofread your resume. Ask someone you trust to double-check it for you. I recommend reading it out loud, too. For me, that's the single best way to catch missed words and grammatical gaffes.

Resume Red Flags

Delete these from your resume now:

- The "Career Objective" section. (Employers don't care about your objectives. They care about theirs.)
- College or high school graduation dates.
- Jobs that lasted less than six months. (This can be a good way to condense an unwieldy resume.) These in-and-out jobs make you look like a flight risk at best and a bad bet at worst. If you can't stay with a company for more than a year or two, it might be a sign that you get bored easily or that you have trouble fitting into the company culture. Take the opportunity to shorten your resume by omitting these short-lived jobs. Be up front about these jobs, though, if asked about them in an interview.
- Outdated tech skills.
- Quirky job titles. Although these can be a conversation icebreaker at a networking event, an offbeat title on your resume can be a turnoff and unsuitable for a more traditional company. A bigger drawback is that the title could jettison you from a recruiter's search criteria. "Wordsmith," for instance, is unlikely to show up in an Applicant Tracking Systems Search for the specific keyword "editor." "Happiness activist" won't turn up in a search for an experienced "activities director."
- Too much personal information.
- "References available upon request." (If you advance in the process, you'll be asked to provide them.)
- Unrelated jobs. If you work in a field unrelated to one you worked in a decade ago, consider excluding the details of

that previous work experience. Include only the years and industries in which you worked, but not the specific employers and positions.

- Lower-level jobs: For jobs you held several years ago that are in the same field but don't reflect your current level, keep descriptions brief or omit.

Showcasing Your Talents

When you're job hunting, you need to be sure that your resume clearly boasts the talents that most employers view as essential these days. Here are general qualities to showcase.

Self-sufficiency

Experienced workers don't need a lot of hand-holding and can hit the ground running. That's precisely what a potential employer is seeking. Independent workers who can get the job done without a lot of direction are highly valued. That you're capable of working independently, able to get along without lots of supervision, and are great at managing your time and keeping a project on track are assets you need to sell with gusto.

To convey that, when describing your work experience, use words such as "managed," "led," "executed," and "delivered," and describe instances when you took the initiative or completed a project with little or no supervision. For example, "Interviewed machine operators and developed multimedia training programs that reduced training time for new hires by 25 percent." Statements like this show rather than tell that you're a self-starter.

Tech-friendly

One of the biggest concerns employers have about older workers is they aren't up to speed with technology and perhaps are unwilling to learn. Prove them wrong.

Here are a few ways to show that you're tech savvy. Mention in your resume any experience with computer hardware and software, especially any hardware and software indicated specifically in the job description for the position you're applying for. Work teleconferencing and webinar technologies into your resume, including Cisco WebEx, Google Hangouts, GoToMeeting, join.me, and TeamViewer. Experience with any of these teleconferencing and collaboration technologies establishes that you're a team player who can work remotely while staying connected.

Maintain an active LinkedIn presence (see Chapter 15) and list your personal LinkedIn URL on your resume just below your e-mail address. Prospective employers can then see for themselves how active you are in relevant industry and professional groups.

Showcase your personal blog or website. If you have your own blog or website, include its URL on your resume, so prospective employers can check it out. Even if they don't visit, the URL shows that you're tech savvy enough to create an online presence.

Problem Solver

When describing your professional accomplishments, add at least one that reveals your ability to identify and solve a problem. For example, you may describe an instance when you noticed that several customers had the same grievance, and you recommended a change in your company's policies or processes that enriched customer satisfaction. Perhaps you found a way to cut the time necessary to perform a certain operation or a way to cut costs.

Communicator

Your resume demonstrates your ability to communicate mostly through its organization and writing. To demonstrate your ability to understand a company's needs based on what you read, therefore, modify your resume to fit both the firm and the job description.

Shape your resume to present the information in a way that makes it easy for the reader to capture your work experience quickly. Aim for sharp, clear job titles, and lively, easy-to-follow descriptions of your job responsibilities. For example, you managed X project or led the team that introduced a new product.

Carefully proofread your resume to eliminate errors. Better yet, have a friend or colleague read it for you and suggest corrections and improvements. An error-free resume shows attention to detail and conveys that you can express yourself clearly in writing.

Visionary

Most employers are looking for candidates who are innovative thinkers. You need to be able to develop and pitch new ways of doing things and navigating challenges. When describing your experience or skills, be sure to include at least one instance when you conceived of a new idea or a way of doing something. Perhaps you read customer posts online that inspired an idea for a new product or service, or maybe you read something about a competitor that opened up new prospects for your organization. Try to think of any ideas you may have had that either made or saved your organization time or money or improved it in some way.

Lifelong Learner

Include recent education, training, and certifications. Presenting yourself as a lifelong learner demonstrates that you're modest enough to accept instruction, open to new ideas and views, and eager and willing to learn new things and develop yourself.

I would be remiss not to add these essential tips:

- **There is no I in resume.** Of course, your resume is all about you, but what employers really want to see is what you can do for them as mirrored in what you've done in the past. I recommend that you refrain from using the word "I." For example, instead of saying, "I managed," just use verbs in a bullet point: "Managed" X project, "Oversaw," "Created," "Designed," Initiated," and so on.
- **Adjust for a career change.** When you're looking to change careers, play up your skills, not your positions. List past employers, but tweak your resume to focus less on jobs and more on the skills needed to do the work. Then, too, be certain your resume displays the precise skills you possess that are relevant to the job you're after.
- **Be honest.** The stress to stand out in a sea of candidates may entice job seekers to be less than honest on their resumes and when interviewing, but is it worth the risk? A recent CareerBuilder survey found that more than three in four HR managers report having caught a lie on a resume, in addition to embellishments. The most common lies include
  - Embellished skill set
  - Embellished responsibilities
  - Dates of employment
  - Job title
  - Academic degree
  - Companies worked for
  - Accolades/awards

What Do Employers Really Want?

Here are five things that HR managers in the CareerBuilder survey say make them more likely to pay attention to a resume and application:

1. Resume has been customized to their open position
2. Skill sets are listed first on the resume
3. Cover letter is included with the resume
4. Application is addressed to the specific hiring manager
5. Resume includes a link to a candidate's blog, portfolio, or website

Filming a Video Resume

Video resumes are gaining in acceptance among job seekers, employers, and recruiters. Although they're no substitute for a traditional resume, a quality video resume serves as a nice addition to a cover letter and resume, sets you apart from the crowd, helps you build a bond with prospective employers before they have a chance to meet you, and offers you another opportunity to prove your mastery of contemporary technology.

Not all jobs merit video resumes. But if you're in a line of work where all eyes are on you—sales, public speaking, tourism, or fundraising, for instance—a video resume is a chance to show off your persona and your talents. It also shows a future employer that you're not daunted by technology.

- Buy a good-quality consumer HD camera to record your video. Then upload your file to your computer. Most computers have editing software to help you edit and produce your video resume.
- Be the star. Although some individuals have used animations, slide shows, and other artistic approaches effectively, you're usually better off simply speaking to the camera—assuming, of course, you're comfortable with it.
- Report to wardrobe. Dress professionally as if you were going to an in-person interview. These videos are traditionally shot from the waist up, so slip into your full costume to set the mood. Style your hair. Ladies: Use a little extra lipstick and makeup because the camera can wash you out. Go easy on the

jewelry. Men: Make sure ties are straightened and shirts are pressed. Watch for stray hairs drifting about on your collar.

- Prepare your pitch and rehearse. Review sample videos, and write a script. You don't have to memorize it, but outline your talking points. Practice what you're going to say. This isn't a long segment. Think of it as a 60-second commercial, a sound bite with some snap to it. It can run longer but certainly no longer than three minutes. Begin by introducing yourself with your full name, say what you do, and briefly describe the type of position you're seeking. Speak clearly, confidently and, conversationally—not too fast but with a punch of energy.

- Check the set. You don't want any background noise, such as a barking dog. Be aware of what's behind you. Some healthy plants or fresh flowers in a vase are good. A bookcase makes a great background, but screen it for any trashy novels. You may opt for a wall hanging that says something about you, such as a framed award you've won. A photo of you actually doing the kind of job you're seeking is another possibility.

- Sit in the light and speak to the camera. If you're using a laptop with a built-in camera, set the computer so that the lens is at eye level. You want light on the front of your face. If your room has a window, face it, or put a small light on the desk in front of you. Gaze straight into the camera as if you're looking into your interviewer's eyes. Talk directly to him or her—your choice of gender.

- Pay attention to your body language. No hair twirling around your finger, lip biting, squinting, or excessive blinking. Don't slouch. Try to appear animated and energized. Feel free to smile, as long as you can smile without it seeming phony.

- End on a strong note. End your video with something simple like, "Thank you for considering me for the job." Smile, and keep looking into the camera until you stop recording.

- Take two . . . or three. Plan to run through a few practice recording sessions. Ask your friends or family to critique the video. Save the version you like to your desktop.

- Distribute your video—selectively. You may want to upload your video on YouTube to provide easy access to it, but upload it as Unlisted, so it's more likely to be viewed only by those people you tell about it. Include a link to your video resume in both your paper and online resumes. Put it up on your own website, if you have one. Send the link to your networking contacts. Upload it to your LinkedIn profile and any other job boards that support videos. For more bells and whistles, check out presenter sites such as Prezi.com.

Writing a Killer Cover Letter

The significance of the cover letter varies by organization. Many large organizations forgo the cover letter and simply use automated systems to process resumes and match candidates to needs within their organizations. For others, the cover letter is a key part of the application and is used as an acid test to determine how well a candidate understands the needs of the organization and can communicate in writing. For these organizations, your cover letter is the key that opens the door for your resume.

Unless the job posting states otherwise, or you're submitting your resume on a site that includes no option for including a cover letter, always include one with your resume. This is your chance to sell yourself. A well-crafted cover letter demonstrates what you bring to the organization and why you're the best candidate for the job. It showcases your skills, experience, and achievements and highlights their relevance to the organization's needs. Here's how you do that.

First, read the job description of the position you're applying for. Research the industry and your prospective employer. Visit the company's website. Visit the websites of the company's top competitors. Visit Glassdoor, Manta, and ZoomInfo, where you can dig up additional information. Find out who your supervisor is likely to be and look the person up on LinkedIn. If you need to get past a hiring manager, try to find out who that person is and look her there, too. The more you know about your audience, the better able you are to appeal to that individual on a personal level.

Drafting Your Cover Letter

Your cover letter should be no longer than one page and typically organized by using the following three sections:

- Introduction: In the first paragraph, tell the employer what position you're applying for, why you're applying for it, and (if applicable) who referred you. For example, "Your need for a detail-oriented person with years of experience in strategic communication is precisely what I am in a position to offer and is timed perfectly for my decision to pursue my goal of working for [organization name]."

- ○ Don't write: "I am writing to submit my resume for the position of. . ."

- Next, describe your skills in a way that matches your skills to the needs of the organization. Use this opportunity to highlight training, education, and skills mentioned in your resume that are particularly relevant to the position you're applying for and the organization's needs. It helps to write an elevator speech—a concise 30-second summary of who you are, what you do, and what you'd like to do professionally. You can use elements of your elevator speech in your cover letter.

- In the last paragraph, express your eagerness to meet with the person to discuss your qualifications and the organization's needs in deeper detail. For example, "For further details, please refer to my resume (attached). I look forward to meeting with you in person to discuss the position and my qualifications in depth."

Fine-tuning Your Cover Letter

Once the first draft is done, here are a few suggestions on how to fine-tune your cover letter:

- Address your letter to a specific person, not just a title or department. You may need to do some research or call the organization to find out the name of the person who's in charge of filling the position or screening applicants.

- In the first paragraph, refer to the exact position you're applying for, including a reference code if the job description provides one.

- Include key words and phrases in your cover letter that match those used in your resume, just in case the organization uses an automated system for screening cover letters and resumes.

- Write brief paragraphs or use a bulleted list to present details. Leaving plenty of white space makes your cover letter more appealing and easier to read.

- Be direct and succinct. For example, instead of writing, "As was mentioned in the job description for this position, your company is in need of a team-oriented individual with a background in marketing and communications. As you can see from the details in my resume, my qualifications make me perfectly suited to that position," write something like this, "Your company needs a team player with experience in marketing and communications. I am that person."
- Share your draft cover letter with friends who will give you their honest reactions. Does your letter feel interesting? Does it make the reader want to know more about you? Revise as needed.
- Proofread your cover letter several times and have someone else check it as well.

Sidestep Common Mistakes

After examining hundreds of cover letters and resumes and speaking with dozens of people in human resources and others in charge of screening applicants, I developed the following list of common mistakes you should avoid when writing a cover letter:

- Don't send out a generic cover letter regardless of the position. Tailor each cover letter (and resume) to the specific position.
- Don't waste space on phrases such as "I am writing to . . . ," "Let me introduce myself," and so on. Get to the point.
- Don't merely repeat the contents of your resume. Instead, highlight your skills and achievements that address the organization's needs and the qualifications for the position.
- Don't call attention to your age by citing your 20, 30, or 40 years of experience. Instead, use words like "extensive" or "significant" to describe your experience.
- Don't include your salary requirements unless the organization specifically requests this information. Save the salary discussion until you're close to being offered the job.

For additional guidance in structuring and writing cover letters, check out AARP's resources at aarp.org/work.

Lining Up Your References in Advance

Potential employers are liable to ask for professional references to check your previous employment and to get a sense of what type of employee you are. They may also ask for personal references to learn more about you. Some employers may ask for the accurate number of years you've known someone and in what capacity—for example, a previous manager or coworker you've known for more than a decade. I suggest that before applying for any openings, pick four or five people willing to serve as your references.

- Bosses, coworkers, professors, and former customers and clients are good choices, but be certain they think positively of you or are at least neutral about your job performance with their company.
- Contact your references before you provide their contact information to see if they're willing to put in a good word for you. You might need to revive your reference's memory about the job you held while working with them. If your potential reference is agreeable, then ask what times and what phone number is best for someone to reach him or her.
- When listing a previous employer, check with human resources that all information in your personnel file is correct.
- Give your reference the background on the potential employer, why you're attracted to the position, and why you think your skills are a good fit. Forward him or her a copy of your resume and the job description, so they are prepared.
- Let your references know when you share their contact information with a potential employer.
- Each time your reference supports you with a recommendation, send a thank-you letter or at the very least an e-mail message. It's good manners and will keep the good juju flowing.
- If you land the job, call or e-mail your references to thank them. You might even treat them to a lunch or a cup of coffee and pass along your new contact information.

According to an SHRM survey, more than eight of 10 human resource professionals said that they regularly conduct reference checks for professional, executive, administrative, and technical positions. And here's what most of them want to know:

- Dates of employment—did you really work the dates you said you did?
- If it's a former boss, would she hire you back?
- What are your strengths and weaknesses, and how might they apply to the job at hand?

If you know that a reference check will be electronic—that is, the potential employer sends an online survey for references to fill out—let them know and review how they might check those boxes. It's human nature to answer more emotionlessly when responding to an electronic form. When asked to rate a person's reliability on a scale of 1 to 5, a reference might check 4, thinking that's a truthful evaluation, but that 4 can sink your chances of landing the job. Let your references know of the risks so they can take those into reflection when entering their responses.

CHAPTER

Job Hunting and Social Media

■ ■ ■

My friend Susan, who was looking for a full-time position, called to tell me she had just heard about a great job at a company where she had always wanted to work. The hitch: She wasn't sure she knew anyone working there, who might be able to get her resume flagged if she sent it via the company's job board on its website. She knew that I often said that without a genuine insider, zapping a resume online is like aiming an arrow in the air and letting it soar with no target in sight.

She tapped into her LinkedIn account to conduct a search and see if she knew anyone at the firm. Turns out she did, so she e-mailed her connection and asked for advice about getting her resume noticed by someone in the human resources department. That got the ball rolling. It took several weeks, but she did get invited in for an interview and, soon after, landed the position.

I admit it doesn't always work quite so smoothly. But you can't rule out the possibility that if you're one of the many older Americans working, or planning to work, you need to get on board with a social media footprint.

Most job searches nowadays are via the internet. Yep, social media platforms such as Facebook, LinkedIn, and Twitter have transformed how you job hunt. As I have noted, you must be comfortable with computers, basic software programs, web navigation, e-mail, and mobile technology.

There's a view out there that once you cross over the big 5–0, you resist learning new technology. Not cool. For those of you who are looking to switch into a new career or build a small business, it's even more important to prove them wrong.

In today's job-hunting world, it's typical to e-mail your resume to companies and to upload them to job boards found on sites such as careerbuilder.com, dice.com, flexjobs.com, indeed.com, monster.com, and remote.co. It's a given that you also need a social networking profile to support it. Online networking and rah-rah self-promotion through social media channels are increasingly important tools to finding a job. It's a little awkward for many of us, but with practice it gets easier.

You may very well choose to ignore it. Do so at your peril. The importance of social media is not to be taken lightly. If you spend some time, you can really build out a diverse network of contacts. I try to add a few new contacts each week.

Most job searches these days are at least started on the internet—specifically, social media platforms such as LinkedIn and Twitter. It's a way to help recruiters find you.

"Social media is one of the easiest ways to accomplish several key factors that help people land jobs," says Miriam Salpeter, a job search and social media coach, and owner of Keppie Careers. As a pro in this area, she told me how she advises her clients. Here are Salpeter's tips on how you benefit from being proactive online:

- **Grow a community of people who know, like, and trust you.** Expanding your network has always proven crucial for job seekers.
- **Learn new information.** Social media is an ongoing source of professional development opportunities. This is so important, as it allows you to keep up-to-date with what's new in a field.
- **Demonstrate expertise.** There's no easier way to showcase what you know to a broad audience of potential colleagues, networking contacts, and hiring managers than via social media. Be found. If you are "perfect for the job" and no one knows, you won't go far! Social media makes it easier for people to learn about you, and that's necessary to land a job.

I know from personal experience that it takes practice to be able to converse clearly and efficiently online. It takes the repetition of doing it every day. It needs to become a habit. Start by taking simple actions. You can share your know-how by posting a link to an article related to your area of work on your Facebook, LinkedIn, or Twitter page with your own short commentary, or chime in on a LinkedIn group discussion, even if it means merely checking the "Like" button.

When hiring managers see that you're using social media, it can help alleviate any worry they may have about you being an applicant who is woefully behind the times. If you are using LinkedIn, have a blog perhaps, and are even semi-active on your Twitter account, it's going to be hard for people to think that you're not comfortable with communicating online. I'm not saying you'll have overnight success in your job search by tapping into social media, and it can zap your time, but in today's marketplace you'd be foolish to ignore it.

Consider this: More than 90 percent of recruiters say they view applicants' social media profiles before making a decision. By building a strong online persona, you gain a competitive edge over a majority of job seekers who avoid these valuable resources.

That said, how helpful social media is in landing a job depends on who you ask. According to a survey by JobVite, almost all employers use LinkedIn to research, vet, and recruit employees. Nearly half of job seekers used social media in the search for their most recent job; of those, 67 percent used Facebook and 35 percent used Twitter. Fifty-nine percent of those surveyed have used social media to assess the company culture of a potential employer.

A 2016 study by the Society for Human Resource Management (SHRM) found that 84 percent of employers use social networks to recruit, a sharp increase from the 56 percent who reported doing so in 2011.

Nevertheless, "The Long Road Back: Struggling to Find Work after Unemployment," AARP's survey sponsored by the AARP Public Policy Institute's Future of Work@50 initiative, found that for those who had been unemployed in the last five years, the most effective way to find a new job was reaching out to a network of contacts, followed by asking relatives and friends about jobs, contacting employers directly, using a headhunter, and consulting professional associations. Interestingly, "used online social networks" didn't make the top five list of most effective means of finding a job. Only 20 percent used online social networks. Of those, just 45 percent of the reemployed said doing so was very or somewhat effective.

I'm not certain about why this disconnect exists, but it could be that online social media job hunting might be better suited to some professions than others. LinkedIn is clearly more aligned with a professional, white-collar job than positions for skill-based workers. That said, social media outreach will make a difference for many of you.

To help you steer through the latest landscape, here are five must-do social media moves.

1. **Become a LinkedIn member.** I view LinkedIn as a key social media tool for most job seekers. For companies, it's where recruiters go these days when they have a job to fill. For you, it's a fast way to build a far-reaching professional network. Networking rules. Employers hire people they know and people they know. You need to make a personal connection at a company where you want to work. LinkedIn has a tool that shows you exactly who in your network of connections works at a company where you might be interested in applying. I can't lay its importance on thick enough. Stay active on LinkedIn. Join alumni and industry groups. Try connecting to a few new people each day. Follow experts in your industry.

   It's easy to create a profile. For me, my LinkedIn profile is my working resume. It lets anyone who wants to know about my background, awards, interests, and so on see it all in a straightforward format that I can tweak easily.

   Don't be bashful about posting your interests and volunteer activities. A well-rounded profile creates an impression of who you are and how you balance your personal and professional life. I'm an active member of LinkedIn groups that relate to my current work, alma mater, past employers, and more. I comment on posts from others and add in my own posts.

   I recommend writing your own personal note when you send a request to people to invite them to connect with you on LinkedIn. The site automatically pops up a generic note, but it only takes a second to write your own. It's friendlier and a good way to remind someone of how you know each other in a more direct way than when you were colleagues at such and such company or classmates, or that you met at a recent networking event.

There's more window dressing to apply on LinkedIn once you're up and rolling. You can add a PowerPoint presentation, a video clip of yourself, or a speech. You can connect your Twitter account stream, so that all your LinkedIn updates are tweeted. I do that. Saves a step. There's a vast amount of information you can cull to paint a portrait of who you are, and you can do it one step at a time as you get more comfortable with steering around the site.

Recruiters look at the summary of your LinkedIn profile for a snapshot of your career history, connections, and recommendations, and that can make or break their decision whether to call you for an interview. This is your big chance to pitch yourself in your best possible light.

Add your LinkedIn profile web address to the bottom signature line on your outgoing e-mail, too. (I put my Twitter handle and my website on mine as well.)

Basic accounts are free. You fill out your profile, listing key words and skills that apply to the job you're searching for. Those words help recruiters find you online in a snap. Add a professional headshot. Ask ex-colleagues, previous bosses, and clients to write recommendations. You can research companies and individuals you want to target, connect with former associates, and let them know when you're looking for new opportunities.

To help you get rolling, LinkedIn has a Help Center that offers directions for creating a profile. See more on LinkedIn below and also please pick up a copy of my book, AARP's *Getting the Job You Want after 50 for Dummies,* for a deeper dive into how to navigate these sites.

2. **Sign up for a Twitter account and apps.** I'm a Twitter fan for a bunch of reasons, but one selling point is that there's no need for a personal introduction or recommendation, which you need with LinkedIn. Just by following their tweets, you can get the scoop on people you may wind up interviewing with or tapping for mentoring advice. You can also share

ideas and tips with other job seekers and pros. Plus, you're always expanding your network. (You don't have to follow everyone who follows you—choose those who interest you).

As with LinkedIn, you'll want to add a headshot that looks professional. For your username, always use your actual name or a shortened form. Include where you live and what kind of work you do. It has to be short and to the point.

You can also download Twitter-related apps that help you job-hunt. One to check out is CareerArc.com. You fill out an online form describing the kinds of job opportunity you're looking for and where, and the site tweets you matches and updates via Twitter, e-mail, or text message.

You need to do more on social media than follow people. It's important to participate in real-time online chats. Especially if you're on Twitter, you need to have regular—albeit brief—online conversations. Check out weekly Twitter chats like #jobhuntchat, one of the largest regular chat groups on Twitter dedicated to job search; #careerchat is another to stop by.

On these chats, you can find information about employment trends and firms that are hiring and network with recruiters and other job seekers. Several conversations are running at the same time, so home in on the one that's up your alley. Chats are all live, and you use the # (hashtag) tied to a certain discussion to keep track of the conversation or ask a question. Sometimes sponsors post transcripts.

Retweet others. Trust me, we all love to know someone is paying attention to what we tweet. It builds a virtual admiration society that is almost akin to friendship. You can also create lists of people, or firms who you want to keep a bead on, so you can quickly find what their latest tweets are and they aren't buried in your Twitter stream.

Otherwise, it can be tough to weed through all the tweets coming down the pike. I have a handful of lists that I make a habit of checking daily.

3. **Join Facebook.** If you aren't on the platform already, and you set your privacy settings properly and highlight your work experience and education on your profile, the site

has lots to offer. Check out *My Facebook for Seniors* (AARP. org/TechBooks) and see below for more on Facebook's job search feature.

It's okay to list your hobbies and comment on or post articles you find interesting, but keep it in good taste. Think of Facebook as a way to let people learn a little about you. It can open doors to great conversations in a job interview, too. Plus, you might even find you are building your network with people who know you from high school and college. That's been my experience. Trust me, they can turn out to be great sources when you're job hunting. You never know where you might get an introduction to a potential employer, or hear of a job opening.

4. **Tap into virtual job fairs.** It's all there online: company recruiters, experts, and so forth. For example, AARP offers virtual career fairs. Attending employers have included the American Red Cross, Apple, AT&T, The Hartford, Rockwell Automation, Jackson Hewitt, Mindteck, Toys R Us, and UnitedHealth Group, to name a few. You can find virtual job events like this by doing a Google search. A search for virtual job fairs for veterans, for instance, shows links to events sponsored by the Military Officers Association of America and Virtual Job Scout (virtualjobscout.org), sponsored by the U.S. Chamber of Commerce Foundation's Hiring Our Heroes. More on virtual career fairs in Chapter 17.

5. **Use apps.** You start by adding your accounts on Facebook and LinkedIn to your smartphone.

Want help getting up to speed? Adult education centers, community colleges, local libraries, and the Osher Life Long Learning Institute offer classes that can help you with smart-phones and smartphone apps, among other gadgets. AARP has lots of how-tos on its website. You might also tap into a how-to video on LinkedIn.com and YouTube from CNET, the tech website.

For social media help, pick up a copy of AARP's *My Social Media for Seniors,* at AARP.org/techbooks or wherever books are sold.

Why I Recommend You Stay on Top of Social Media

1. You can learn about job openings.
2. You build your network of people who may be able to help you get your foot in the door for an interview.
3. Employers are looking. They do their due diligence on you the same way you do your sleuthing on them. They will search your profile online to see if you're a good fit for their company and get a sense of who you are outside of your working world—are you a team player, do you have a sense of humor, are you an animal lover, what are your hobbies, and so on. They also are checking to see if your information is consistent across all of the social media platforms. So be sure to list work experience with your most sought-after skills.
4. It's a great way to market yourself. Think Sales 101. I suggest that you keep LinkedIn status updates and any sharing of posts there strictly professional. Facebook posts can be more personal, but do include some work-oriented updates related to your career. Instagram can be a mix of both personal and professional snaps.

Keep in mind that there is another sales job at foot here: When you post online, say, a comment or your profile, you are showing your written communication skills. Pay attention to punctuation, spelling, and grammar. Don't be sloppy. If you catch an error, it's easy to either delete the post on Twitter or edit it in LinkedIn and Facebook.

The Nuts and Bolts of Creating Your Social Media Profile

Each site has its own profile feature that allows you to insert different types and quantities of information. On every one, I urge you to include a professional photo and your name. Add a website or blog if you have one, work history, education, and so forth.

Kerry's LinkedIn Cheat Sheet

1. **Create an appealing headline.**
   Your headline is the text that appears near the top of your profile, just below your name. When employers run a LinkedIn search, the search results display names, photos, and headlines. Your headline can be up to 120 characters long, and I suggest you make the most of those 120 characters.

To edit your headline, mouse over that area of your profile and click the pen icon that appears next to your headline. A pop-up appears, prompting you to enter your professional headline.

Click in the box and type a headline that describes exactly what you do or want to do professionally. For instance, mine reads National Keynote Speaker, Career/Retirement/Personal Finance Expert/Strategist, Bestselling Author. Make sure your professional headline highlights any key words you want to use to promote yourself. You might also look at other profiles of people who currently hold the job you want.

If you're job hunting, I advise including some signal that you're actively looking for employment, perhaps "Actively seeking a position as X." This signals to recruiters and hiring managers that you're on the market. Another route is to place your preferred job title in your headline and then use your summary to remark that you're looking for a certain position.

2. **Write a LinkedIn summary.**

This is the place to tell your story in your own voice. It's your written sizzle reel.

- Write one or two brief paragraphs. Emphasize your main skills and examples of achievements.
- Write in the first or third person. Use the first person—I, me, and my—to add a personal touch, or describe yourself in the third person—he, she, him, her—to make your summary sound more objective. Neither option is better or worse, but pick one and stick to it.
- Emphasize skills more than experience. By concentrating on skills, you increase your horizons, because skills developed in one area of expertise may transfer, or as I like to say, redeploy, to another.
- If you're currently on a job hunt, wrap up with a sentence that starts with something like, "I am looking for new opportunities . . ." followed by a description of the position you're seeking. For example, "I am currently looking for an opportunity to use my skills in writing and analysis in the field of finance."

Although you can include a section to your profile for volunteer gigs, I would tuck a mention of any volunteer work that you're passionate about in your summary. This gives you an opening to spell out what motivates you and the type of work that energizes you (because this is what you do even when you're not getting a paycheck), and to make clear what the skills you've developed in that capacity in career/professional terms. You were a project manager, for example. You don't have to specifically say the work was not for pay, of course, but list the name of the nonprofit. It can just be one line: "I am passionate about the work I did with [nonprofit organization], where I [description of skills or accomplishments]."

3. Conduct preliminary research.

Before you start to build out your profile, do some initial research to find out what other people in your field and position have done with their profile.

Pay attention to the key words they use that you might include in your summary and profile. With a little snooping, you can come away with some great models to use as a foundation to help you create your profile.

4. Detail your job experience.

Pull up or print out a copy of your resume. Enter your work history. For each position you held, mouse over the Experience section, click +Add Position, enter your information in the resulting form, and click Save. Include positions you held for six months or longer and go back at least 15 or 20 years, with the most detail in the ones you held in the last ten years. Your experience and longevity in the workplace is what distinguishes you in a positive way.

Use proper job titles. Don't try to be creative by using a job title such as Money Guru or Sales Slam-Dunker. You may want to tweak your title to make it more descriptive of what you did or want to do.

Keep it snappy. When describing job responsibilities, skills, and accomplishments in the Description box, always lead with verbs and keep them punchy; for example, "Led

strategy," "Developed budget," "Managed . . . ," "Devised . . . ,"
"Created . . . ," and so on.

- ○ Include accomplishments. In the Description area, be sure
  to mention measureable accomplishments as you did on
  your resume; for example, "Completed key project two
  months ahead of schedule," or "Outperformed projections
  by 40 percent," or "Increased sales by 20 percent."
- ○ Reorder positions tactically. Arrange your positions in
  reverse chronological order with your most recent position first, unless you have good reason to do otherwise. For
  example, if you're looking for a particular position, you
  may want to list previous positions in which you excelled in
  skills required by the position you're seeking.

Add the volunteer section and add any volunteer positions you've held. (The option to add sections is just below
your profile photo.) According to LinkedIn, 42 percent of
hiring managers surveyed said they view volunteer experience as equivalent to formal work experience. It can set you
apart from other candidates.

Volunteer work can be a great icebreaker. True story:
One woman I know who was hiring is a dog lover and saw two
candidates on LinkedIn who were qualified. One of them
volunteered at the ASPCA. Guess who got the job.

By adding the "Volunteer and Causes" section to your
LinkedIn profile, you can share your volunteer experience
and if you are interested in skills-based volunteering or joining a board. This helps nonprofits find you and helps your
network keep your interests top of mind when thinking of
potential volunteers and board members. LinkedIn also has a
section called the "Volunteer Marketplace," that helps members find board and volunteer opportunities.

5. **Add your educational background.**

Letting LinkedIn know the diplomas and degrees you've
earned does more than boost your profile in the eyes of
recruiters and potential employers. It also helps you get connected with people who attended the same schools. Based on
the information you enter about the schools you attended,
LinkedIn can recommend people you know who may be on

LinkedIn and get you connected. Skipping graduation dates doesn't disguise your age, but I don't put mine on my profile. Other experts think it offers a point of connection with possible hiring managers who might be peers.

6. **List your skills.**

LinkedIn permits you to list up to 50 skills or areas of expertise. Your connections on LinkedIn can then choose to endorse you. To add skills, scroll down to the Skills & Endorsements section of your profile and click +Add a Skill. Click in the What Are Your Areas of Expertise? box, type a skill or area of expertise, and click Add. You can drag and drop skills to arrange them in their order of importance or put the skills most relevant to the job you're seeking first. Otherwise, LinkedIn lists your skills in the order in which they're most highly endorsed.

Keep in mind that if you're targeting a specific job or job title in your search, you may want to choose words that match those used in job descriptions for positions you'd like to apply for. When you're listing your skills, check the "I Want to be Endorsed" option.

7. **Add other important sections to your profile.**

The more details you include in your profile, the better. Here are a few of the available sections you should consider adding:
- Causes you care about
- Certifications
- Courses: Include seminars, classes, workshops, and other educational achievements to show that you're a lifelong learner and dedicated to self-improvement.
- Honors and awards
- Languages
- Organizations
- Publications

If you're in a creative profession in which employers or clients review work samples as part of their evaluation process, add media samples to your profile. You can add documents, presentations, videos, and so on to the Summary, Education, and Experience sections of your profile.

8. **Keep it current.**

Completing your LinkedIn profile doesn't mean you're done. One of the biggest mistakes people make on LinkedIn is letting their profile stagnate. Update it periodically with new projects, awards, and so on.

9. **Give and receive recommendations and endorsements.**

When you're trying to impress employers, what you say about yourself isn't half as important as what others who've worked alongside you say about you. LinkedIn provides two ways for colleagues, bosses, clients, and others on LinkedIn to vouch for you:

   ○ Recommendations: A recommendation is a written statement by a LinkedIn member vouching for the quality of your work or the services or products you offer. They may come from former teachers, mentors, managers, colleagues, coworkers, or clients. Positive recommendations give recruiters and employers more reason to trust one candidate over another who doesn't come as highly recommended.

   ○ Endorsements: An endorsement is an acknowledgment by a LinkedIn member that you have a skill you claim to have. Your LinkedIn connections can endorse your skills with a click of the mouse, making them much easier to give.

   One way to encourage your connections to give recommendations and endorsements is to write positive recommendations for them and endorse their skills. To give a recommendation to one of your LinkedIn connections, click Connections near the top of any LinkedIn page, click the connection you want to endorse or recommend, scroll down to the Endorsements or Recommendations section, and follow the on-screen cues to endorse a skill or recommend your connection. When you do, your connection is notified and is likely to reciprocate by endorsing your skills or recommending you.

10. **Get involved in LinkedIn Groups.**

You can find LinkedIn groups related to specific organization and industries, certain professions, schools you attended, past employers, and a wide range of other interests.

You can even create your own group. To find groups you may be interested in, type in your interest in the search bar near the top of any LinkedIn page, and click Groups. LinkedIn displays a list of groups that match your search entry. Click the group's name to find out more about it and, if you're interested in joining the group, click the Join button. If you choose to join a private group, the group manager needs to approve your request before you can engage with the group; this may take a few minutes to hours or even days.

After you join a group, you can and should engage with others, but before you post anything, I suggest that you hang out for a while and read some of the discussions to get a feel for the group's culture.

Whenever you or other members of a group post a discussion topic, it appears in the group and in the discussions feed on your Groups page. Below every discussion is a link you can click to "Like" the post, comment on it, or follow the discussion.

In addition to helping you grow your LinkedIn network and engage with other professionals in your field, groups offer the following perks:

○ Lets you keep up with the latest trends and technologies in your field.
○ Gives you an opportunity to establish yourself as an expert in your field. The group page lists the top contributors, which is instantly recognized by any recruiters or employers who visit the group.
○ Allows you to connect with professionals in your field in a less formal forum. You never know where that spark of something you have in common make come into play.
○ Demonstrate that you're willing to learn new things.
○ Provide you with another opportunity to post fresh content. According to LinkedIn, if you share once a week, you increase your chances of having your profile viewed by a recruiter tenfold.

11. **Follow companies and individuals.**

LinkedIn allows you to follow companies and certain high-profile individuals on LinkedIn without necessarily establishing a LinkedIn connection. Following a company offers the following benefits:

○ Keeps you in the loop about anything new that's going on at the company or in the industry. This information can come in handy as you compose a cover letter and resume or prepare for an interview.

○ Lets you know who you know. When you visit the company's page, a box on the right shows your connections at that company. If you're seeking employment with that company, these connections can be very helpful in getting the inside scoop about a job or what the company is like.

○ Lets you keep an eye on who's being hired and who's departing. If someone's leaving the position you want, this could be the perfect opportunity to get in touch with the company's HR department.

To find a company you want to follow, search for the company by name. When you find a company you want to follow, click its +Follow button. (One caveat: Linkedin does change its options regularly, so you may need to use the search bar for help.)

You can also follow thought leaders—high-profile individuals who publish popular articles regularly. For now, to follow a person or company, click Follow on their profile page. If you don't see a Follow button, click the More icon on the top portion of the person's profile. Select Follow from the dropdown. This is a relatively new feature that lets LinkedIn members follow people they want to learn from and may want to connect with in the future without establishing a formal connection, and to keep thought leaders from being inundated with invitations to connect.

I connect only with friends or people I've met in person or worked with professionally. That LinkedIn "connection" is part of my brand and reflects on me, my online identity, so I want to be linked publically only to people I know and respect.

But not everyone shares my philosophy about accepting invitations. Many people figure the more connections, the better. So follow your own counsel on this one.

Finding Job Postings on LinkedIn

Any company can pay to post a job on LinkedIn, making it one of today's leading job boards. To check job postings, click Jobs near the top of your LinkedIn page. Scroll down the page to view job postings that LinkedIn recommends based on information you entered in your profile, your LinkedIn connections, and on your job search preferences. You can change your job search preferences for location, company size, and industries:

1. Under What Location(s) Would You Like to Work In, enter your preferred locations (city and state) and click Next.
2. Select the industries you're interested in and click Finish.
3. Click Close. LinkedIn displays job postings that match your job search preferences.

When you find a job that sounds interesting, click it. The job page that appears typically has a button you can click to apply on LinkedIn or go directly to the organization's website to apply. It also shows whether any of your first-degree LinkedIn connections work for the company.

Practicing Online Etiquette

Here are a few good manners to put into practice:

- Read lots of posts to get a sense of the group dynamic before posting anything.
  - Be agreeable. No ranting or raving.
- Look for opportunities to add something valuable to a discussion, something that helps others in the group.
  - Stick to the topic at hand.
- If you have to disagree, do it with caution and respect. Probably best to let it go.
  - Don't share jokes. Being funny online is tough and dicey.
  - Be brief. This is not your personal soapbox.
- Don't type in ALL CAPS ever, because it is the same as yelling.

Tweeting Your Way to a New Job

Tweeting your way to your next job might seem a little implausible. But having a professional presence on Twitter can lead you to employment openings and connect you with recruiters. And it can validate online savvy that will assure hiring managers that you're at ease with technology.

How It Might Work for You

Suppose you're an architect looking for work. You tweet about developments in the industry and follow people who are doing the same. Over time you build up a network that keeps you informed in detail about the business and job openings, and puts you in touch with other people who share your love for the profession.

When a job opens, you may well first hear of it on Twitter. And, who knows, one of your followers who's hiring may decide the best fit for the job is you—the person who's been tweeting all that sharp stuff about the business.

LinkedIn gets the lion's share of attention in online job networking. But Twitter offers an inside track. Plus, starting off is easier—no need to create an in-depth profile listing your job history and more.

Getting Started

1. **Create a Twitter identity that highlights your professional goals.** Head to twitter.com and click the sign-up button. Choose your Twitter username, or handle, judiciously. It's great if you can use your full name, but if it's taken, play around a little to find a good one. Avoid anything kitschy.

   This is business if you're job hunting. It's not a personal page for your friends. So upload a close-up, good-quality profile photo, with a brief, targeted description of who you are professionally.

   Use the short bio space to describe what you want out of your next career move. For example: "As an accountant with over 20 years' experience, I'm looking for a position in a nonprofit organization."

   If you have a LinkedIn profile or website or blog address, link to it. And consider throwing in a (very) quick personal addendum to round you out as a human being. My account, for example, says "Passion: Horses."

2. **Follow the right folks.** Go to the websites of companies where you might want to work and then become their follower.

Follow leaders in the industry you've targeted. Before you know it, you'll be following a smorgasbord of industry bigwigs, bloggers, job boards, magazines, recruiters, professional networks, alumni associations, and human resources personnel.

Your screen will fill up regularly with their tweets. Watch for job listings, but also for broadcasts that can mean jobs. For instance, if a business gets new funding, introduces a new product, or opens an office or plant in a new region, it's a sign it may be looking for new employees.

3. **Plug into job feeds.** Twitter has loads of job feeds for particular companies, industries, and locations. Conduct a Twitter search to find relevant job feeds. For example, search for "microsoft jobs," and you find several feeds for jobs at Microsoft, including @MicrosoftJobs, @MicrosoftJobsUS, and @MicrosoftJobsNL. Search for "jobs chicago," and you find @JobsChicago, @ChicagoWebJobs, and @Jobs4CHI.

   Search Twitter for job feeds and follow the ones you like, such as twitter.com/jobsintech and twitter.com/hrcrossing. Every day, thousands of jobs are posted on Twitter, often long before they appear on more traditional job boards.

   Also, tap Twitter apps. CareerArc, for example, delivers targeted job openings directly to you. Type in the job title you're interested in or the skills you have, along with the city, state, and zip code of where you'd like to work, choose the desired delivery method, and click "Send Me Job Matches."

4. **Ramp up your Twitter etiquette.** Twitter doesn't have many official rules beyond the restriction that, for now, tweets can be no longer than 140 text characters.

   But here's how to be respected in this medium. Read the posts of users you follow and tweet a reply only when you have something worthwhile to add. Try to post, share, or retweet several items each day. Make sure that the content you're sharing (or even clicking on as a "Like") supports the image you want to convey. Never retweet something without reading it first.

   Use a hashtag (#) before any key words in your tweet (no space between # and the word) so that your tweet will show up in the Twitter feeds of users who are interested in the topic but may not be following you. A limit of two hashtags per post is best. Whenever you're referencing another Twitter user, type @ and then the person's username (no space after @) so that the person knows you named him or her.

The best way to bond with people you don't know is to follow them, retweet them, and reply to their comments. But don't tweet to an individual. Instead, use the messages feature.

Set aside time at least twice a day to participate online—perhaps an hour in total for Twitter and your other social media sites. Set a clock if you think you'll get sucked in for too long.

Finally, while online job hunting is useful, you still need to push back from the computer and go to real-world networking events or grab a coffee with someone to ask for advice and introductions. Yes, I know it sounds old-fashioned, but there's no substitute for meeting face-to-face and shaking hands. Real-time connections have staying power.

Follow Companies You're Interested In

Organizations, hiring managers, and others are more likely to be interested in you if you show an honest interest in them, and one small way you can do that is to "Follow" or "Like" them on networking sites, including Facebook, Google +, Instagram, LinkedIn, Pinterest, and Twitter. Following an organization not only shows you care about the organization, but it also keeps you well versed in what the organization is up to and perhaps even what's going on in the industry. This information comes in handy when you need to submit a resume and cover letter or prepare for an interview.

Even if you don't want to follow them, you might use search engines like Google and Bing to research organizations and key personnel. Go to www.google.com and search for an organization you may be interested in working for. Click the link to the organization's website, and you'll find loads of information about the organization and what it does. Most organizations have an About page where you can find valuable information about the company, its leaders, its mission statement, and more.

Create a Google News Alert for the Organization

Visit an organization's page on LinkedIn, and notice off to the right a panel that allows you to filter people you're already connected to at that organization.

After you "Like" an organization on Facebook, anything posted by that organization pops up in your Newsfeed.

After you "follow" an organization on Twitter, its tweets appear in your Twitter feed. Some large organizations, such as IBM, have numerous divisions you can choose to follow as well.

Five Ways to Manage Your Online Reputation

Job hunting is a two-way street. While you're researching potential employers and learning all you can about the hiring managers who'll be interviewing you, they're checking you out, too.

According to CareerBuilder's 2016 social media recruitment survey, 60 percent of employers use social networking sites to research job candidates, up from 11 percent a decade ago, when the survey was first conducted.

"Tools such as Facebook and Twitter enable employers to get a glimpse of who candidates are outside the confines of a resume or cover letter," points out Rosemary Haefner, chief human resources officer of CareerBuilder.

And employers put stock in what they find—or don't. More than two in five employers said they are less likely to interview job candidates if they're unable to find information about the person online. And nearly half of hiring managers who screen candidates via social networks said they've found information that caused them not to hire a person, according to the CareerBuilder survey.

So have you paid the proper attention to your online reputation? Simply put, if you're looking for a job, you ignore the digital "you" at your peril.

Invisibility indicates that you're not up to speed with technology and the online world. And digital dirt, well, that can really give the wrong impression. The biggest turnoffs that CareerBuilder cited were inappropriate photographs or videos; signs that the candidate is binge-drinking or using drugs; bigoted comments related to race, religion, or gender; bad-mouthing of previous employers or fellow employees; and poor communication skills.

So to put your best foot forward online, here are five things you need to do.

1. Know your digital identity.

Chances are your digital identity is pretty complex. Some of it you create—at a minimum you should have pages on LinkedIn and Facebook. Some of it is created by your friends when they post comments and photos you're in. And some of it is created by total strangers—the staff at schools you attended, the DMV, former workplaces, the local newspaper, et cetera.

Your first task is to know what's out there. So do what employers do when they begin researching you online: conduct a basic search of your name and its variations, such as with and without your middle name or initial. If your name is not unusual, you may get mainly material about other people who share it. So be creative in drilling down to material about yourself—try your name plus your school or hometown or last employer.

When you've narrowed things down, click on the top 10 to 20 links. Read carefully. You're looking at what a prospective employer can see.

Now, some of the other people who popped up during your search may seem to an employer to be you, though they're not. "Pay attention to avoid a mistaken online identity," says Susan P. Joyce, an online job search expert. "Your reputation and job search can be damaged by that person."

In an extreme case—someone with your name, say, was convicted of fraud in your town last month—you may want to be proactive and inform a potential employer that you're not this person.

But keep in mind that if your doppelgänger's entry appears far down a search results list, it's probably not going to bite you.

Still, if you're troubled, think about creating a "clean" professional name for your social media sites. It might be JohnHannon, JohnWHannon, or JohnWilliamHannon. You do this by searching variations of your name until you find one without anything negative associated with it. Then claim it on LinkedIn and other social media sites. Use it going forward on your resume, e-mail address, and job applications.

It can take some time to redo what you already have in place, but the basic change can be as simple as replacing your middle name with an initial, according to Joyce.

2. **Scrub the social media pages that are yours.**

Look over everything on your social media timelines and remove any dirt that you wouldn't want employers or recruiters to see. If you can't delete it yourself, contact the site manager and request to have it removed.

Check out Facebook posts that you're tagged in and untag yourself if the post contains any content, including photos, that is unprofessional.

On Twitter, you can review mentions on your profile name and discover tweets by others that mention you. If you can't remove an uncomplimentary comment or photo, you can at least prepare a response should a potential employer ask you about it.

Just because you're being vigilant with what you put online about yourself doesn't mean your friends are. Keep an eye on what others are posting on your profile and what you're tagged in. Consider asking for cooperation from people who are serial offenders in terms of putting up offensive stuff.

Create a free Google Alert for your name so you'll be notified via e-mail whenever anything is posted about you (or someone with your name) online.

3. **Fine-tune your privacy.**

Though you want to be visible online to a potential employer, every social media and networking channel has privacy settings that let you restrict how visible you are. In some cases, you can limit what other people share about you. With most services, you click an icon in the upper right corner of the opening screen for a menu that includes a privacy settings option.

Social media sites change their privacy systems often, and sometimes this leads to a change in your personal settings. It's good practice to review the privacy settings for all of your accounts regularly.

4. Be active on the platforms you've committed to.

Make a point of posting comments or articles, retweeting, or sharing on your social media sites daily to keep them current and relevant. This shows that you're up to speed with your industry and connected with leaders in your field. Be certain, though, that the content you're sharing (or even clicking "Like" on) supports the image you want to deliver to a potential employer. Never share something without reading it carefully first.

Adding fresh content regularly has a second payoff: it helps assure that when someone searches for you by name, the top of the search results page will include links to content that you posted.

Although you need to be careful about what you post, you don't want to be so reined in that prospective employers can't find a playful or creative side to you. Hiring managers look for a proper professional image, but they also want to get a bead on what makes you run and your level of comfort and engagement on social media channels.

Calculated posts on your accounts at Facebook, Google+, LinkedIn, Twitter, and even Pinterest can craft a richer picture of you. About a third of employers who screen candidates via social networks found information that caused them to hire a candidate, according to LinkedIn, and this included content that showed personality and interests confirming the person was a good fit for the company culture.

For me, I might retweet an article by *New York Times* sports writer Joe Drape on horse racing, or one about the sports teams of my hometown, Pittsburgh. I also periodically pop up in pictures of where I'm traveling on Facebook.

Taken together, these posts can help people understand who I am and decide whether I'm a good fit for their company culture. It also might give a hiring manager an icebreaker for interviews. I had a great interview with someone who became a new client after we both commented on pictures of our Labrador retrievers that we had posted on Facebook. I'm not sure how dogs fit in with personal branding, but they've always seemed to work well for me.

Tout Your Accomplishments

Bragging online is not in poor taste, if it's properly presented. For instance, there's a place on your LinkedIn profile to add all those sweet bits from professional acknowledgments to awards.

Engaging with the Community

Although I encourage you to use social media and networks as an influential tool for finding and landing that dream job, getting a job shouldn't be the motivator for connecting with others. If it is, you're probably going to come across as anxious and self-absorbed.

For valuable advice in finding and landing the job you want, consider following one or more of the experts sampled here:

Job Search

@Absolutely_Abby
@AlisonDoyle
@AvidCareerist
@CareerPivot
@CareerRocketeer
@DawnRasmussen
@dorothydalton
@JobHuntOrg
@JoshuaWaldman
@Keppie_Careers
@KerryHannon
@NancyCollamer
@PhyllisMufson
@Social_Hire
@Tonyrestell
@YouTern and
@YouTernMark

Resumes, Cover Letters, and More

@JulieWalraven
@jobjenny
@LisaRangel
@ResumeExpert
@resumeservice
@SandraJTResumes

Career

@Beverlyejones
@careersherpa
@dailymuse
@DorieClark
@encoreorg
@JohnTarnoff
@Macs_List
@MaggieMistal

@MHynesPDX
@NextAvenue
@Sixtyandme
@ThisChairRocks
@WorkCoachCafe

Human Resources

@hrbartender
@realevilhrlady
@SabrinaLBaker
@SteveBoese

Personal Branding

@DanSchawbel
@megguiseppi

Job Boards

@Coolworks
@Flexjobs
@Glassdoor
@GovLoop
@MonsterCareers
@retirementjobs

CHAPTER

16

Navigating the Job Search Boards

■ ■ ■

J ob postings via online jobs boards can be a top-notch source of intelligence about who's hiring for what jobs and where. But keep in mind that most employers still hire the old-fashioned way—they fill jobs either internally or through referrals. In other words, they hire people they know, or people who know people they know. If you know a company where you'd like to work, your first stop should be the firm's website careers section. You can usually apply directly via the site.

Next stop, surfing the big boards. Keep focused and don't apply to jobs scattershot. Online boards are not the be-all and end-all to finding a job, but they are a great first stop to see what's out there and what qualifications you might need for the positions that interest you.

Be realistic, though. It will help when the frustration kicks in after zapping resumes into the black hole. "Fewer than 20 percent of jobs are filled by someone responding to an online job posting," advises Susan P. Joyce, editor of Job-Hunt and WorkCoachCafe .com. You'll need to continue with personal networking—outreach to people you know in the real world—which remains at the root of a successful job hunt. That said, 20 percent is one out of five, so you may not want to skip this chapter.

To get the most out of job boards, you have to know how to navigate the latest features beyond creating an account and uploading a resume.

This chapter provides an overview of your options and how to use them, including the inside scoop on best ways to apply for government jobs.

Job Boards and Apps

Online job boards and their mobile apps let you stay on your search all day and even, if you choose, all night, wherever you may be. They alert you pronto when a position is posted that might be for you. You can zap your resume to a hiring manager straight from your device with a few taps of the finger.

Following are the leading boards and apps to consider.

AARP.org/Jobs

AARP has a database of jobs. You can also see the AARP Employer Pledge program, a national initiative to direct job seekers to employers who value—and are hiring—experienced workers. More than 300 employers have signed the pledge, including AlliedBarton, American Red Cross, AT&T, Charles Schwab, CVS Caremark, General Mills, Google, Kimberly-Clark, ManpowerGroup, National Institutes of Health (NIH), New York Life Insurance, Scripps Health, and Wells Fargo. The companies are listed on the site, and you can click each firm for current openings. Also check out AARP .org/work for lots more on jobs and job-hunting.

Best Feature

Postings from companies who appreciate experienced workers.

CareerBuilder.com

CareerBuilder is one of the largest boards, providing job listings, resume posting, and career advice and resources to job seekers. It pulls from career sites of more than 1,000 partners, including 300 newspapers and leading portals.

Best Feature

Extensive postings and smart career advice.

Facebook

We think of Facebook as a social place with friends, but it has a growing jobs board as well (facebook.com/jobs). The Jobs link is on the left column of your desktop or laptop homepage, under the Explore section.

If you find a posting that appeals to you, tap the Apply Now button. This takes you over to the employer's Facebook page. Hit Apply Now again, and up pops a page with your name and any education or employment history that you've made public on your Facebook page. There's also a text box where you can Introduce Yourself in 1,000 characters.

When you hit Send, the information goes to the employer as a Facebook message. If people there like the looks of you, they can set up an interview in that same way.

Tips

If you're interested in a company, be sure to "Like" its Facebook page. Flesh out your Facebook profile with jobs, education, volunteer work, and contact info. Make yourself stand out. You might, for instance, fill in that item that many of us leave blank, your favorite quote. And keep in mind your privacy settings—employers will be able to see anything you've designated as public on your profile.

Best Feature

Ability to send an employer a personal precis based on your Facebook profile, rather than having to create a new profile and upload a resume.

Glassdoor.com

This website offers job listings and reviews of more than 600,000 companies worldwide, CEO approval ratings, salary reports, interview reviews and questions, benefits reviews, and more. Users sign up through their e-mail addresses or Facebook or Google accounts.

The search filter scans through millions of listings on the site to find potential jobs for you based on location, salary, company size, and job title. Find something you like? You can apply directly. Those are standard features in job apps, but Glassdoor goes further than many in letting you *understand* a company that has an opening that interests you.

For a start, you can peruse reviews of the company by current and former employees, and the numbers are enormous. When last checked, the Home Depot entry had over 15,000 employee reviews, which gave the company an overall rating of 3.5 stars (out of five) as a place to work. There's also data on such things as how many employees like a company's CEO, how it ranks with others based on employee benefits, and types of companies you should never work for. Curious about the look and feel of a particular workplace? You can browse for snapshots from employees' cameras.

You have to keep in mind the limitations of online reviews about anything—people tend to go to the trouble of posting a review when they want to gripe, not sing praise. Still, the review feature can give you an insider's peek at working at a particular company. And Glassdoor maintains a policy of not allowing employers to delete or alter reviews.

Best Feature

Standout tools for researching a potential employer.

Google

Google lets you search for jobs across most of the major online job boards like CareerBuilder, Facebook, LinkedIn, Monster, and others. Google also includes job listings its finds on a company's homepage.

The goal is to give job seekers a one-stop way to see which jobs are available without having to go to numerous sites and stumbling on duplicate postings. On the Google search bar, you type in is a query like "freelance writing jobs in Pittsburgh," "marketing jobs in Washington, D.C.," or whatever your fancy is. The search result page is broad but you winnow it down by such criteria as contractor, full-time, or part-time positions.

You can filter jobs by type of company, title, location, when they were posted, and employer. You can also create notification alerts for when a new job is posted that matches your ideal position.

Once you find a job posting you're interested in, Google links you to the job site to start the application process. For jobs that appeared on multiple sites, Google connects you to the one with the most complete job posting. You are also able to access Glassdoor and Indeed ratings for a company.

Best Feature

The sheer scope and breadth of the job postings and ability to customize search.

Indeed.com

With Indeed.com, you can sort job postings by criteria such as geography, industry, experience, or salary. You can also post your resume after creating an account and read reviews by current and former employees rating work-life balance, compensation and benefits, and job culture.

Indeed's Job Trends button (indeed.com/jobtrends) analyzes its millions of job postings to show which industries are hiring, job titles, top locations, and top keyword searches. You can click to exact job postings, sort by salary, and get new jobs sent to you by e-mail from that search.

Indeed gathers job listings based on your settings—industry, salary, and more—from all the major online job boards, newspaper classifieds, associations, and company career pages into one location for you to access. If you are using the app, you can find openings in towns nearby based on your device's GPS telling it where you are. Set up e-mail alerts to be dinged when new jobs pop up in a certain category.

When you find a job you like, you can save it so you can apply later when you've got time to focus. Or, if you have uploaded your resume, you can send it in straightaway with a customized message attached. The app keeps a record of each job you apply for.

Best Feature

Vast listing of potential jobs.

Job-Hunt.org

This free online guide focuses on providing job seekers over 50 with articles written by experts covering topics ranging from finding contract jobs to interviewing tips, avoiding job scams, working with recruiters, and the best ways to use LinkedIn and Google for job searches.

Best Feature

Great articles and advice on the nuts and bolts of job search.

Jobr

Jobr is an app exclusively for your tablet or smartphone. The big job board Monster scooped up this fast-growing start-up tool (jobr. jobrapp.com). It works like a hip dating app. After you set up a profile and upload your resume, you type in the kind of job you're looking for—sales, say—and your location to get rolling. As potential jobs land on your screen, you swipe left to dismiss and move along and swipe right to apply—as you would a potential romantic match.

You'll do well to go slow, however. If you swipe left, you may never see the job again. If you swipe right, you may be applying for the job prematurely without really considering if it's up your alley and how you might make yourself stand out. The simple fact is that job seeking requires thoughtful consideration.

To help you navigate, the app provides a virtual "career concierge" that answers your questions as you go.

Best Feature

Speedy hook-ups, and quick answers from that concierge helper when you get tripped up.

Monster.com

One of the original job boards, Monster has expanded to include many resources. You can search for and apply for jobs online, post a resume, review company profiles, and get salary information and career advice.

LinkedIn

LinkedIn's Jobs link appears on the header of your profile page. Click on the icon and you'll be transferred to a page listing jobs LinkedIn believes may interest you, based on experience listed in your profile and companies where you have contacts. This makes LinkedIn a leader in working your connections for a referral.

Under the Update Preferences tab, you can check a box to let recruiters know you're on the market. You type in a short (300 characters max) introduction laying out what you're pursuing. This feature is meant to be private, meaning no one in your public connections is to know you're engaging with recruiters. But the site does warn: "We take steps to not show your current company that you're open, but can't guarantee that we can identify every recruiter affiliated with your company."

While the basic LinkedIn Job Search is free, the site also offers a Premium subscription at $29.99 per month with features that evaluate you against other job applicants for the position, provide specific salary information, and bump you to the top of recruiter lists as a featured applicant.

Best Features

That heads-up to recruiters that you're on the prowl. And alerts about which LinkedIn connections have contacts at a company where you'd like to work.

LinkUp

LinkUp (linkup.com) lists jobs that are found only on company websites. This helps you search in what's sometimes called the hidden job market. The fact is that the major job search engines rely on employers taking the initiative to provide them with lists of jobs they're trying to fill. That means the engines don't have jobs that are "hiding in plain sight" on the websites of employers who for whatever reason don't want to list with the big engines. LinkUp is updated daily and currently has more than three million jobs.

Best Feature

Access to jobs that may still be under the radar.

Snagajob

Snagajob (snagajob.com) specializes in connecting you with hourly employment. You'll find a range of jobs such as cashier, delivery driver, restaurant greeter, security guard, and more. Click on links to Houston or San Francisco and you'll find by-the-hour opportunities in those cities.

You can search for local job openings and have "Daily Job Matches" update sent directly to you. You can filter positions by schedule (part time, seasonal, summer) and type of job (automotive, construction, food and restaurant) and distance from your home. The app has a map function to show you the company's location.

While Snagajob lists many jobs that require just a click to apply, with others you have to go through the longer process of applying on the company's website.

Best Feature

Local, hourly jobs take center stage.

Switch

Switch (switchapp.com) is an up-and-coming app for your smartphone or tablet, but it's still specialized in scope. It primarily matches jobs seekers in New York City and the San Francisco Bay Area with employers offering tech- and media-related jobs. But it's expanding to other industries and cities.

This app encourages you to upload your LinkedIn profile and resume. Once you're on board, Switch recommends jobs daily based on your background and location. As with Jobr, you swipe right to show you're interested in a job, and left to pass.

But here you're anonymous. If you express interest, hiring managers see only your professional profile—not your name or contact information. If they like it, you're instantly connected with them so that you can do a virtual chat about the opening.

Switch's discreet platform generally allows you to be on the market without the concern that a current employer or client will hear about it (though you can never be 100 percent sure word won't leak). Your profile is automatically excluded from being sent to companies that are on your profile.

Best Feature

Anonymous matches without the fuss of cover letters and applications.

ZipRecruiter

ZipRecruiter Job Search (ziprecruiter.com) started in 2010 as a platform where small businesses can post jobs, but it has grown considerably and now aggregates listings from more than 100 job boards.

You complete a profile on the site and upload a resume and cover letter, which you can edit as you go along, to customize to the needs of particular employers. You're able to bookmark a job that interests you, and then apply for it later once you're on your home computer. You can also set custom alerts for up to 20 types of jobs, with daily notifications sent your way.

You can opt in to a database of active job seekers through which thousands of employers and recruiters can search for people with your skills and (you hope) designate you as one to be contacted. You'll get status updates, such as when your resume has been viewed, which can give you important impressions for how your resume and experience are playing in the market.

Best Features

A wide range of flexible kinds of work, and the ability to get noticed by recruiters.

Five Pitfalls of an Online Job Search

Job boards are great for conducting research, but be aware of the following potential drawbacks:

- Online job postings aren't always removed in a timely fashion, so the job opening may no longer exist by the time you discover it.
- Recruiters sometimes post jobs to determine whether the description is alluring for job seekers. If too few people respond, they change it and the true posting goes live a few days or even weeks later.
- Sometimes recruiters put up fake posts to gather resumes for future headhunting searches.
- Employers may post jobs to satisfy the public posting requirement before hiring the in-house applicant who already has been chosen.
- Scammers collect resumes and other information from job seekers.

Helpful Tip

Salary.com and PayScale.com both help you research salary levels where you live and for the position you're seeking. PayScale lets you run a personal salary report and has a tool to help you find the best job suited for your needs. The database filters jobs based on criteria such as salary, location, education, and flexibility. LinkedIn (linkedin.com/salary) also has a detailed breakdown of salaries by job title and location.

Additional websites to consider visiting:

- **Craigslist** (craigslist.org) doesn't focus on jobs, but it's worth checking out for local and part-time jobs. Fifty+ job seekers have definitely found success with it. That said, be especially careful on Craigslist because anyone can post a job opening. Research the employer carefully before sending any sensitive information, and don't go to your initial interview alone.
- **O*NET OnLine** (onetonline.org) is the Occupational Information Network, sponsored by the U.S. Department of Labor. It includes multiple search tools, summary and detailed occupational reports, occupational outlook information, and direct links to job postings, apprenticeship programs, and salary information.
- **Mynextmove.org** is part of O*Net and is geared toward those who are new to using web tools. The site offers an online interest inventory and includes a list of occupations that match the user's interest profile.
- **National Older Worker Career Center** (nowcc.org) is a non-profit organization dedicated to promoting experienced workers as a "valuable and critical component of the nation's workforce." Mouse over Applicants near the top of the opening page, and click Current Openings to browse job openings listed by state and find a link to submit your application.
- **Retiredbrains.com** is an online job board specializing in part-time gigs. It shows thousands of jobs for those over 50.
- **Retirementjobs.com** is geared toward full-time positions for 50+ job seekers.
- **Seniorjobbank.org** is a career site with a jobs board for boomers and seniors that links to companies through Indeed.com.
- **Seniors4hire.org** is a site where job seekers can submit a resume, post a description of their model job, or apply for posted jobs.

There are plenty of smaller, niche-focused job sites that are worth considering.

- **CrunchBoard.com** is one of the more popular job boards for internet and technology jobs.
- **Dice.com** is a leading site for tech job seekers. You can search by company, job title, keyword, and location. There's also career advice and tech news for job seekers.

- **Doximity.com** is the largest professional network for U.S. healthcare professionals.
- **Engineeringdaily.net** lists jobs in engineering.
- **HealthJobsNationwide.com** is for healthcare jobs.
- **Mediabistro.com** lists jobs in journalism and other media.
- **Salesgravy.com** features an area for sales talent sourcing and recruiting. Click the "Search Sales Jobs" link in the upper-right corner of the home page to log in and search.
- **Work At Home Vintage Employees** (wahve.com) is a site for professionals "phasing" into retirement who work from home for insurance firms. Most positions are long term, but some are short term for projects that are a minimum of three months. Positions range from bookkeeper to claims support and customer service representatives.
- **Workforce50.com** has a search tool, managed by Indeed, to find jobs for older, experienced workers.
- **The Write Jobs** (writejobs.info) has writing jobs.

Visit the websites of professional organizations in your field to see whether the site has a job board or links to other sites that post relevant jobs.

To find local job boards in your area, search the internet for your city, state, or county, followed by "jobs." For example, DCJobs.com caters to job seekers in Washington, D.C.

See Chapter 1, page 17, for additional sites to help you find part-time work and Chapter 2, page 68, for a list of work-from-home job boards.

Looking into Government Jobs

Government jobs are often available at the federal, state, county, and municipal levels. The largest employer in the United States is the federal government, which employs more than 2,723,000 people.

Employment in the state and local government sector is projected to increase by 929,000, to reach just over 20 million in 2022. This increase is more than two-and-a-half times the increase seen in the 2002 to 2012 period.

To find out what's available, do the following:

- Visit USAJobs.gov to search for jobs by keyword, job title, government agency, and location, or start at usa.gov, track down the government agency you want to look for, and check its list of openings. Most agencies have their own job boards, and you may see additional positions on those sites that you don't see on the broader site. In most cases, you still have to go through USAJobs to apply, but some positions are exempt from the competitive system and allow for more direct hiring.

- Visit GovernmentJobs.com to search specifically for jobs posted by employers in the public sector. You can search by job title or key word and by location, or browse jobs by category or location.
- Search for your state's website, access it, and then poke around to find job-related links. You may find links for jobs in education or a more general jobs or human resources link that leads to an area where state job opportunities are posted.
- Search for your county's or city's website, access it, and look for job links. Less populated counties and municipalities are less likely to have their own websites or to post jobs on those sites, but it's worth a try.

You can also tap into government-related websites such as Go Government (gogovernment.org), which can help you research federal agencies and government careers, and Best Places to Work in the Federal Government (bestplacestowork.org). GovLoop (govloop.com) is another site to visit. There's also a job board there featuring thousands of government jobs from auditing to communications to program management.

Go Directly to the Agency's Website

After pinpointing the agency you're aiming for, check out its job board directly, which may contain additional job openings that aren't posted on USAJobs.gov. You still need to apply on USAJobs.gov, but these positions may be exempt from requirements for posting jobs there.

Apply

Even if you find and eventually secure the job through your networking efforts, you need to jump through this hoop. Regardless of where the job is posted and how you find out about it, you must apply for openings on USAJobs.gov.

Visit College Websites . . . to Find a Job

College towns and colleges, which tend to be recession resistant, are often great places to live and work in the 50+ years. In addition to supplying ample jobs for people not yet ready to clock out, colleges offer affordable entertainment, sports, and lifelong learning opportunities.

In fact, they account for nine in a list of 25 Best Places to Retire that *Forbes* recently compiled. The publication notes that these towns have "increased cultural and learning opportunities."

Each year, a new class of students moves in, helping keep the economy bustling. Booming research centers and incubators for start-ups are common in the towns. Put it all together and you have a wide and attractive range of jobs and opportunities.

Another consideration: A growing number of institutions such as Bucknell University in Lewisburg, PA, and West Virginia University in Morgantown, WV, have signed AARP's employer pledge, which among other things commits them to be age-blind in hiring decisions.

Here's the Forbes list, by the way: Athens, GA (University of Georgia), Bethlehem, PA (Lehigh, Moravian), Boise, ID (Boise State), Clemson, SC (Clemson), Harrisonburg, VA (James Madison), Iowa City, IA (University of Iowa), Lawrence, KS (University of Kansas), Lincoln, NE (University of Nebraska), and San Marcos, TX (Texas State).

You can get started by checking a school's HR page. Broaden your search by looking off-campus to the surrounding community. The big job board Indeed has a category for college town jobs listing a range of opportunities.

As with any job search, boots on the ground is often the way to go. Go there and ask around. Explore the websites of colleges and universities that interest you and click the link for jobs or human resources to see what's available. Nearly every higher education facility in the nation posts its openings on its website for all to see. Or check the site HigherEdJobs (higheredjobs.com). You can screen by location, institution, job title, category, and full- or part-time positions.

Many colleges rely on temporary workers in a broad range of functions. For example, at the University of Virginia recent postings for temporary positions on its job board included work in accounting, administrative assistance for deans, customer service and IT support. There were also openings for custodians, house-keepers, landscapers, masons, electricians and plumbers.

Broaden your search to employer's websites in the community. College towns are hotbeds of arts culture. There are museums, music clubs and theaters. Some even have minor league baseball teams, such as Durham, NC, home to Duke University, my alma mater. The Durham Bulls offer plenty of seasonal jobs. These include positions in promotions, tending customers in the Ballpark Corner Store, ushering fans to their seats, and helping maintain the field.

You can find other jobs with a cultural flavor in arts organizations, such as sales positions in museum gift shops and box offices in theaters. There is also full-time work in fundraising, selling seasonal subscriptions, coordinating events, editing publicity materials, and more.

University towns often have start-up incubators that are linked with the school. Experts who can help on a consulting basis are frequently in demand in lieu of hiring full-time staffers, a fiscal stretch for early-stage entrepreneurs. Could you assist with such challenges as navigating licensing agreements, securing patents, or making sense of government regulations? Most independent contractors parachute in to problem-solve or work on a specific project.

Taking Extra Precautions with Online Job Postings

Be careful when replying to online job postings, especially on generic classified sites, such as Craigslist, because anyone can post a job listing. Look for the following warning signs:

- Any posting that demands sensitive personal or financial information, such as your Social Security number or a credit card number. Work-from-home postings are notorious for phishing expeditions (gathering personal and financial information to lift your identity or worse), charging to get started, and promising payment that never comes.
- Requests to e-mail your response to a free e-mail address ending in gmail.com or yahoo.com, for example, instead of to a company e-mail address ending in something like wiley.com or ibm.com.

- A link that redirects you to somewhere other than the place shown in the link. You can usually mouse over the link and look in the status bar near the bottom of your web browser or e-mail window to see the actual address of where the link will take you; if it differs from the address in the link itself, don't click the link.
- A job listing that requires payment to gain access to additional information or to qualify for consideration.

When first responding to a generic job listing via e-mail, share only your name and e-mail address. Signify your interest in the position and ask for the organization's name, physical address, and phone number so you can do your own background check to make sure the organization is valid.

CHAPTER 17

Tapping Others for Help

■ ■ ■

It takes a village, as the saying goes. Finding a job, as I've stressed throughout this book, can often depend on who you know—someone who can tell you about a potential opportunity, or who can put in a good word for you inside a company, who knows someone who knows someone.

But it goes deeper than that. Having someone you trust at your back can go a long way to keeping you going when the depression of rejection wears you down. Another person who is not a family member or close friend—a career counselor, a coach, or a fellow job seeker—can keep you motivated.

And whether or not you're on the job hunt right now, you can't afford to be content with your network. Your circle has to keep expanding and strengthening. Much like lifetime learning is an essential ingredient in our lives and careers, so is an ever-expanding roster of people who touch our lives. Nurturing existing relationships and meeting new people can keep our lives interesting on multiple levels. Who doesn't love swapping stories, learning from one another? It's the magic of the human connection.

In truth, you never know when your network will come through for work purposes. My own daily networking is often not about finding a job at all, but it builds a foundation that over time has produced results not just in terms of professional opportunities but personal rewards of helping someone else and sending that good

277

karma out into the world. I never expect to be thanked for my individual efforts, and you should never help someone for that reason, but my experience has been that when you do good works, good things do come back to you when you least expect it and often from where you least expect it.

It doesn't take a huge effort. I write a quick note of congratulations when I find out someone in my group has had a child (or a grandchild these days,) a wedding in the family, or a promotion, or I send condolences if someone has had a loss. If I read a book I think someone would enjoy, I pop that person a quick heads-up. I try to introduce people to one another if I think they might make a connection, either personal or professional. It makes me feel good to do so. That goodwill generally comes back to me in spades, even though I never have an agenda or an expectation. The truth is I still get writing assignments from colleagues I worked with three decades ago because we have stayed connected in some fashion—mostly online in recent years. We have all changed jobs professionally over the years, but we still reach back to tap each other's expertise and offer paying jobs, or pass along ones we have heard about that they might be right for, whenever we can.

I keep people in my circles up to date on my life, too—within reason. This is often via my Facebook, Instagram, or LinkedIn pages. Every so often I seek advice or ask for help to solve a problem, like finding an expert to interview or someone to reach out to at a company I am interested in working with.

And sure, a lot of your networking, like plenty of your job search maneuvers, can be conducted by computer or phone, but nothing beats connecting with someone new face to face.

Networking in Action

I interviewed Debra Dixon, a principal with TwinLogic Strategies, a small lobbying firm in Washington, D.C., for a column I wrote for *The New York Times* on how women over 50 can stay on top of their career game. She recently made a pivot from the government to the private sector. In many ways, her instinctive networking ability has been the key to her success.

Now in her 50s, Dixon had worked for Representative Xavier Becerra (D-CA) for approximately 17 years, initially as his legislative director and trade counsel, and then as his chief of staff, until she was appointed to serve as chief of staff for the U.S. Department of Education's Office of Planning, Evaluation and Policy Development in 2014. Two years later, she was hired by Elizabeth Frazee, the founder of TwinLogic Strategies.

When she realized it was time to move out of government service, she hit her network hard. "I reached out in every direction, 360-degrees, side-to-side and up-and-down," she says. "You never know where opportunities will present themselves, or how someone that you've mentored, or helped along the way might return the favor."

Frazee was a contact from Dixon's early days working in government. "It was a conscious networking back then because she was a Republican and I was a Democrat," says Dixon, "and we both wanted to get to know someone from the other party. We stayed in touch over the years, and now she's my boss."

Although the women had been in touch periodically, interestingly, Dixon is convinced it was when she brushed up her LinkedIn page that she came across Frazee's radar again.

Strong professional and social connections, like the one Dixon and Frazee have held and nurtured over the years, underpin career longevity. "We underestimate the power of our networks," says Debra Whitman, AARP's chief public policy officer. "You can't be complacent."

Even when you have no agenda, when a connection—whether it's a new contact, an ex-colleague, or a friend—takes a new job, or you want to show them something you're doing, or share an article they might find interesting, send a quick e-mail, she says. "It makes people think of you."

And you need to look beyond people your age for potential relationships that might pay off in the years ahead. "I always encourage my older clients to have younger people in their network," says Jayne Mattson of Keystone Associates, a career-management firm in Boston. "They are the ones who are going to be hiring you."

Mattson, now in her 60s, teamed up with a millennial, Molly F. Sullivan, to found Career Engage Boston. The nonprofit provides career development programs for early- to mid-career professionals, including mentoring opportunities, webinars, and seminars on career-related topics such as setting goals, finding your perfect job, changing careers, and writing resumes.

The ticket for many of us is to find someone who has some power to open a door, to really believe in their value, according to Sylvia Ann Hewlett, an economist and the founder and CEO of the Center for Talent Innovation, co-director of the Women's Leadership Program at the Columbia Business School, and author of *Forget a Mentor, Find a Sponsor: The New Way to Fast-Track Your Career.*

"I needed to take sponsorship much more seriously, for instance, as I sought to seek funding for the think tank that I founded at age 56 and my consulting firm that I founded at age 59," says Hewlett. "I was able to convince folks that I had lots of runway left and I had some fantastic ideas. It was my incredible network, who chose to back what I did, and that has made the difference."

Hewlett rallied her network for her ventures by "literally dusting off my Rolodex," she says. "The great news is that if you've been a professional for a number years, you have all kinds of acquaintances, or former college friends, parents of friends of your children, maybe even your children's friends, depending on your age. You almost don't realize the network you've got. One woman I connected with was wife of minister of the Unitarian church I attended. She turned out to be connected with a company that became one of my big funders."

Networking for Skilled-Trade Jobs

The importance of networking holds true for all lines of work. One way to look for a range of blue-collar professional jobs—from cabinetry to construction work to masonry, plumbing, and home contracting work—is by developing relationships with business owners in your area who can connect you with possible clients. For example, if you're a home contractor, you might build a camaraderie with local real estate agents. They can pass your name along to their sellers, who, in turn, might use your services to help get a home prepped for sale with small repairs and facelifts such as quartz kitchen countertops or a reglazed tub. A new buyer of a fixer-upper project, too, might be a potential client.

Whether you're a skilled artisan, tradesperson, or hair stylist, your work might easily lend itself to visual showcasing to people you are friends with, or who follow you, via an online professional portfolio of photos on sites such as Facebook, Instagram, Pinterest and, yes, LinkedIn.

You can build your brand and reputation online and market your services by posting images of completed projects. Encourage satisfied customers to tout your talents. Consider recording and posting a YouTube video of a work project from start to finish featuring your specialized skills and process. Wear your pride in your workmanship and show it off.

Face-to-face networking, such as joining trade associations affiliated with your line of work and perhaps a labor union, is a must, whether you're a landscaper, house painter, plumber, or tiler. Talking to people in your community is fundamental to adding new clients. Word of mouth is what will bring you new work. That means also reaching out to people who belong to your religious organization, connecting with other parents at your kid's (or grandkid's) sporting events, doing volunteer work, and getting involved with your local chamber of commerce.

Consider searching for work in your city on Jobcase.com, a website aimed at helping a range of workers from carpenters to housekeepers to masons to security guards find jobs.

Join Networking and Job-Hunting Groups

Seek out a local networking group for people in your occupation, or start your own if you can't find one that suits. Joining a group, job club, or Meetup.com group for job seekers can keep you top of trends and potentially learn about job openings. Studies have shown that these kinds of support groups are beneficial because you feel accountable to group members and you can share leads. Even better, from a psychological viewpoint, these can be a great way to get out of your house if you're not working.

You might also be able to connect with locals who have similar interests on Meetup.com. Some groups target boomers and may arrange hikes in local parks, group dog walks, volunteer outings, or trips to area museums. Although these are nonwork events, you never know where you might meet someone who can turn you on to a job opening. Meantime, it's a stress-free setting where you bond over shared interests, which is a great way to grow a new friendship and, in turn, your network.

Importantly, some Meetup groups are explicitly for crafters, entrepreneurs, real estate professionals, sales and marketing representatives, small business owners, and more. Search your city on Meetup.com to find one near you.

You might also join a formal networking group. These groups vary depending on where you live, but you generally have several to choose from, including Business Networking International, Kiwanis, LeTip, MasterMind Groups, Optimists, Rotary, Women in Business Networking, your local chamber of commerce or convention and visitor's bureau, and local merchant associations.

There are others that aren't career-oriented, but helpful for making new connections. As I mentioned earlier, I'm a member of The Transition Network (thetransitionnetwork.org), a nonprofit networking group for women over 50. It's based in New York, but the group has a chapter in Washington, D.C., where I live. Peer groups like this are a great way to fight the nervousness barrier that can stand in the way of building new contacts and friends. It's a safe, welcoming environment, and the events tend to be fairly intimate.

I also am involved in my alumni groups in the city and make a point of attending various events from lectures to volunteer outings where there is a range of ages of both genders and professions. Book clubs, and sports or hobby-oriented organizations like knitting groups and biking, running, or walking clubs, can also smooth the way to new friendships and opportunities that can rise from these connections.

When you're ready to circulate, here are my top six networking tips to help you make the most of a network event:

- **Show up.** If you hear of a local event that sounds intriguing, push yourself to make room in your schedule. If possible, review the RSVP list to see if you know anyone attending, or if there are people you want to be sure to meet. Then do a quick review of their LinkedIn profile to gather background for questions. Make certain your own online accounts at Facebook, LinkedIn, and Twitter tell the same story about you as your resume does. If you're in full job-hunting mode, rehearse your elevator speech of who you are, what you're doing right now, and what kind of position you're seeking.
- **Show up early.** The best time to schmooze is before things get rolling. Plus the low noise level in the room will be more conducive to conversation.
- **Build relationships.** As you're chatting, remember that networking isn't about finding someone to help you get a job

today. It's a process of developing contacts gradually over time through people who connect with and trust each other.

- **Be curious.** Networking is not work. It's about being interested in what other people are doing and being open to learning from them. Ask questions and try to get people to talk about themselves. Spend twice as much time listening as you do talking. Try to use the other person's name once or twice during your conversation. People like to hear their names and at the same time it will help you remember it.

- **Set goals.** Before heading to a new event, tell yourself that you'll try to meet three or four new people and get their contact information. Afterward, jot down on your smartphone notes app who you met, where you met, and what you discussed.

- **Follow up.** The day after the event, send a note to your new connections, telling them how much you enjoyed meeting them and proposing a future date to get together informally, if you want to.

E-mail works fine, but, hey, if you've got a personal notecard, send it. These days, people rarely receive mail other than bills, junk, and magazines, so your recipient will be pleased to get your card.

Building Your Networking Muscle

I asked John Tarnoff, the career coach and author of that first-rate book *Boomer Reinvention: How to Create Your Dream Career Over 50*, how people should build their networking muscle. This is what he told me:

> *The biggest obstacle is people think of themselves as bad networkers or too shy. Fear is the obstacle. I understand that. I am actually a shy person. There are days when I look at an appointment and ask myself: 'Do I really want to talk to people and meet people?' Inevitably, if I force myself out the door, I'm fine within 5 minutes.*
>
> *If you have a problem with meeting someone new, especially at an event, just smile and start asking questions. It can be as simple as: 'So how far did you have to drive to get here tonight?' Or: 'Tell me, why are you here?' It can be a pickup line. 'Love that tie.' 'Where did you get those glasses?' The goal is to find something to say as a pretext of breaking the ice.*

The second thing is to be of service to someone. At this point in your life, have faith that all the knowledge you have will allow you to be helpful to someone at that event. Find somebody who needs you to help them. It gets you out of your head and completely restores your faith in yourself. Helping people out is an amazingly reinforcing experience.

Check Out Your College Career Center

It sounds like a longshot, but you may find help from your school's placement office or career center decades after you walked off with your diploma. Many colleges and graduate schools have special relationships with businesses who recruit through the college. Career center staff can help you revamp your resume and cover letter. They may also provide you with an online account where you can post your profile and resume, access online podcast seminars or webinars, view job and internship listings with contact information, sign up for career center appointments, and get the latest news on job fairs and recruiter visits. There are also active alumni lists for networking purposes.

Many schools offer free career coaching and welcome alums back at job fairs and for employer informational meetings. Some schools assist alumni in setting up interviews. You can brush up on job-hunting skills (free of charge in most cases) and link to a vast network of people inclined to lend a hand. Consider it added value—a degree that keeps giving back. I used to always tell my dad that my degree was worth far, far more than he paid in tuition. He loved hearing that, and it had the added benefit of being true.

Search for your school on LinkedIn and tap into your alma mater's LinkedIn network for additional connections. At my alma mater, Duke University, alumni can view more than 150,000 profiles of Duke classmates by logging in to its Duke Alumni career networking site (alumni.duke.edu/benefits/career-networking). Using this private network, alumni and students can search for connections in specific industries or companies, identify potential mentors, find alumni career coaches, and expand their personal and professional contacts. Several alumni groups cater to specific career pursuits via networking and educational events

For example, the D.C. Politics and Policy Network is a group of alumni working on legislative and policy issues in government, nonprofit organizations, and the private sector. Duke Entertainment,

Media and Arts Network (DEMAN) is Duke's network dedicated to nurturing and developing passions and careers in the arts, media, and entertainment industries. You can connect with DEMAN on Facebook and LinkedIn.

Similarly, Duke Global Entrepreneurship Network (DukeGEN), is an active alumni group that provides energy and support to Duke entrepreneurs. You can connect with DukeGEN on Facebook, LinkedIn, and Twitter.

Get my drift? Head to your alma mater's career center's website and see what's available.

Network Your Way to a New Job

Be patient. Bill Valentine's is donor relations manager at the United Way of Central and Northeastern Connecticut. He left his position as a customer service manager at the financial services firm ING in November 2013.

He had a 16-week fellowship with the Encore!Connecticut program. Run by the University of Connecticut's Nonprofit Leadership Program, it helps professionals, mostly those 50+, make the transition to jobs in the state's nonprofit sector.

During his fellowship, Valentine had 35 networking meetings. That led to four formal job interviews, two with the United Way. "Not one of those networking meetings was a waste of time. I met someone. I learned something," he says.

Pairing Up with a Mentor or Sponsor

If you've decided to change careers, hang out a shingle as a free-lancer, or start your own business, I recommend finding a mentor or sponsor to guide you, as Sylvia Ann Hewlett advises. Spending time and learning from someone who's been there and done that is invaluable. Almost universally, the people I know who have made a successful transition to new work after age 50 had at least one person they could turn to when the ground got unsteady, or they had setbacks.

Look for someone who knows the ins and outs of the new line of work. A mentor or sponsor can play numerous roles, from teaching you the ropes to boosting your confidence and endorsing you to potential employers or customers.

These kinds of relationships don't take off with a snap of your fingers. It's a process of developing your relationship over a period of time, as Dixon did. A good mentoring relationship grows progressively.

Who to turn to? Start by making a list of the people in your network who could possibly offer you the guidance you need. After settling on a few people, ask them for specific advice about an issue or problem you're facing. You might have different mentors or gurus for different areas you need counseling in.

Ease into the relationship. At some point, you may want to schedule regular meetings, even if only to have a cup of coffee and touch base on how things are going. Remember, this is a two-way street. See if there is something you can do to help them in some way. Keep in mind that if you really expect people to step out for you, you need to be confident that your performance also will reflect back in a positive way on them, and that they will benefit in some way from your success. There has to be a win-win proposition.

Mentorships and sponsorships often morph into mutually beneficial friendships. The main reason most mentors and sponsors say they take the time to counsel and help is the intangible pleasure they get in paying it forward.

Be clear about your goals. Write them down to help you focus on what you hope to achieve. You may have a certain business task at hand, something as simple as wanting someone to give you advice on how to spruce up your image for a job interview. Or you may want the inside scoop on which people at a certain organization to approach about getting a job there. Or perhaps you're looking for someone who can help you learn the ropes of a new business area or skill and will let you job-shadow them to get an idea of what it's like behind the curtain.

How I Tapped a Virtual Mentor

If you can't find someone in your professional and social circles who fits the bill, or just want another expert at your back, consider hiring a virtual mentor who can offer direction. Virtual mentoring can be less intimate, but it can still deliver the advice you need to find the job you want.

To get connected with a virtual mentor, contact a mentor matchmaking firm such as PivotPlanet (pivotplanet.com), which serves people looking to pivot from an existing career to another. PivotPlanet's goal is to offer easy access to expert advisors in hundreds of fields, from acupuncture to financial planning to landscape design. It's networking and counseling for job seekers of all stripes—from aspiring entrepreneurs to people burned out in the corporate cubicle and baby boomers planning encore careers—at a fraction of the cost of hiring a career coach. One-hour sessions via videoconference or phone typically range from $40 to $125. In-person mentorship sessions are also available.

It's easy to get started. You type in the type of work you want to explore, and choose from the list of advisors resulting from your search. You can also click Find an Advisor, at the top of the page, to browse advisors by career type, job title, or any key word.

Compare advisors by reading their biographies, watching their videos, scanning their photo galleries, and reading client reviews. Once you set up an account, you send a message to an advisor requesting a one-hour conference and provide up to 10 times and dates that work for you. Work directly with PivotPlanet staff to schedule a full-day or half-day in-person session. Have a list of questions ready to go and a pad and pen for note taking, or tape the session.

I've used the individual services of one of its mentors, who lives in Florida, hundreds of miles from my home in Washington, D.C., to hone my public speaking goals and business plan. I found my one-on-one sessions incredibly useful and empowering, and the hourly fee well worth it. The mentor and I are now Facebook friends and LinkedIn contacts. I feel I know him personally. I've seen pictures of his home and his outdoor grill (he loves to cook) and his wife and dog. You get it. We're building a connection, and it's been meaningful to me to watch and observe his professional work on LinkedIn and more.

Explore Reverse Mentoring

Multigenerational workforces are here to stay and that's a good thing. And as workers stay on the job beyond what was once traditional retirement, it's even more important to find ways to accept mentoring help from those younger than us—what's known as reverse mentoring. It's especially effective when the mentor and mentee complement one another; for example, when the younger person is more tech savvy and the older person knows the business.

For the last several years, I've been in a few reverse-mentoring relationships. One is with someone I now consider a friend who's two decades younger, far hipper, and more attuned to navigating social media. It's nice to have someone I can call or e-mail with a quick question about a new platform—say, how to put up a story on Snapchat—who doesn't treat me like I'm a woefully behind the times. On the flipside, as an author and national columnist, I've helped market her book, introduced her to people who can further her career, and written recommendations.

Many millennials and those coming behind them have an infectious energy and entrepreneurial boldness. Their drive and passion to achieve success can be a great inspiration.

Work with a Career Coach

Studies show that people who work with a coach seem to have better luck finding a job. "You want someone who understands the obstacles and can help guide and motivate you," says Ofer Sharone, a professor at University of Massachusetts Amherst, where he researches and teaches on the topics of career transitions and employment.

If you know you need a change but are hesitant about what to do, a career coach can help you set goals, clearly outline the steps to take you there, and prompt you to make it happen. A coach can also be there for you when you're stuck in a job search. It's easy to slip into a paralysis and depression if the search stretches into months. A good coach can look at your resume and experience from a fresh, unbiased stance, and provide perhaps a new direction, suggest positions and industries you may have overlooked, help you focus, and stay active.

I personally used a coach to give me the kind of impartial help a friend or family member couldn't. I found her through my dog, Zena. She and I met when training our puppies a few years ago.

Countless career coaches representing a wide assortment of styles and philosophies sell their services online, and winnowing down the field entails due diligence. The Life Planning Network (lifeplanningnetwork.org), for example, offers a coach directory geared to midlife workers.

To find the right coach for you, follow these suggestions:

- Look for qualifications. Career coaching is a self-regulated industry and profession. Many coaches have been doing it for years without adding professional designations. But designations indicate formal training and adherence to general standards of professionalism.
- Explore the past career paths of potential coaches. Find out as much as you can about their career paths, both in the coaching field and in the regular work world. Don't be too timid to question potential coaches about their level of expertise for your particular needs.
- Ask for at least three references. Of course, no one is going to hand over the names of clients who didn't love them, but asking for references is an important step in your process. You never know what you might learn when you talk to a reference on the phone. Ask about a potential coach's work style and how she succeeded with other clients starting a new career.
- Find a coach who conducts one-on-one sessions.
- Expect a free initial consultation. After you've narrowed your search, you'll want to interview a few candidates. Never agree to work with a coach without a trial run. This initial session should be gratis.
- Ask about fees. Rates vary significantly, anywhere from $50 to more than $200 per hour. Some coaches require a minimum number of hours. On average, coach–client relationships last from six months to a year. You may sign on for one or two meetings to jump-start your job search. Some coaches provide resources, such as books, and give homework assignments to prepare for future sessions.
- Check out potential coaches' websites or blogs. This should give you insight into their areas of expertise and publications. Search their names on the Web and see if you find uncensored comments written by other clients.
- Get a written agreement. This is a business relationship, so treat it like one with a formal agreement that defines the duties of each party. Verbal agreements can be risky and leave both the client and the coach susceptible to unexpected misunderstandings.

Where to Find a Coach

While fate allowed me to meet my career coach, asking friends for recommendations is a good place to start. You don't need a coach who lives in your town, either. While it's nice to meet in person, most coaches these days work by phone or video conference, say Facetime, Google Hangouts, GoToMeeting, Skype, or Zoom.

Check out online directories. The Life Planning Network (lifeplanningnetwork.org), for example, offers a coach directory geared to midlife workers. Another good place to find a directory of coaches is the International Coach Federation (coachfederation. org). The organization awards a global credential that thousands of coaches hold worldwide. ICF-credentialed coaches have met educational requirements, received specific coach training, and achieved a designated number of experience hours. Two other helpful sites are the Association of Career Professionals International (http:// www.acpinternational.org/).

and the National Career Development Association (ncda.org).

Explore resources for free coaches. Investigate local libraries, community colleges, and the alumni offices of your alma mater for gratis coaching sessions or low-cost workshops and courses. CareerOneStop (careeronestop.org), sponsored by the U.S. Department of Labor, offers coaching and special programs for military members moving into the private sector at various locations around the country. If you're unemployed, your local unemployment office may be able to set you up with free career counseling. These could be small groups as opposed to one-on-one sessions, but they are helpful nonetheless for getting you moving forward.

Where to Find a Coach

Another option for coaching and more help is to seek out a local job center. Operation A.B.L.E of New England (Ability Based on Long Experience) is one example, but do some investigating in your community to see if there might be something similar.

I had the opportunity at a recent conference of the American Society on Aging to meet Joan Cirillo, CEO of Operation A.B.L.E,. It operates in Massachusetts and New Hampshire. I was so inspired I wrote about the group in my PBS Next Avenue column.

Operation A.B.L.E (operationable.net) has offered training and employment to roughly 35,000 people over 45 since 1982. And since 2000, more than 16,000 job seekers over 45 have found positions through the organization's help.

What appeals to me most about A.B.L.E. is it's a multi-tiered program with a variety of services, from offering resources such as job listings and basic computer training, to resume and cover letter tutorials, to help brushing up on interview skills. It also provides access to one-on-one coaching, paid internships and apprenticeships, and networking clubs.

"We're teaching you how to find a job," says Martha Field, program director for the group's ABLE AgeWorks, whose participants are highly skilled, educated, and experienced professionals. "We can't find you a job, but we can make you develop a strategic career outreach plan to know where you're going."

One of A.B.L.E.'s most useful features: a job board linking to regional employers who are supportive of older workers and serve on the group's advisory board. These include Fidelity, Harvard, Massachusetts General Hospital, MIT, The Museum of Fine Arts Boston, and TJX Companies (parent of retailers TJ Maxx and Marshalls).

And A.B.L.E.'s job club helps job seekers network with others like them, supporting one another and keeping one another focused and proactive. In my reporting for my books about finding work after 50 (like *Getting the Job You Want after 50 for Dummies*), I've found that these kinds of job clubs improve the success rate of older workers landing jobs.

A.B.L.E. also offers training courses for particular fields, which is very smart. For example, its 12-week medical office and customer service training program trains students in medical terminology, regulatory information affecting the healthcare industry, and medical office procedures and administration, as well as customer service and communication skills. This program prepares participants for jobs such as patient service coordinator and medical office administrator. Students in the program get assigned to a six-week internship.

Connecting with a Recruiter

A good recruiter gives you the inside track on great jobs—ones that may never have hit your radar. On LinkedIn these days, you can check a box that enables recruiters to find you, as I mentioned in Chapter 15. If you get the gig, the recruiter earns a fee, paid by the employer, for playing matchmaker.

Yet this seemingly symbiotic relationship can be confusing for a job seeker, especially if you've never worked with a recruiter before and aren't sure what the recruiter's role is in getting you hired. Although recruiters may discover you through their networking efforts and learn about you from your colleagues, they are increasingly using the web to track down candidates through social media sites and job boards. That's one of the reasons you should have a strong online presence, as I explained in Chapter 15.

If you want to work with a recruiter as part of your job-hunting strategy, you can track *them* down by using the methods they employ to find their candidates: via networking, referrals from colleagues, and social media.

You can also search the Web for recruiters in your area that serve specific industries. For example, if you enter into the Google search engine the industry you are interested in, "recruiter," then the name of your town, you'll find links to recruitment websites. In most cities, you can find trade associations of executive recruiters that provide a website with their members' names and expertise listed.

Look for a recruiter who has expertise in the industry in which you're interested, and choose one or two who specialize in that field. Recruiters typically prescreen over the phone and then file your resume in their database for future jobs. Remember, recruiters generally work for a finder's fee paid by the employer. The recruiter works for the employer, not for you. Recruiters, for the most part, are salespeople. It's about closing the deal.

Recruiters who contact you are often simply casting about to pull together a batch of potential candidates for a client. They may actually know very little about your work experience and current situation beyond what they've seen on your social media profile and online resume.

Ask up front if the recruiter has a specific job in mind for you, and be clear about the salary you require. Prepare to answer detailed questions about your resume, job experience, and any gaps.

You may be asked for a list of references. And he or she may need to know if you have any issues with relocation. If you have to travel to get to an interview, be clear on who's paying the travel expenses.

Depending on the job opening and employer, the recruiter will probably ask if you're willing to agree to a drug test and to checks of your criminal background, references, educational background, and credit.

And unless it's part of the job description, this is not the time to ask about telecommuting policies or other flextime options. Save that for after you get an offer. Moreover, resume writing is not a recruiter's job, but good recruiters may help fine-tune your resume for the certain job they are trying to fill.

Checking Out Job Fairs

One way to meet with potential employers is at a job fair. To attend a brick-and-mortar job fair, you're typically required to pay a small entrance fee. To gain the full value of these in-person events, do the following:

- Research the companies at the fair. Review ahead of time the roster of employers participating and what kinds of jobs are available. Go to company websites and their social media pages, and search Google News (news.google.com) and the firm's name to find out any recent news. This will help you get a better sense of the organization and understand more about it should you have a chance to speak to one of the representatives at the fair about a position.
- Dress in proper business attire and be well groomed. First impressions count. Although you probably won't have an interview per se, prepare as if you will.
- In addition to connecting with company reps, introduce yourself to other job seekers.
  - Tell them what you do, and ask what they do.
  - Share contact information.
  - If you make a good connection, you may agree to share leads with a fellow job seeker.
- Be sure to have your contact information stored in your smartphone, so you can directly text or e-mail it to anyone who is interested, or go the old-fashioned way and carry a simple business card that includes your name, target job title, expertise, and contact information. Use a plain-type font, such as Arial or Helvetica. Make sure the size is big enough to read without squinting.
- Carry twice as many copies of your resume as there are exhibitors. You generally leave one at a company's booth and hand one to anyone you speak to directly. If you have a few

293

versions of your resume geared to specific jobs, bring along copies of each. It's smart to have your virtual resume ready to share as well.

- Visit as many booths as you can. Smaller companies may be a better bet than the bigger names.
- Always show your interest in a company by first asking about vacancies the company is looking to fill and asking any specific questions about the firm that show you've done your research. Then you can deliver your elevator pitch if it makes sense to do so.
- If a company mentions a position that appeals to you, but the resume you have tucked in your bag isn't geared to that specific job, hold off handing over your resume. You can send a resume in a day or two after you've had a chance to tweak it.
- Ask for business cards or virtual contacts from every company representative you speak to, so you can follow up with an e-mail and a call within a week.
- Be realistic. Not many people actually get hired via job fairs. Employers mine these events to gather resumes that potentially lead to future phone and in-person interviews. The networking and educational opportunities these fairs offer are far-reaching. You never know where the connections may lead.
- Always send thank-you e-mails to anyone you talked to, and be sure to attach your resume to the e-mail. Reference something from your conversation with them as a reminder of who you are.

Virtual Career Fairs

For the 50+ jobseeker, partaking in a virtual career fair sends a strong signal that you are tech savvy—a chief factor for many hiring managers.

Virtual career fairs should be approached as seriously as you would an in-person interview, even if you are sitting in your home office.

To find an online career event that's geared to your job search, canvass job board websites, including Brazen Careerist (brazen-careerist.com) and Monster (monster.com), for upcoming fairs. LinkedIn, industry groups, military associations, and membership associations such as AARP can also direct you to upcoming job fairs they're sponsoring or are connected to in some fashion. (Some companies offer their own virtual fairs. Check their websites or social media accounts.) See which businesses have a booth with job openings and a recruiter or hiring manager available during the fair hours.

To make the most of the job fair, follow these suggestions before, during, and after the fair:

- Do your research on the various employers on the attendee roster as you would an in-person fair.
- Update your resume and social media accounts. When you register, you'll probably need to produce a profile and upload a photo and a basic resume. Tweak your resume, or, better yet, create several versions of it to match jobs you want. Save each resume on your desktop so you'll have it ready to shoot to a recruiter.
- Get your computer ready. Generally speaking, a Mac or PC desktop or laptop is fine. After registering, you'll likely receive a confirmation e-mail with instructions to see whether your computer meets system requirements.
- Keep your conversations professional and focused. Your goal is to connect with all the companies you have on your list. These can be instantaneous conversations, so be careful to keep it formal. Use "Mr." and "Ms." Avoid emoticons and watch for typos. Post sticky notes on your desk to remind you of your three core selling points. These will help you stay focused when a conversation gets rolling. Be patient for a response. With lots of questions coming in from other job seekers, the recruiter may be slow to answer.
- Be prepared for an impromptu video interview. Recruiters may ask if you can launch into a video interview, usually Skype, on the spot. This means that you need to understand in advance how these virtual interviews work. Check out my tips for a video interview in Chapter 18.
- Surf the chat rooms and expert career-pro advice sessions. Stop by not just the firm's "booth" but also its chat room. Recruiters and hiring managers are often accessible there. In chat rooms and educational sessions, you're able to read

what other participants post, learn from the answers to others' questions, and read more from the hiring managers staffing the booth about the company culture and more.

- Send thank-you e-mails, just as you would for a live job fair.

Attitude Counts

One final note: In this chapter, I have explored a multitude of ways the human touch can help you in your job hunt, but none of these interactions will pay dividends if you don't have a great job search attitude.

Dorian Mintzer, a terrific life coach based in Boston, and Renée Rosenberg, a career transition expert and mental health counselor from New York City, shared with me their message of how to stay positive. It's a can-do message similar to what I preach and have written about for AARP, *Forbes,* and Next Avenue and in my AARP books, including *Getting the Job You Want after 50* and *Love Your Job: The New Rules for Career Happiness.* And Mintzer has a special message for those of us who are 50+.

"It's easy to let ageism myths be internalized, leading to self-sabotage during the job search," Mintzer tells me. "It's important to be aware of our own attitudes about aging and what messages we're sending to others about ourselves. We can become our own worst enemy."

Start by asking, "What am I passionate about?" says Mintzer. Then, she notes, dig deeper to "assess what you really want from a job, what are your needs, skills and values." It's all about knowing that you're really good at something and then being able to market yourself based on that—articulately telling hiring managers about the results your strengths and skills produced, Mintzer includes.

"You have to know what you have achieved in your years of experience and really own it," Rosenberg added.

Run with a good crowd. As you're looking for work, stay away from negative people and seek out positive role models in their 50s, 60s, and 70s who are working and productive, the women advised. "They can serve as inspirational mentors," says Mintzer.

You might want to look for a job-search buddy who is also trying to find work. Then, keep each other optimistic and confident. For example, practice telling your sales story to one another, so you're prepared to sell yourself in an interview.

Force yourself to network regularly. "Part of a downward spiral is not feeling connected to others," says Mintzer. "Don't isolate. Join networking groups."

"Academic research convincingly shows that more than half of all jobs come through a network," Chris Farrell, the author of *Unretirement: How Baby Boomers Are Changing the Way We Think about Work, Community, and the Good Life,* told me. He suspects, as I do, that the percentage is even higher for workers 60 or older.

So meet with as many people as possible. Glean their insights and their recommendations of companies or nonprofits you might want to consider learning more about, or openings they may know of. Always ask the most critical question, says Farrell: "Who else should I talk to?"

Prospects can crop up in improbable places—not to be maudlin, but even on sad occasions. "At the wake of a former colleague, I was talking with my former boss and two former co-workers as we waited in line," says Susan P. Joyce, online job search specialist and editor of Job-Hunt.org and WorkCoachCafe.com. "We had all been laid off. My former boss had a new job and needed to hire people he knew and could trust. So, he talked with the two of them and ended up hiring them."

Mintzer and Rosenberg are especially bullish about joining LinkedIn groups in your field and being active in LinkedIn conversations.

Finally, maintain a sense of humor. "Laugh a lot," counsels Rosenberg. "Laughter energizes you," seconds Mintzer, with a grin.

CHAPTER

Great Job Interview Tips

■ ■ ■

You can make all the great impressions in the world on paper, but where the magic happens is when you meet someone face-to-face. Once you get the nod for an interview, it's show time.

In this chapter, I provide some interviewing advice that can boost your image and your chances of nabbing the position. There are no do-overs in the interview process, so you have to get this right the first time out of the gate.

Before you start the process, practice your patter. One way is to have a friend or partner act as an interviewer and run through a dress rehearsal in your living room. You can also rig up your own mock interview with Skype, a smartphone that has video capability, or a video camera and tripod stand. Ask a friend to lob questions your way. If you have a video recording, you can review it to see where you can improve your delivery and responses.

Another effective exercise is to use an online job interview simulator. You may be able to access simulators through your alma mater's career center, a professional organization you belong to, or a job-search site. A simulator enables you to practice answering interview questions at home, using a computer with internet access, a webcam or built-in camera in your computer, and a microphone.

You may also be able to engage in mock interviews by using a smartphone app. Check out the following sites and apps:

- Interview4 (interview4.com/job-candidates)
- Interview Simulation (thiswaytocpa.com/career-tools/ interview-simulation)
- InterviewStream Prep (interviewstream.com/ interviewstream-prep)
- Monster.com Interviews (available at itunes.apple.com)
- My Interview Simulator (myinterviewsimulator.com)

When you record your interview, you'll be able to evaluate your answers, facial expressions, and body language. If you're conducting your interviews online or using an app, see if the site or software you're using has an option to record. After each interview, watch and critique your performance, so you can work on improving areas of weakness.

Although some people are naturals, most require training and practice to master the art of the job interview. To get the training and practice you need, consider the following options:

- Join Toastmasters. Since 1924, Toastmasters International has helped people from all walks of life improve their speaking skills and self-confidence in front of an audience. Most meetings consist of about 20 people who meet weekly for an hour or two. Participants practice and learn skills of effective speech: focus, organization, language, vocal variety, and body language. You learn how to focus your attention away from your own anxieties and concentrate on your message and your audience, which goes a long way toward acing an interview.
- Take a public speaking course. You can find public speaking courses at your local community college. Most courses cover techniques for managing communication anxiety, speaking clearly, tuning into your body language, and much more.
- Sign up for an acting class, or an improvisational comedy workshop. If you have a secret yearning to be a *Saturday Night Live* cast member and develop interviewing skills at the same time, sign up for an improv comedy workshop. These workshops help you build your confidence and stage presence.
- Work with a coach. A good career coach can give you feedback and offer advice to sharpen your presentation.

Much of what makes a great interview is intuitive. It's chemistry between two people. Each situation is unique. And regardless of how practiced you are, there's plenty of room for improvement when you're in the hot seat.

I'm not going to even try to tell you how to actually answer some of the more bizarre questions that interviewers are tossing out these days. The job website Glassdoor.com published a list of 25 oddball interview questions from 2016 that interview candidates shared.

Here are a few:

- "If I gave you $40,000 to start a business, what would you start?" Asked at Hubspot.
- "If you were a brand, what would be your motto?" Asked at Boston Consulting Group.
- "How many basketballs would fit in this room?" Asked at Delta Air Lines.

I'm sticking to the old-fashioned nuts and bolts of an interview. The things you can control. The interviewer is leading the dance, but if you're prepared, you can follow along smoothly and with confidence.

Few events in life are more nerve-racking than a job interview. You're onstage, alone, in the spotlight, with strangers grilling you to determine whether you're the best person for a job that—who knows?—could set you on a path to work you love.

"Interviews are interviews: They're scary, intimidating, and we have a lot riding on them," says John Tarnoff, a Los Angeles–based career coach. They can be even more unnerving if you're a late-career job-switcher who hasn't sat in the interview seat for 10 or 20 years.

So here's a road map to acing an interview.

Check out the potential employer. Start by going to its website. The About page will typically give you information about history, mission, and people. Read the news or press releases page. Also check the company's LinkedIn and Facebook pages, and follow it on Twitter.

Of course, you don't want to rely entirely on what the employer says about itself. Search for it on the Web and set up Google News alerts about it. Read discussions to get up to speed on what people connected to this workplace are talking about.

See if your LinkedIn network has an inside connection. If someone in your network works for the organization, or previously did, contact that person to find out more and possibly obtain the contacts of people in the department you hope to join.

Check out your interviewers. LinkedIn pages and a Google search should provide some personal background on them. Sure, employers hire for skills, but they also want to have a connection with you. Find out where people went to school and worked.

Give yourself a "faith lift." Okay, you understand the organization. Now understand yourself. If you've been out of work for a while, you might be underestimating your own value. Take time to reflect on your best moments, the circumstances you shine in. Query people you trust to remind you of all those talents and skills you've honed over the years. Ask them to list two or three things you're really good at.

Practice your pitch. Get comfortable answering interview questions. They're likely to include "Tell me about yourself," "What are your strengths and weaknesses," and "Why are you a good fit for the job," says Jayne Mattson, senior vice president of Keystone Associates, a career management consulting firm headquartered in Boston. You'll need to "provide concrete examples of your work. This will show the value you will bring to the organization," Mattson says.

Make a list of points you want to convey and then practice how to bring them up if the interviewer doesn't ask about them.

Think up questions to ask about the organization. Thoughtful questions fill out your own knowledge of an organization, but they can also convey seriousness to the interviewer. But make sure they aren't answered on, say, the employer's website. You'll look like you didn't do your homework.

If you have trouble tooting your own horn and find that you're getting down on yourself, ask people you trust who know you well to help you develop your highlight reel and remind you of all those talents and skills you've honed throughout the years. Ask them to list two or three things you're really good at. After reading the positive comments, you'll have the swagger you need.

Confidence is crucial to acing an interview. To project confidence, you need to be comfortable in your own skin. Research and preparation help, but you can do more to hone your presentation skills.

I encourage you to approach this meeting as you would a conversation with someone you want to know better and whom you want to know more about you. Look forward to the interview, not with a sense of dread, but with enthusiasm. This is an opportunity to meet and get to know a new colleague, someone who shares your goals and is committed, as you are, to the organization's success. You're teaming up with your interviewers to find out whether you and your prospective employer are a good match. You're allies, not adversaries.

Don't forget to eat. When the day of the interview arrives, start with a high-protein breakfast. Avoid sugary or starchy foods that tend to give you a quick sugar high. Drink water, but not too much. If you feel better after exercise, perform your normal routine.

Dress appropriately. If it's a "business casual" office, what does that really mean? I lean toward the more formal approach, even if you're told that everyone wears blue jeans and sneakers. Pick something that you feel good in and that's comfortable. Skip the super-high heels or open-toe shoes. You do want polished footwear, though. If you're all scuffed, buy new shoes or pay for a professional's elbow grease. Shoes count.

Take the time to really look in the mirror before you head out. A quick pit stop in the office building's restroom, or the coffee shop next door, before you enter the firm's actual domain is a good idea. Check for rogue dog hairs, missed buttons, undone zippers, or bits of bagel in your teeth.

True story: I once interviewed for a job with aluminum foil wrapped around all the brass buttons on my red blazer. I had pulled it straight from the cleaner's bag without checking. Yikes. The interviewer never mentioned it. I still laugh sheepishly about it today. I got the job, but ahem, attention to details, please.

Don't be late. Your interview starts way before you shake hands. Arrive 10 or 15 minutes early. It's more than a case of punctuality, too. When you arrive early, you have a chance to take a breath and center yourself. It removes one layer of stress. If you're skating in under the bell, it's probably evident in the tension-taut lines of your face and your damp handshake.

Begin your interview at the door. Greet the receptionist with the same respect as you will the person who is interviewing you. You're on stage from the instant you state your name at the front desk.

Most one-on-one job interviews last between 25 and 30 minutes, so your total on-site performance time is precious. Since it's short and sweet, milk every minute of it, from the waiting room onward.

Turn off your cell phone. Don't spend your time in the on-deck area gabbing on your cell, for example, or responding to e-mails, or even tweeting. Focus on why you're there. It's okay to review a list of questions you want to ask. Soak up the office atmosphere. Look around. It will give you clues to whether this is a place you might want to hang your hat. Remind yourself that you're here to find out whether the place is a good fit for you; it's not just about selling yourself to the organization. As you're waiting, take some slow, deep breaths.

Start with a relaxed meet and greet. Step up with a firm one-handed handshake. Two hands can be a little forthright and maybe even too familiar. Kick off the first few minutes of your interview as you would a conversation with someone you've just met at a reception. Keep it relaxed and conversational, yet professional and not too personal. Direct eye contact is important. My standard advice: Commenting on wall décor or a desk accessory is acceptable, but saying you like someone's tie or shoes may be stepping over the line.

I personally like to scan wall and desk photographs, say, and see if I can find a common bond. A framed image of a Labrador retriever or a horse always sets an instant connection for me. These initial moments are where the chemistry between the interviewer and you can spark. Think speed dating.

Offer your paper resume before you sit down. Presenting an actual resume to an interviewer is akin to bringing a gift to a host or hostess. You're passing along something of value in exchange for the invitation to meet and his or her time. By taking it out in the opening moments of the interview, it becomes an interactive asset. If there are areas or responsibilities that you want to emphasize or explain, the interview is your chance to draw attention to them.

People often think if something is on their resume the significance is clear to the interviewer, but those bullet points don't always speak for themselves.

Follow the leader. Synch up with the interviewer's rhythm. It's important to go at his or her tempo. Don't try too hard and talk too fast. Answer concisely and with a confident, calm manner. Pause before you respond—even repeat the question if need be—to buy yourself some moments to gather a measured answer.

Watch your language (body language, that is). Leaning forward can cue that you're interested. Look people in the eyes when you're talking to them. I'm not trying to sound like your mother, but this is important. It's fine to glance upward, or off to the side, if you're forming a thought, but a clear, direct gaze portrays candor and sincerity. But don't stare.

Your body language counts here, so pay attention. No slouching. Sit straight, take some deep breaths, and relax. Stroking your neck and throat unconsciously can make you look nervous. A confident, loose (unclenched) fist lightly tucked under your chin is okay in small doses. Pressing your fingertips together in a steeple formation is also a simple sign of self-assurance, but don't overdo it. Be careful about folding your arms across your chest. You might think it makes you look serious, but it can come off as a defensive stance.

If you've got a point you want to play up, a hand gesture is fine, but keep those to a minimum. Your best move is to keep your hands laced together with your thumbs on top, sitting calmly in your lap, or propped lightly on the arms of the chair. Avoid twisting and spinning your pen, rings, necklace, or bracelets. You might even do this inadvertently, so be mindful of what your hands are up to. It sends an interviewer a signal of nerves or even anxiety.

Keep focused on your interviewers and the reality that you're sitting in that chair to sell solutions to their problems or challenges, not what you want to say next about yourself. At the core of a job interview, it's about them, not about you. Listen closely to what they're saying.

Don't give rapid, off-the-top-of-your-head answers. This isn't *Jeopardy!*. There's no race to push the buzzer. Answer concisely; don't ramble. Try for a confident, calm manner. You want to show that you're decisive, organized, and clear-thinking. Don't talk so much that you go on for 10 minutes answering one question. Crisp and to-the-point answers allow interviewers to get to all their questions and gather as much knowledge about you as they can.

Also be sure to ask what they see as the biggest problem that someone in the job needs to solve. If you have some ideas of what can be done to address that, here is your moment. You can also file it away to slip into your thank-you note.

Be enthused, but not fawning. You're a pro, remember. Show your passion. You don't want to jump up and down on your chair, obviously, but don't be afraid to express your feelings about the job and your fit in assertive terms.

Act interested and dignified. Interviewers really want to know what interests and intrigues you about their company, too. Be forthright and clear about why you are motivated by what the organization does and the challenges of the position you're interviewing for, plus why you think you would be a good fit with their culture.

It's a two-way street. Yes, you're there to sell yourself, but they're selling the job, too. It also makes them feel good about their own good fortune to work there. Even the most jaded hiring manager has a glimmer of insecurity.

Subtly slip into the conversation that you've done your background check—information you've gleaned from the Google news alert for the company and the specific industry you've already set up. This insider know-how will show that you're aware of the state of their business right now. It will make it easier to respond to questions about why the job is something that's a good match for both of you—that you have the key skills to solve their challenges today and moving forward.

Stick to your main selling points. It's easy to veer off topic in an interview. At home, write down and practice three main selling points about yourself to help you stay focused. Have specific examples that highlight your strengths to share with the interviewer.

I recommend that toward the end of the interview, you click through your mental checklist to make sure you've covered each of your topic points during your discussion. If not, don't leave until you have. If you sense the interviewer is wrapping things up, politely interject that you want to make sure you mention X, Y, or Z, and why.

Be sensitive to younger interviewers. Refrain from telling war stories about how things used to be. Interact in the same way you would with a person of your own generation.

Don't be thrown off if asked if you think you're overqualified for a position. You might be. Here's your canned answer: What matters to you at this stage is having the opportunity to work with top people in a firm whose values and products you trust and where your experience can be used in a significant way.

Keep in mind, however, that no one wants to hire someone who will in time resent working at something they feel is less than their talents, or for pay lower than what they believe they merit. You can't blame them. This is a tricky area, and you must be comfortable with the repercussions. It's easy to say it will be okay, but what's that really going to feel like if it comes to pass? Can your ego handle it?

Use your mentoring skills as a selling point. This is often a backdoor way of dealing with the concerns someone might have about how you will deal with the younger-boss dilemma. If you can slip it into the conversation, explain how mentoring has always been a part of your work and management style. It's a process that you have benefited from over the years as a mentee and a mentor and hope you can continue to give back by guiding less-experienced co-workers. And, importantly, you're open to learning from them, too. Again, mentoring helps both people.

Final questions. In the end, your interviewer will probably ask if you have any questions for them. Be prepared with at least two or three to toss out. Otherwise, you look as if you're not all that interested. But whatever you do, don't bring up salary at this stage. Save that for your next visit—either in person or on the phone, when they're close to making a selection.

Here are a few things you might want answered if they haven't already been covered in the course of your discussion: "What do you think are the key elements of the job? What are the firm's goals for the division the job is in? Why is the position open?"

(You may have to use your judgment whether this last question is appropriate. It's possible that it will make the interviewer defensive.) "Is it a new job or did someone leave the company? Is the interview process just getting rolling, or is it wrapping up? What's a typical day like, or is there such a thing?"

If this person would be your boss, and you feel at ease, you might ask, "What's your management style? Why did you come to work here? What challenges make you excited to come to work each day? What do you like the most about working here?" These kinds of questions let somebody see that you're genuinely attracted to the job, plus you can get a better read on what's next in the hiring process, and if it's a company you would fit with.

Ask for a business card. This one is up for grabs. I hear from younger workers that business cards are passé, so use your judgment. For me, in this age of e-mail, a business card seems a little quaint, but it's a tangible gift exchange. You can leave yours, while accepting a card in return with appreciation. It intrinsically shows you're interested in the interviewer's contact information, as well as the job. Ask if they prefer to be contacted via phone, e-mail, or text.

Good manners count. No hugs here. Go for a firm handshake, look your interviewer straight in his or her eyes with a warm smile, and offer genuine thanks for their time. And call me old-fashioned, but never forget to write a thank-you note to everyone you interviewed with.

I'm a stickler for thank-you notes in all aspects of my life. I learned the power of a proper note from a book, *White Gloves and Party Manners,* that my mother gave me when I was a child. It's an etiquette guide for young people, first published in 1965 and written by Marjabelle Young Stewart and Ann Buchwald (wife of Art Buchwald).

A thank-you note is simple and classy, and just might make you stand apart among a roster of applicants. I personally like a handwritten one, but an e-mail works today.

You can thank your interviewer by e-mail within the hour, from your smartphone. In many cases, the immediacy is welcomed and effective. And send a handwritten thank-you note the same day.

It's not wrong to do both, particularly if there's additional material you'd like to share with the interviewer, or if there were any questions you stumbled on or didn't answer well before you left. Use your correspondence to wrap up and leave a positive impression.

Then, relax! "Win or lose, as important and maybe even life-saving as getting this gig may be, it is ultimately out of your control," Tarnoff points out. What's important is that you've done your best.

And while I'm thinking of it, thanks for taking the time to read my book. I appreciate it.

Personality Plus

Depending on what type of job you're seeking, employers are looking for different characteristics, so keep these in mind when you're psyching yourself up for your interviews:

- **Curiosity:** An enthusiasm to learn new things and find solutions conveys an eagerness to learn. Ask questions about the company and its services, products, customers, competition, and so on to demonstrate your natural curiosity. Don't ask a potential employer questions you already know the answers to, because you'll come across as being clueless. After all, you should have done some research about the company prior to the interview. Let your natural curiosity prevail.

- **Insight:** An understanding of the company, what it does, how it functions, and what its challenges are helps you demonstrate your ability to gain insight into an organization. Research helps you develop the type of insight you need to demonstrate.

- **Engagement:** Your ability to carry on an intelligent conversation with the interviewers demonstrates engagement. Listen carefully to what they say and respond thoughtfully to show that you heard, understood, and are able to formulate a relevant response. If you're introduced to others in the organization, greet them respectfully, ask how they're doing, and listen to what they say. Engagement is all about showing that you care.

- **Intellect:** Brainpower never goes out of style, and again, doing your homework prior to the interview can provide the framework of understanding about the organization to answer and ask questions in an intelligent manner. Maintaining eye contact, speaking clearly, and using proper English also convey a certain level of intelligence and sophistication.

- **Creativity:** The aptitude for being inventive and original in your thinking is a magic ingredient. You may be able to demonstrate creativity as you respond to questions, or if given an opportunity to talk about a way you creatively solved a problem or met a challenge for a previous employer. Don't try to force creativity into the conversation, but take advantage of any sensible opportunity to do so.

- **Drive and determination:** Grit and purpose are core attributes for a successful employee. Interviewers want to see a whatever-it-takes attitude. Be prepared to discuss situations at work or in your personal life when you faced adversity or experienced a setback and managed to overcome it.

- **Efficiency:** How productive are you? A key attribute employers seek is someone who is effective in his or her work with good organization skills.

- **Open-mindedness:** A willingness to try new ways of doing things and a tolerance for taking risks are valuable attributes in team members and leaders. When answering questions that call on you to consider a certain option, think about your answer carefully. Unless the option requires you to do something criminal or unethical, give it careful consideration.
- **Passion for the organization:** Interviewers want to see that you love the company and what it does as much as they do and that you're committed to its success. You can demonstrate your passion for the organization by researching it carefully; following it on Facebook, LinkedIn, and Twitter; and mentioning specifically what you like most about the organization during the interview. Be prepared to explain why you want to work for the organization and what you can do to help it further its mission.
- **Passion for the role:** Being an engaged employee comes down to loving your work and your job. No employer wants to hire someone who's resentful of taking on a role they feel is beneath them or they're overqualified for, nor do they want to hire someone who treats the position as a stepping stone to what they really want. Talk passionately about the work you do and the work you'd like to do for the organization. Discuss how you want to immerse yourself in the job and really make a career out of it. Engaging with professional organizations, such as professional groups and relevant LinkedIn discussion groups, also demonstrates passion for what you do.
- **Punctuality:** Employers look for people who are reliable and they can count on.
- **Team player:** In the end, whether or not you get tapped for a job often comes down to a hiring manager's gut sense of how well you will play with the other kids. Someone who is willing and happy to chip in and works easily and collaboratively with others is highly valued.

Things to Avoid

Just as important as what you should do is what you should not.

- Acting arrogant: Humility rules the day. Employers want people on their team who work well with others and don't hold themselves above anyone else. You should be confident and have swagger, as I like to urge older workers, but never go egotistic. If you believe in yourself, you don't need this haughty crutch.

- Dropping names: It's okay to name names of people you may know in common or those big players in your industry whom you've worked with recently, but this technique is generally a turnoff and suggests insecurity.
- Bringing up compensation too early: Wait for signs that the organization wants you before thinking about how much they're willing to pay to get you. Besides, if you bring up the topic too soon, you may end up low-balling yourself. For more on negotiation, see Chapter 20.
- Focusing too much on yourself: Focus not on what your employer can do for you. Focus on what you can do for your employer. After your prospective employer decides that you're the best candidate for the job, you can shift your focus to getting what you want.
- Not being engaging enough: Although you don't want to chatter away about yourself for any extended amount of time, being stiff and standoffish is just as bad. Take the time to dance.
- Twisting the facts: You have nothing to gain from exaggerating or massaging the truth, whether it pertains to past jobs and responsibilities, graduation dates, experience, or simply your age. Honesty is nothing to play around with. After being caught in a lie, you may not be able to restore your credibility or regain your composure.

Acing the Telephone Interview

To improve your performance on a telephone interview, follow these suggestions:

- Use a landline phone, if possible. Avoid spotty cell phone and VoIP (Voice over Internet Protocol) connections. A landline removes the technical difficulties that may unnerve you during the interview.
- Pick a quiet location. Find a comfortable place without distractions from people, pets, music, and street noise. If you're home, inform everyone in the household that you're going to be on a very important phone call and are not to be disturbed.
- Turn off other phones and mute the speakers on your computer. You don't want anything ringing or dinging in the background.

- Lay out a copy of your resume and the job description. You may need to refer to details from these documents during the call, but don't read off of them, because reading can sound stiff.
- Have paper and pen handy. Jot down notes during the conversation, if that helps you follow the conversation and keep track of what's been said. However, if note taking interferes with your ability to listen and respond, then keep it to a minimum. You should still have paper and pen handy, just in case.
- Have a drink nearby. A glass of water is best, or a cup of coffee or tea if you're looking for a little caffeine bump. Keeping your whistle wet helps you steer clear of throat clearing, which is awkward and ruins the flow of conversation. And if you haven't said anything in a while, warm up your voice before the phone rings.
- Smile. Interviewers can hear a smile over the phone. You'll sound upbeat and convey a sense that you're happy to have the opportunity to discuss the opening. Smile especially when you answer the phone and greet the caller, when you talk about your work and what you're passionate about, and when you ask questions about the company. Put a mirror in front of yourself, so you can make sure you're smiling.
- Pay attention to your posture. Stand or sit up straight during the call. I prefer standing. I think it makes my voice sound stronger and more energetic. I even walk while the interviewer is talking.
- Be ready to go 10 minutes ahead of time. You don't want to sound hurried.
- Answer professionally. When the phone rings, smile and greet the caller with something like, "Hi, this is [name]." If you know who's calling (from Caller ID), consider following up with "Is this [name]?" Don't try to pretend that you don't know who's calling, because that can make you sound phony.
- Listen carefully before you speak. Pause before you answer to gather your thoughts. Then talk. Try to answer each question in two minutes or less. Otherwise, your interviewer may tune out. Because you can't see the person, it's tempting to fill in any pauses in the conversation, but rein it in.
- Enunciate your words and don't speak too fast. Projecting your voice distinctly and enthusiastically is fundamental.

- Avoid fillers such as "like," "you know," and "um." Use precise language to communicate your thoughts. Remind yourself that short pauses are acceptable and much preferred over fillers that can make you sound less sophisticated.
- End on an up note. If you really want the job, finish your conversation by saying, "Thanks for the call. I'm very interested in what we've discussed today and would appreciate the opportunity to meet you in person. What's the next step?" Think of this as your call to action.

Starring in Skype or Video Interviews

Virtual interviews are rapidly becoming more commonplace. Video interviews involve talking live with an interviewer via Skype, Zoom, or other videoconferencing technology or video-recording responses to questions from a recorded interviewer.

These tips can help you become comfortable with these interview formats and ace your interview:

- Check your equipment. You'll need a dependable internet connection, a webcam, and a microphone. If possible, use an Ethernet cable to connect to the internet and turn off Wi-Fi, so your connection is faster and more reliable.
- Perform a background check. Look at what will appear behind you. If it's a clutter-fest with file folders and paper piles, or even personal items such as pictures from your vacation, do a clean sweep. Having a painting, bookcase, or attractive plant in the background is best, but make sure the painting and books are tasteful.
- Adjust the lighting. You want soft light illuminating your face. Think of those klieg lights that shine on television anchors' faces. If your room has a window, face it, or put a lamp on the desk in front of you. Avoid backlit scenarios that put you in a shadow and glaring front-lighting that makes you squint.
- Experiment with the interview platform. If it's a live video interview, you may need to download the application software and set up an account. If it's a prerecorded interviewer, you'll receive instructions ahead of time about what's needed to participate.

- Reboot your computer. Rebooting ensures that you're not running applications that may interrupt the interview. Exit any applications set up to automatically run whenever you start your computer.
- Adjust your webcam and chair. Position them so you're in the middle (horizontally) and the top of your head is near the top of the screen. You should be looking up slightly at the camera, a position that helps define your chin and subtly conveys a message of strength and confidence.
- Do a dry run. Practice with a friend or family member on the platform you'll be using or something similar. With Skype, you can record it to review. This also helps with figuring out just how loud you need to talk and how to position your webcam.
- Dress for an in-person interview. Solid colors are best. Avoid white. Don't forget some makeup, even if you're a guy. It takes the shine off your skin.
- Have a cheat sheet. Sticky notes on your screen can remind you of talking points you want to be sure to highlight about your experience and why you're a good fit for the job as well as questions about the firm and the position. Have your resume and the job description handy, too.
- Try your best to look into the camera when talking. You'll be tempted to look at yourself or the interviewers on the screen, instead, but doing so breaks eye contact with the interviewers. Remember, their eyes are the camera.
- Smile when appropriate. Smiling provides a big boost for your video presence and energizes the interview. Try warming up ahead of time by thinking of something funny to make you laugh, or grinning at yourself in a mirror to loosen up your facial muscles. Smile especially during the meet and greet.
- Moderate your body language. Breathe deeply and slowly and relax. Keep your shoulders back and your hands quiet. No hair spinning around your pinky, lip chewing, squinting your eyes, or overblinking.
- Raise technical issues, if necessary. If something goes awry— say, your internet connection blips out, or you're having trouble with your computer's camera or microphone—speak up. If it happens during a recorded interview, just abort and contact the recruiter to explain and reschedule.

- Say thanks. End your interview by saying, "Thank you for considering me for the job. I look forward to hearing from you." Smile, and continue eyeing the camera until the recording or interview stops.

Being a Winner in Automated Interviews

Automated interviews are those in which a recorded interviewer asks questions, and you're given a set amount of time to record each answer. Video recruiting firms, such as HireVue and WePow, call it "modern recruiting" and have signed on clients including Geico, Hilton Worldwide, Nike, and Walmart to develop digital interviews with candidates.

Many candidates, especially older candidates, who tend to be more accustomed to interacting with people than performing in front of a webcam, may have a tough time with automated interviews. Establishing rapport with interviewers when you have to answer in two minutes or less can be quite a challenge. And you can't look around someone's office for impromptu conversation starters.

It really is more like acting than interviewing, so rehearse. Sit yourself in front of your webcam, set it up to record, and practice answering questions until you're comfortable with the format. Watch and critique your recorded responses to improve your delivery. All the suggestions in the previous section for video interviews apply to automated interviews as well.

CHAPTER

Special Job Circumstances

■ ■ ■

We all have plenty of unique circumstances when it comes to job hunting, but these three situations seem to impact a wide swath of job seekers I've met along the road for interviews and counseling: workers who are looking for jobs with the federal government, transitioning from the military to the civilian workforce, and job hunting with a physical limitation. All surely come with their own set of challenges and smart tactics to succeed. Here's a roundup of my best advice in each category.

Finding a Job with the Federal Government

I talked a little about government jobs in Chapter 16, "Navigating the Job Search Boards," but let me delve a little deeper, since there are a lot of jobs out there that may suit your needs.

Chat with virtually anyone who has pursued a job with the federal government, and he or she will tell you the hiring procedure can be agonizingly slow and bureaucratic.

There are plenty of motives to want to work in the public sector, so don't be deterred if this is your calling. According to the Partnership for Public Service (ourpublicservice.org), a nonprofit, nonpartisan organization, federal agencies are struggling to recruit and hire vital talent. Due to competition for top candidates, many of the brightest employees in critical fields like cybersecurity, science, technology, engineering, and math are choosing other employers over the federal government.

It's genuinely challenging for government to attract and hire mid- and senior-level talent from outside government, who could bring fresh perspectives and innovations from other sectors to solve federal challenges.

Even if you don't live in or around Washington, D.C., or have no wish to, that's okay—four out of five federal government jobs are based outside the nation's capital. In fact, more than 50,000 government employees work abroad.

And consider this: Health and retirement benefits tend to be more substantial than in the private sector, and there are often openings for telecommuting and flextime at many agencies. Pay is competitive with the private and nonprofit sectors: mid-level job wages can run from $50,000 to more than $100,000 a year.

The trick is to discover how to traverse the system. Here's how to start your government job search.

1. Follow Your Heart

The federal government is a gigantic pool of hundreds of agencies and departments. Search for job openings by agency, job type, location, or salary range on the USAJobs.gov site or at Govloop.com. There's a wide range of openings for people with an assortment of skills and experience—from accountants, attorneys, and architects to information technology (IT) workers, vendor management specialists, and healthcare workers at agencies such as the National Institutes of Health.

One way to cut through the clutter is to contemplate what matters most to you and where your know-how will best suit. "When we talk to our 100,000-plus members about what they love most about their government job, it comes down to mission and a sense of purpose," says Steve Ressler, founder and president of GovLoop, a social networking and resource site for government workers. Learn about the various agencies by attending events sponsored by government-related associations such as the American Council for Technology and Industry Advisory Council (ACT-IAC), the Partnership for Public Service, and the International City/County Management Association (ICMA), to name a few. You can also tap into government-related websites such as Government Executive (Govex.com).

Two other useful sites sponsored by the Partnership for Public Service are GoGovernment.org, which can help you research federal agencies and government careers, and Best Places to Work in the Federal Government (bestplacestowork.org).

Don't simply say, "I'm an accountant and want to go to work as an accountant in government." Every agency has a need for accountants and budget analysts, so narrow your scope a little bit.

2. Network, Network, Network

Although the application procedure is inflexible, it helps to reach out to anyone you know who works for the federal government. You want to get a sense of what it's like from someone working there now. The culture and environment make a difference.

Start by tapping your LinkedIn account to connect with people you know who work in or with the federal government, and join groups associated with the agencies that are attractive to you.

Check out your alumni connections, too. You might hear about openings in advance of an official job posting. Plus, having someone who can draw attention to your application can be a big benefit. The career or alumni center at your college or university may have a link with the government agency where you're applying.

If you've recently graduated from a degree or certification program, check out the Recent Graduates Program on the USAJobs site. This is meant for individuals who've graduated with an associate, bachelor's, master's, professional, doctoral, vocational, or technical degree or certificate from qualifying educational institutions. To be eligible, applicants must apply within two years of degree or certificate completion.

One exception: Veterans, due to their military service obligation, have up to six years after completing a degree or certificate program to apply. For federal employment information for veterans, go to the Office of Personnel Management's FedsHireVets website, fedshirevets.gov.

3. Get Your Resume Ship Shape

Resumes and applications for most jobs are generally directed through USAJobs. The specific language in the job descriptions and postings themselves can often read like a foreign language. And you will need to use specific keywords from the postings in your resume. You also will need to expand your resume that you send to private sector employers. And don't be surprised if you're obliged to write essays, too. The more facts you can share about your work and your results, the better.

Don't freak. There's help out there to lead you through the federal job resume-building route. On USAJobs, there's a tutorial on how to reformat your resume (as a PDF) and other tips. You begin with a regular resume that has all the data required by the agencies, and then you can fine-tune up to five different ones for different job openings. You also can sign up for job-posting alerts. "It's not rocket science," says Ressler. "[Your resume] should easily be formatted in a couple hours."

Ressler's organization, GovLoop (govloop.com), offers a free resume tool kit. The Go Government site and the Job-Hunt site's Guide to Federal Government Job Search (job-hunt.org/federal-government-job-search/federal-job-search) are other good resources for finding help with applications and revamping resumes.

4. Head to an Agency's Website

Once you have identified the agency you're targeting, check out its job board. Most agencies have their own job boards, and you may see additional positions on those sites that you don't see on the broader site. In most cases, you still have to go through USAJobs to apply, but there are spots that are excused from the competitive system and allow for more direct hiring.

5. Start with Temporary Assignments

These are often available through political appointments, or term appointments, where you're doing work for a short term or on a specific project for a year or more. Term appointments are listed on USAJobs.

The Presidential Innovation Fellows program recruits high achievers in the technology field for a yearlong shift in federal service. There are also government-sponsored fellowship programs such as Code for America (codeforamerica.org), which seeks our tech industry professionals to help 100+ local governments serve their communities better. Fuse Corps (fusecorps.org) is a nonprofit that places leaders from the private sector into local government for one-year stints. USE Fellows are mid-career professionals with 15 or more years of private sector experience who are looking to transition their careers for greater social impact.

There's also the Agriculture Conservation Experienced Services Program of the U.S. Department of Agriculture, and the EPA's Senior Environmental Employment Program. These two programs are operated by the National Older Worker Career Center, a non-profit based in Arlington, Virginia. NOWCC posts the job and reviews potential candidates; the agencies meet with the individuals and make choices. NOWCC does the background check and, once the person is hired, handles the paperwork. To learn more, visit the job-postings area of the NOWCC site.

Other groups doing comparable work to NOWCC are the National Asian Pacific Center on Aging, National Association for Hispanic Elderly, National Caucus and Center on Black Aged, National Council on Aging, and Senior Service America.

6. Be Determined

You've got to hang with it and know that the process is not a short one. It's time consuming.

It can easily take four months or longer to get an offer. This varies from one agency to the next, but 80 to 90 days between application and hiring is the norm. "I always encourage prospective job applicants to make sure they apply to numerous jobs over a series of months and give it time," Ressler advises. "When I conducted a personal government job search, I applied to 40 jobs over three months," he says. "I got four interviews and two offers. The time from first application to starting the position I took was approximately three months."

Acing Federal Job Applications

Before you can apply, you must create an account at the USAJobs website. Then click Profile and enter the details requested. Tabs at the top of the Profile area enable you to enter Contact Information, Hiring Eligibility, Other (your preferences, such as willingness to travel and whether you want full- or part-time work), and Demographic.

After that's done, click Resumes, and create a new resume or upload an existing one. For help, you can go to the bottom of the page and click Sample Resume or What to Include for extra details.

I suggest using the site's resume builder to add your resume rather than uploading it, so the information in a format that's acceptable to the automated screening system.

Next, you can do a job search using the Keyword and Location boxes at the top of any page. Click on a job that interests you. Read about it. Then if you are game to apply, tweak your resume to fit. As with applying for a private sector job, you'll find most of the keywords you need in the Overview, Duties, and Qualifications & Evaluations section of the posting.

The Resource Center on the site has tutorials to help with the nuts and bolts of the process. GovLoop also offers a free resume toolkit (www.govloop.com/groups/rockyourresume) that may also help. AsI mentioned above, for additional help with applications and revamping resumes, check out Go Government (gogovernment.org) and Job-Hunt.org's Guide to Federal Government Job Search (https://www.job-hunt.org/federal-government-job-search/federal-job-search.shtml).

Individuals with disabilities, veterans, students, and recent graduates, and senior executives might qualify for special attention.

Transitioning from Military to Civilian Jobs

When Destiny Burns retired after a 20-year military career as a Navy intelligence communications officer with posts around the world from Japan to the Persian Gulf, she segued to business development positions for large defense contractors, such as General Dynamics and Northrop Grumman, in Washington, D.C.

But it's not always that easy to slide into a great job post from the armed services. You'd think that employers would be tripping over themselves to hire you. After all, you served your country, you're a team player, you probably received specialized training, you gained valuable life experience. Above all, you've got a record of "sticking with it."

The reality, however, is that some employers are reluctant to hire you. Some fear you'll be prone to post-traumatic stress disorder (PTSD) and suicide, or have other mental or physical illnesses that will compromise your ability to do the job.

Others mistakenly believe that as a veteran, you'll require closer supervision than other candidates, because you're used to following orders. Moreover, employers may not understand how your experience and skills qualify you for their current openings.

"Few employers have many vets or understand anything about the military," laments consultant Patra Frame, a U.S. Air Force veteran and founder of Strategies for Human Resources in Alexandria, Virginia. Her organization specializes in helping military people transition to civilian life.

Employers "do not know what to expect, what skills are common, what the difference is between enlisted and officers," she explains. "You may need to do more to help prospective employers understand how your job skills, experience, and character transfer to the position and meet the employer's needs."

So here are eight steps to help you make the jump from military service to the civilian 9 to 5.

1. **Self-examination.** Serving in the military for 20 years "means in most cases you have never written a resume, attended a job interview, or applied for a job," says Diane Hudson, a career coach and resume writer who specializes in training and coaching vets. (She's also Job-Hunt's expert for placing veterans.)

   So start by making two lists. The first lays out the character attributes from your military experience that you'll want to showcase in your job search. This list might include such things as "leadership," "highly educated," "healthy/fit," "drug-free," and "Department of Defense clearance."

Veteran Job Sites

As a veteran, you can take advantage of all job-search websites and apps. But there are quite a few sites devoted exclusively to helping veterans. Have a look at these:

CareerOneStop.org
Dol.gov/vets/
FedsHireVets.gov
HireHeroesUSA.org
HireVeterans.com
Military.com
MilitaryHire.com
MyNextMove.org
Transition Assistance Online (taonline.com)
vacareers.va.gov/veterans/employment-coordination.asp
VetJobs.com

Create a catalog of your precise skills: accounting, engineering, computer software maintenance, security, logistics, and so forth. Dig around online to get an idea how many of your skills are sought after. Sometimes a first job is with a company that does defense contracting, as it was with Burns.

Look at your skill set and past experience as transferable to lots of different challenges and fields. Think of it as redirecting or redeploying many of the skills you already have in place. Look inside and answer some important questions: What am I best at? Ask friends and colleagues, too.

Hudson cites the case of an infantryman who'd served in the Army for 23 years and retired at the rank of E-9/command sergeant major. "He felt he had no skills or direct value to offer corporate America," recalls Hudson. "He said he operated tanks, weapons, and dug ditches."

Together they determined that he'd also directly supervised, trained, and evaluated 40 personnel, supporting over 2,000 troops in four countries, with an inventory list of 1,500 line items and material assets valued at $65 million, including large vehicles. His areas of expertise included personnel management, logistics, and operations.

The soldier later accepted a management position with a major retailer as a logistics expert. He had oversight supervisory responsibility for several hundred employees and multiple warehouses, says Hudson. "He doubled his salary and banked his military retirement pay."

2. **Translate your military credentials into "civilian speak."** "It is not just a job change but also a major culture change," Hudson says. "Learn the civilian or corporate equivalent language for your military acronyms, jargon, ranks [and] service."

Most industry professionals don't know, for instance, that a Military Occupational Specialty (MOS) is an area of expertise. They may not grasp the difference between a captain in the Army (junior officer) and a captain in the Navy (senior officer).

Believe it or not, there are websites that can translate the language of your former world into things civilians can understand. These sites include O*Net Resources Center and Military to Federal Jobs Crosswalk. Your old role as a deputy commander, for example, might be rendered as equivalent to executive vice president of special projects for a large company.

Use this civilian language without fail on your resume and your LinkedIn and other social media profiles. And, of course, in interviews.

3. **Explore government programs**. The U.S. Department of Veterans Affairs Transition Assistance Program should be your last stop in uniform. It offers a range of workshops that help you explore your skills and job interests, write a resume, and understand what civilian employers are looking for.

Three optional workshops—Career Technical Training Track, Education Track, and Entrepreneurship Track—are also available. Service members can elect to attend one, two, or all three.

4. **Seek out employers that go out of their way to hire veterans.** Many companies have specific programs to take on people who have served. Often their official websites make this clear. These employers include AT&T, Bank of America, Boeing, Cisco Systems, Citibank, Comcast, CVS Caremark, Deloitte, General Electric, Google, Hewlett-Packard, SAP, Walt Disney, and Xerox.

Federal agencies hire under the terms of a Veterans Preference program. This doesn't, of course, guarantee you a job. Basically it means that your military service will tip a job decision in your direction if you're qualified and other factors with competing applicants are equal.

5. **Find a mentor.** The nonprofit American Corporate Partners (acp-usa.org) offers veterans tools for career growth through mentoring, career counseling, and networking. Its mentoring program is open to all currently serving and recently separated veterans (including members of the Reserve and National Guard) who have served on active duty for at least 180 days since September 11, 2001. Spouses of veterans killed on duty and spouses of severely wounded post-9/11 veterans can also take part.

Much of the advice is parlayed via an online bulletin board where HR experts and seasoned professionals give advice in response to specific workplace and education questions posed by military vets of all stripes and ages. But ACP also pairs specific vets with corporate execs in more traditional mentor–protégé relationships. Employees from such enterprises as Bloomberg, Fidelity, IBM, PNC, and TIAA now participate.

6. **Network.** Reconnect with past peers and bosses on LinkedIn and other social media sites.

    Or look for military-focused groups. The Military Officers Association of America hosts military career fairs around the country and has a job board on its website as well as an interactive tool to help you prepare for interviews. It has a LinkedIn Career Networking group. The events and information are open to active-duty, retired, former, and National Guard/Reserve service members of all ranks and their spouses, as well as government employees.

7. **Skill up.** You learned a lot in uniform, but you can always learn more. Myriad programs give former military people a leg up in that task. The Veteran Education Benefits User's Guide (military.com/education/money-for-school/veteran-education-benefits-users-guide.html), published by AccreditedOnlineColleges.org, will lead you to grants, scholarships, and other educational resources.

8. **Ace the interview.** When you get called in for a sit-down with a hiring manager, draw on your old military confidence. But be sure that your words are from the civilian world. Don't worry about coming off as stiff. "Few military are as formal as many civilians expect, although the tendency to say sir and ma'am is hard to break," says Frame with a laugh.

Seven Smart Job-Hunting Tips for Adults with Disabilities

To be honest, finding a job when you have a disability is similar to finding a job when you don't. You have to network, search the job boards, tailor your resume to the position, establish a strong, upbeat online identity, submit job applications, and be a star in your interviews.

Whether you're dealing with a vision or hearing impairment, or some other physical or cognitive limitation—arthritis, perhaps, or PTSD—disability can add special challenges to finding a job.

Even if your condition doesn't undermine your ability to do a job, the fact is that many potential employers will have worries. But you can prove them wrong—and in making your case you'll have special protections under the Americans with Disabilities Act.

Consider these seven smart ways to navigate your job search.

1. **Check out websites geared to disabled and older workers.** For instance, you may want to look for jobs that allow you to work at home. Sites like Flexjobs.com and Remote.co are good places to start. Disability.gov has exhaustive info about U.S. government disability programs and employment. Look at the Department of Labor's Job Accommodation Network and GettingHired.com, a disability employment site featuring postings from such companies as Hilton Worldwide Inc. and energy provider Exelon Corp.

   If you're receiving disability benefits from Social Security, look into its Ticket to Work program (ssa.gov/work/). You may qualify for free employment help such as career counseling and job placement and training.

2. **Tap into the federal government's job board.** Go to USAJobs. gov and click on the link for people with disabilities. You can set up a profile and receive alerts for government jobs that are specifically for people in your situation.

3. **Find a mentor.** Connect with someone who has comparable issues and holds a job that appeals to you. Ask how the person obtained the job and does it well despite the disability. The nearest chapter of the national association that deals with your condition might be able to put you in touch with a mentor.

4. **Do a reality check.** You've found an opening. Now ask yourself: Can I do the job? Truthfully, will you be not only comfortable with the work, but good at it? If you have knee or hip issues, for example, you might do well to avoid a job in retail that includes long periods of standing. Likewise for one with a commute that requires lengthy walks to and from a bus stop.

For some people, the challenge is cognitive issues, such as problem solving, editing, and writing on a computer, says Rosalind Joffe, a career coach for people living with chronic health conditions. "For others, it can be such things as vision," she says. "When thinking about a new job, you want to keep in mind these limits, but focus on what you can do. If you only focus on your limits, it's difficult to find the courage and resilience to look for a job at all."

So, before you put your hat in the ring, dissect the job description carefully to figure out requirements beyond formal skills and certifications. The Bureau of Labor Statistics's *Occupational Outlook Handbook* is a good resource for this task.

5. **Consider when—and if—to discuss your disability.** "If you can do the job as described, without any work-arounds," says Joffe, "then ask yourself what makes you want to discuss your health condition and the limitations it puts on you." There may, in fact, be no reason to bring it up.

The Americans with Disabilities Act bars an employer from denying you a job just because you have a disability. To protect you, detailed rules say what the employer can and can't ask, and when—for instance, the employer can't ask disability-related questions or require medical exams until after you've been given a conditional job offer. You can find the full details on the ADA website (ada.gov).

Even if you have an obvious condition, most experts agree that disclosing a disability in a resume or cover letter can work against you, at least in the initial stages when an employer is paring down a stack of applications. Your first objective is to get invited in for an interview to show what you have to offer.

If there's something physically noticeable or an issue such as accessibility for a wheelchair, consider letting your interviewer know in advance, after the meeting date is set.

That's the advice of Kate Williams, head of the Employment Immersion Program at LightHouse for the Blind and Visually Impaired in San Francisco. You don't want surprises when you come through the door. "You want the hiring manager to look at your skills and your talents," she says. "You should be defined by your ability, not your disability."

6. **Polish your interview performance.** There's no reason you shouldn't discuss the proverbial elephant in the room if you're comfortable doing so. It gives you the power to make the case why, disability or not, you're the best person for the job.

   If you'll need to handle certain duties differently than other employees, be sure you can easily explain any work-arounds and particular accommodations such as a special computer screen, desk, or speech recognition software.

   If there's a gap on your resume due to a medical-related issue, be prepared to show how you continued building your skills through such activities as volunteer work or certification courses.

   Before you come in, practice. Ask a friend or family member to sit down with you and hear your pitch.

   In short, the best way for you to stand out is to demonstrate that you can do the job and are genuinely interested in the company and opportunity.

7. **Adopt a chin-up attitude.** "You have to get out of the 'I can't do it, I'm not capable' mentality," Williams advises. "If you don't project the belief that you can do the job, no one else will believe it."

   Kate Williams, now in her 70s, is blind, due to a progressive congenital eye disease that began to slowly erode her vision at 47. "It was devastating to me," Williams told me. "But I realized that I just had to learn to do things differently if I wanted to keep working. Today, I have an opportunity to let people know that life is not being defined by your disability, but your ability."

   Williams also won the Purpose Prize (now the AARP Purpose Prize) in 2014—awarded to Americans age 60 and older who are making an impact.

How Employment May Affect Your Disability Benefits

If you're receiving Social Security disability benefits, you need to look into how employment may impact your Supplemental Security Income (SSI) and Medicaid coverage.

Here are the basics:

If you take a job, you must report any income you earn to the Social Security Administration (SSA). Earning some income doesn't automatically reduce or stop your benefits.

- The SSA offers people with disabilities a trial work period, which allows you to test your ability to work for up to nine months in a 60-month period. You receive your full benefits regardless of how much you earn. After the trial period, you have 36 months to work, during which time you receive benefits for any month you work and receive earnings that aren't considered "substantial." In 2017, "substantial" meant not over $1,170 per month or $1,950 for workers who are blind." Check out the SSA's publication "Working While Disabled— How We Can Help" (www.socialsecurity.gov/pubs/EN-05– 10095.pdf) for more about SSI work incentives.
- If you receive Medicaid, your coverage will continue even after your SSI payments stop until your income reaches a certain level, which varies by state. Contact the SSA to find out what that income level is for your state. To remain eligible for Medicaid in most states, you must
    - need Medicaid in order to work,
    - be unable to afford similar healthcare coverage without SSI,
    - still be disabled, and
    - meet all other requirements for SSI eligibility.

Organizations That Can Help

Here are a few job hunting resources for assistance in your search:

ABILITYJobs.com (abilityjobs.com) The Job Seeker link offers a place to post your resume, view job postings, set up job alerts, and create a job seeker account.

American Foundation for the Blind (afb.org) is the go-to place on the Web to start your job search if you're visually impaired. In the Resources section, you can create a profile, register with CareerConnect, explore careers, connect with a mentor, and get help with interviewing skills, resume building, and disability disclosure.

CareerOneStop (careeronestop.org) is sponsored by the U.S. Department of Labor. Scroll down and click Workers with Disabilities to access a page where you can find out more about the Americans with Disabilities Act, job-search resources, interview tips, insight on when and how to disclose a disability, job accommodations, vocational rehabilitation, and more.

disABLEDperson.com is designed specifically for people with disabilities and the companies seeking to hire them. Search for jobs, peruse jobs by category and location, set up job alerts, and read educational articles to help you in your job search.

Getting Hired (gettinghired.com) is dedicated to people with disabilities and employers looking to hire them. Search by job title, key words, location, and category. The site also features a Career Tools section with articles, a career assessment, job recommendations, and interview training.

NIB (National Industries for the Blind) (nib.org) provides job listings, a resume builder, links to state resources, and much more.

RecruitDisability.org allows you to screen for jobs by job title, key word, and location; browse jobs by category; build and post your resume; set up job alerts; and compare salaries based on industry, function, location, and more. It also has articles to help with your job search.

SourceAmerica (sourceamerica.org) is a source of job opportunities for "people with significant disabilities." The organization and its partners deliver training to people with disabilities, help them find jobs, and enable them to be successful at work. It is one of only two non-profit agencies that support the AbilityOne Program, a federal program designed to provide employment opportunities to people who are blind or have other significant disabilities.

Think Beyond the Label (thinkbeyondthelabel.com) lets you search for jobs by key word, job title, industry, and location and sort your search results by date.

USAJobs.gov is the place to go to find out about and apply for jobs with the federal government. Visit opm.gov/policy-data-oversight/disability-employment for details about getting a job with the federal government when you have a disability.

Don't overlook state and local resources. Search the Web for [your state] or [your city] or [your county] followed by "jobs disabilities" or "jobs disabled" to find links to state and local resources.

20

Negotiating Pay

■ ■ ■

For many of us considering a new job, pay is where the rubber meets the road. Your starting salary or initial hourly wage is not only important for now, but it also will impact your future income potential, since future raises will be based on that figure.

Then too, if you feel the salary or hourly pay offered is too low—and frankly, it may very well be less than you made in your previous job—you understandably can feel slighted and undervalued. It's disturbing. It's not unusual to feel resentful, even. But asking for more can feel awkward.

You need a job, and you probably want *that* job. You don't want to shut the door on the opportunity. But you don't want to feel you're taking a step back. You feel trapped.

I get it. I don't have a magic wand, but I do have some advice that can help you tackle this critical step in landing a great job that's right for you.

The most angst-ridden stage of a job hunt is often the feared salary question you must answer on an application, or even in your interview discussion with a potential employer. Typically, the query is to learn what your previous job paid and what pay range you're seeking. Employers want to get a sense of whether you might take the job as a placeholder and jump ship when one that meets your expectations comes along. Be honest; you might. They also can use the information to weed out applicants who they consider to be pricey.

The big conundrum experienced workers looking for a job face is even as they expect a certain salary, employers consider them too expensive.

And in some ways, it's understandable. Your salary and health insurance, if you're lucky enough to find a job with health insurance, is a financial concern for the company.

I'm not going to gloss over this issue of pay shortfalls. It's a reality. In the survey "The Long Road Back: Struggling to Find Work after Unemployment," the AARP Public Policy Institute found that almost half of people ages 45 to 64 who were unemployed for some time during the five years prior to the report are making less than they used to in their former jobs.

I hear this all the time. Many workers over 50 who I have studied and interviewed express their frustration at being devalued by potential employers, and it gnaws at them. They reject job after job and sit waiting for the perfect one to come along. And the longer they wait, the bigger the gap between jobs. That's not good. The longer you are out of work, the harder it is to get a new position— and it's a red flag for hiring managers.

The truth is, a younger, less experienced worker may not hesitate at a salary that to you seems offensive and is a profound cut from what you earned in your last position. They have the future upside ahead and know the experience they gain will make them more valuable in the years to come.

For you, it can come down to a matter of pride. And if the offer is below your expectations, it's hard to accept. Your ego is bruised.

If you do accept the salary offered, sidestepping your inner irritation may prove uncomfortable. Trust me—you have to make peace with this issue from the get-go. But if it's a position you truly want, negotiating can help you find common ground.

Step 1: Practice Patience

My big-picture advice is to be confident and prepared when the time comes to discuss salary, but to hold your horses. Never accept an offer at face value. Keep quiet even if you feel the pressure to respond immediately.

Negotiating on the spot is never a good idea. When given a job offer, ask how long you have to consider it and arrange a time to deliver your answer. Remember, taking a job is a huge decision and you shouldn't feel forced to accept an offer in a heartbeat.

If you receive an offer in person, remember that your body language is essential to the negotiation process. You need to sit quietly and be relaxed; no nervous twitching allowed. Whether it's by phone or in person, the steady, firm tone of your voice and the words you choose should convey you believe you're worth what you're asking for.

You don't want to whine or sound desperate or anxious, or be too quick to reply, as I said. Nor do you want to come across as put off and insulted. Keep in mind that your potential employer has devoted time and energy interviewing and doing their due diligence on you. If it has come this far, it is rarely eager to start the search over again.

So hit the pause button. When you're ready to deliver your response, put your poker face on, get centered, and negotiate from a position of strength, believing in your value and clear about your expectations and what the position ultimately means to you.

Look at the Big Picture

You may be able to find ways to sweeten the offer around the edges. See if you can bump up your benefits; for example, more flextime or telecommuting, a signing bonus, more vacation days, new workplace development, educational opportunities, and other perks like bringing your dog to work. (Kidding—although that would work for me!)

A flexible workday, job sharing, or telecommuting might be more valuable to you now, giving you more time to do the things you really want to do at this stage of your life, such as travel or hobbies. Health insurance, retirement savings plans, and paid time off can play a significant role in determining your perfect job. Working for a company or nonprofit with a mission that matters to you may easily make up for a gap in pay.

Other options: Try asking for a pay review in three or six months, tuition reimbursement, parking allowance, or transportation passes. Those sorts of benefits may make a lower salary more, well, acceptable.

Consider what core benefits you need and which ones you can live without. In addition to health coverage and vacation time, traditional benefits can include sick leave, short- and long-term disability insurance, life insurance, survivor income, stock options, and retirement plans. If your spouse or partner has health benefits through his or her employer, for example, you may not need them, and that can be a bargaining chip to trade for something else you want, such as more vacation days.

Research Salary Ranges

Do your due diligence. Job postings rarely mention salary, so the first step in landing the salary you're after is to do your homework. Search for what the position, or one close to it, is likely to pay where you live using Glassdoor.com, LinkedIn.com, PayScale.com, and Salary.com, as well as the Economic Research Institute. For government jobs, check the U.S. Office of Personnel Management. If you are interested in a nonprofit, check out the organization's latest online tax filing (Form 990) to see how much its key employees and executives earn.

Glassdoor, for instance, has a database of millions of company reviews, CEO approval ratings, salary reports, interview reviews and questions, benefits reviews, office photos, and more. This intelligence is shared by the employees past and present. PayScale.com uses crowdsourcing and big data technologies to assemble its real-time database of more than 54 million individual salary profiles. Salary.com provides salary information for thousands of job titles. Check out LinkedIn salary screens at linkedin.com/salary/.

Network with people who are in your line of work to understand what the going rate is. It's tough to get people to disclose what they make, but you might be able to suss out some hypothetical ranges. Just ask, all they can say is they don't know.

A company *can* ask you what you made at your last job. In most cities, a hiring manager can legally ask your salary history and your salary requirements, although you are not mandated to give it. If you do answer, don't lie.

The issue of past pay is not to be taken lightly, particularly for women, who still make around 79 cents to the dollar a man makes, according to the U.S. Census Bureau. In New York City, the City Council tackled the issue by voting in the spring of 2017 to prohibit employers from asking job seekers about previous salaries to help "break the cycle of gender pay inequity by reducing the likelihood that a person will be prejudiced by prior salary levels." This is good news.

If you're working with a recruiter hired by the company, you can be more straightforward about salary than if you're dealing directly with the hiring manager. Recruiters know what the market demands and may be able to go back to the employer and say that your salary figure is realistic.

When you fill out a job application, you will likely have to declare your desired salary or hourly pay, or disclose what you made at your last job. A recruiter or hiring manager who calls you may bluntly ask your salary requirements right off the bat.

Keep in mind that employers base pay on the requirements of the job and the availability of qualified job candidates, not what the job seeker was paid in the past, says Susan P. Joyce, online job search expert and editor of Job-Hunt.org and WorkCoachCafe.com.

Since job requirements differ from employer to employer, you never want to walk in with a fixed number in mind of what the job should pay. What's essential is that you know what *you* are willing to accept.

Job Applications and Salary

So, how do you answer inquiries about your salary without turning off a potential employer during the screening process?

If a job application asks you about salary, you can:

1. Enter the salary you'd be happy accepting. If you can add more details, consider modifying that figure by adding something like, "The minimum salary requirement specified is based on anticipated job responsibilities and workload and does not account for other forms of compensation."
2. Give your base salary only for your most recent position. If you get invited in for an interview and salary comes up, explain that you provided your base salary and state other ways you were compensated.
3. If the job description specifies a desired salary range, enter a broad range such as $55,000 to $85,000. Be honest with yourself, though, that the low salary amount is something you can live with and would contemplate accepting.
4. Get imaginative. "If the form accepts alphabetical characters, I've heard people have success with typing in 'negotiable' and even 'confidential,' but most systems require numbers," says Joyce. In that case, your target salary number (hopefully realistic) or a zero seems to work best.

Answering Questions about Pay

When asked about pay in an interview, the best response is to say that since the position is not exactly the same as your last job, you need a little time to understand what the job truly entails before saying what you think a fair salary for the job is likely to be. "Even if the job title is the same, it's seldom an apples-to-apples comparison," Joyce says.

If you are pressed to be more precise, ask what the salary range is and factor that in your response. So if the salary range is $50,000 to $60,000 and you want to make at least $55,000, you're probably best off asking for something between, say, $55,000 and $60,000.

And finally, as I mentioned, think beyond salary. "Most people don't think about negotiating 'total compensation,' which is salary, of course, plus benefits (and more)," Joyce tells me.

So, if you're hitting a salary deal breaker, take a breath and think creatively. Look for those nonfinancial benefits that are hard to put a dollar figure on.

And keep in mind that if you've been out of work for a while, you may need to reconsider your make-it-or-break-it salary request and be candid about what number is going to work for you right now. Here are things to factor in when aligning your salary expectations with a new job.

Accepting Lower Pay

One of the hardest hurdles older workers have is dealing with the preconception from human resource professionals who don't believe you will happily work for less. When you're shifting careers to follow a passion, for example, it should make sense to an employer that if you don't have experience in that field, you will not resent working for less—at least to start. Be prepared to make your case for why you're okay with that, at least in the beginning. This is when negotiating for a performance and salary review in a few months can be a good strategy.

In fact, 82 percent of respondents to a survey by the American Institute for Economic Research reported successfully transitioning to a new career after age 45. Of those respondents who reported that they initially took pay cuts, half of them saw an increase in pay over time after "a period of hard work and persistence."

Less Responsibility for Less Pay

If in your former job you were in a position where you were the manager or foreman of a team of other workers, do some soul-searching and be truthful with yourself. Are you okay making less, for example, if you no longer want to be the one in charge of all that comes along with that responsibility? You may feel less stress and be happier at work if you are in a *nonmanagement* position. It's hard to put a dollar value on that.

And if at this stage of your life some of the big-ticket items, like a kid's college tuition or a mortgage, are behind you, you're free to accept work that may not pay as much but is meaningful to you, or is something you have always wanted to do.

For many workers, this career chapter is one where it's no longer about ego and climbing your way to the top. It's one where you're honestly ready to lose the pressure of managing others. You simply want to get back to basics and concentrate on work you enjoy and honing your own skills.

Yes, this stepping back may not be what we're accustomed to do, but it might be just what will help you find a job you that really love and will satisfy your goals.

"Money is not everything when it comes to our work," says career coach Kathy Caprino. "There are so many other factors that need to be considered. Figure out what your top life priorities are."

If earning a comparable salary to your last job is essential to you from a financial and ego perspective, however, be certain you deserve that pay based on your current skills, not on your years in the workplace. "You need clarity—a solid, realistic understanding of what you have done, what you have to offer, and what you can contribute to an organization, with evidence—proven metrics that illustrate beyond a shadow of a doubt what you're capable of and why someone should jump at hiring you," she says.

How to Negotiate Pay

You theoretically can't negotiate a job offer until you have one. Avoid getting into a detailed salary discussion or attempting to negotiate any condition until you have an offer on the table. For example, expressing during the interview your desire to work from home or have a compressed schedule could sour the deal. Wait to talk about this until you have an offer, and always be sure to learn what the company's policies and perceptions are for what you might want to request.

Negotiate with the Right Person

The person who delivers the offer to you may not be the person with the power or authority to negotiate. Every company has a different set of methods. It's important that you know who has definitive budget approval for the job. While human resources may be the ones who extend the offer, they may not have permission to negotiate.

Use Company Research and Inside Information

During the interview and through networking conversations with company insiders, you may uncover precious information. Perhaps you learn that the company has negotiated vacation time for certain employees or allows some of the team to work from home once a week. Your odds of getting things are better if there is already a precedent in the company or department. Use the information you uncover to your advantage.

To recap: Here are some things you may want to consider negotiating for:

- Job title
- Start date
- Vacation/paid time off (PTO)
- Flextime/job hours
- Remote or virtual work
- Signing or other bonuses
- Level of responsibility
- Relocation expenses
- Professional association dues, subscriptions
- Laptop, mobile phone, home office technology
- Auto (car lease, mileage)
- Training/certification reimbursement
- Severance provisions

Get Your Job Offer in Writing

Once you have reached a final agreement on the terms of the offer, be sure you ask for it in writing. For contractors, this is essential.

You will want this before you begin your first day of work. Managers can change and policies can shift. You want to protect yourself in case anything changes.

Parting Thought

A salary shortfall shouldn't always mean no. Don't get so caught up in status, salaries, and job titles that you become blind to opportunities to move in new directions. This is where financial fitness can give you some wiggle room because you aren't tied to a certain salary in order to pay the bills.

And keep in mind that although no hiring manager wants to hear this, nothing is forever. This job might be one you have for a year or three years or more. But it doesn't have to be your job for the next decade, unless you want it to be.

You may have several jobs over this next chapter of your working life. You may juggle myriad jobs at the same time, as I've said before. That's what this gig economy demands these days for many of us, and each client is a separate negotiation weighing the benefits to you, the time involved, and compensation offered.

You might even choose to accept less in pay because you simply love the person you will be working for. They make you shine and feel good. I've done this and have never regretted it.

It's fluid. There are no hard and fast rules when it comes to negotiating. Pay is personal . . . to you. Only you can value your time and how you choose to spend it.

CHAPTER

Why Part-Time or Contract Work Is Worth It

■ ■ ■

Today was the day. I put away the last vestige of the ho, ho, ho season—the festive bowl of holiday cards with pictures of smiling kids and pets, along with the occasional annual letters detailing whirlwind lives.

As I was taking a final gander, one caught my eye. It was sent by Gwenn Rosener. Rosener's firm, FlexProfessionals LLC (flexprofessionalsllc.com), is a recruiting and staffing company in the Washington, D.C., area that focuses on helping professionals—including retirees who want to continue working—find part-time work with competitive pay. The job seekers she places are typically college-educated workers, have 10-plus years of professional experience, and are eager to work 20 to 30 hours a week at hourly rates. The companies she works with are generally small, fast growing, and looking for experienced employees who can tackle a range of positions, from HR managers, business development and proposal writers, to web designers, analysts, bookkeepers, and office managers—all in part-time or temporary jobs.

Rosener, who was once an Ernst & Young senior manager and holds a Harvard MBA in her back pocket, and her partners, Sheila Murphy and Ellen Grealish, all have executive-level management and consulting backgrounds. Grealish worked at Hewlett-Packard and Andersen Consulting (now Accenture), and Murphy held consulting posts, mostly with government clients, including the U.S. Department of Housing and Urban Development.

The three partners started their business in 2010 and reeled in revenues of $140,000 with a profit of $47,000 that first year, placing CFOs, HR managers, business development and proposal writers, web designers, analysts, bookkeepers, and office managers in part-time or temporary jobs. And their business has been growing ever since.

It doesn't surprise me. Part-time and contract staffing is on the rise. "It's an easy way for employers to get great experienced staff and save money at the same time," says Art Koff, founder of RetiredBrains.com, a job search site for older workers.

That can be good news for many of you, and it's especially true if you're a retiree and need some extra money to boost your current retirement income. Part-time or contract jobs can pay enough to bolster income from investments and Social Security, often without exceeding the limits that would require a reduction in Social Security payments. Even if that happens, those benefits are not truly lost: at your full retirement age, your payment will be increased to account for the benefits withheld. For more about working while receiving Social Security, see *AARP Social Security For Dummies* or contact the Social Security Administration (ssa.gov).

For all types of job seekers, though, there are scores of reasons why part-time or contract work is worth it. Here are a few to ponder:

- It gets you in the door. It may lead to full-time work with an employer eventually. Don't miss the opportunity.
- It gets you decent pay. You can make your experience a plus. Employers are typically willing to pay you generously, providing you have the chops and solve their problem or need quickly. It lets them bypass the hand-holding and learning curve stage that a younger, less experienced, but lower-paid worker might require.
- It builds your professional network. Nurture relationships with co-workers during your assignment. You never know where contacts may lead you, and whom they might be able to refer you to for future jobs.
- It lands you new and *au courant* references for future employers to contact about what you've been up to lately.

- It keeps your resume alive. It's a bone to stave off the disgrace of those gaping holes of idleness in your resume.
- It keeps your skills sharp. You know the mantra: Use it or lose it.
- It gives you something to do. Don't discount this. Having a sense of purpose is a great thing for all kinds of reasons.
- Contract work particularly lets you get psyched about a work project without the pressure of long-term expectations. No job is forever, anyway. This one just might be shorter than most, and that can be tremendously freeing.

You can't expect that part-time or contract positions will lead to a full-time or ongoing position. I know that. If it's a job or a company that turns you on, though, you can subtly let it be known that you'd love an opportunity to be considered for a full-time position should things change. And please, don't take it personally if they don't.

Even if it's just what it claims to be, a part-time or short-term job, you still win, in my experience. First, it might be just the flexible work schedule you're looking for. Second, if it's a permanent, full-time job you really want, it still has your back.

What I mean by that is when you're making money, the truth is you feel better about yourself. You feel valued, and that's cool. It builds confidence. That's far healthier than shooting out resumes and not getting a single response. And seriously, you never know what might come your way when you back away from the computer screen.

Contract Work Is Hot

Contract work typically offers a variable schedule, perhaps lasting a week per month, or a few months each year. It usually offers decent pay and flexible hours, and taps into your professional-level skills. For those looking to switch careers or land a new position, there's an upside here too, as I will explain. From the employer's perspective, hiring temporary workers simply makes sense in many circumstances. Employers can staff up for short-range projects without the price tag of healthcare and other benefits.

And in this employment market, they can attract the crème de la crème. These are often workers who have been downsized or have taken early retirement packages.

I have little doubt that employers' shift to hiring contract workers is not so short term. For older workers who are willing to change their mindset about the security of a permanent, full-time position in the corporate world, these can be win-win. Nothing is secure these days; if you've been downsized, you're well aware of that.

Moreover, from talking with thousands of 50+ job seekers, I know that plenty of you don't have that burning desire to throw all your energy into a new position in the way you once did anyway, lip-service aside. You want work-life balance. Employers might sense that. Your age and compensation demands may pose an obstacle, too.

The pay for contract positions, though, can be top notch. As a contract worker, you can make your years of experience an asset. In many situations, a younger worker isn't going to get the job done quickly and capably without some hands-on training. So employers are typically willing to pay you handsomely, on an interim basis, that is. You don't have to roll over and work for less money—phew!

People who are genuinely seeking a permanent, full-time job, especially those who have been out of work for several months, are missing an opportunity by not accepting contract jobs as a means to an end. This is not a time to be a snob about it, or wear blinders and be trapped by the quaint notion of nailing a full-time gig "just like your old job."

Those days of velvet handcuffs and cushy benefits are virtually gone. This may be your time to weave together your future, perhaps with a patchwork of contract assignments.

You, Inc.

Let's call you self-employed, a consultant, a freelancer, an entrepreneur—You, Inc. Mine is Kerry, Inc. It has a nice ring to it, doesn't it?

As an aside, in fact, I always counsel workers of all ages to consider themselves the CEO of their own small business—even if you have a full-time job. Your primary employer is simply your largest client. I always did side jobs when I had a full-time position. That prepared me for my current self-employed status and gave me a ready list of clients. Not everyone can do this, and you have to be careful not to run afoul of employer rules about outside work, or using company time or supplies in your moonlighting endeavors.

As a career transition strategist, I view contract assignments as a perfect opportunity for a range of job seekers, particularly career switchers. If you're looking to get into a new field, for example, the opportunity to try on different hats, work in various types of businesses, even add new skills and experience, is worth pursuing. With a short-term "dip in the pool" assignment, you can find out if this is something you really want to do.

I always tell people who ask my advice on changing careers to test-drive the job first: moonlight, apprentice, volunteer. If you can get paid for it, go for it. That's the only way you'll know if the new career is all you dreamed it would be.

A final tip: Hone your yarn-spinning. Even if the assignment was the pits, and that's always possible, find a clever way to use the experience in a positive way. It can be a great example of your work ethic, or your ability to helicopter in and solve a problem, or fill a professional need for a company. Make the time spent part of your personal career story. Poetic license.

Replacing a lost income stream today is challenging, even more so if you were financially and psychologically unprepared for your pink slip. But as Henry Ford, founder of Ford Motor Co., said: "Nothing is particularly hard if you divide it into small jobs."

Meet a Contract Worker Turned Full-Time Manager

For nearly four years, Mary Doan, a former chief executive of the advertising agency Saatchi & Saatchi's San Francisco office, earned a living by stringing together short-term marketing director and development consulting stints ranging from new product development to communication strategies to website development, and by being "open to all possibilities," she says. Most of her assignments lasted from three months to about a year.

Her employers included a Silicon Valley start-up that sold solar energy, and nonprofit organizations, such as the San Francisco Food Bank, and Bread and Roses, an organization that brings live music performances to various venues, including senior centers.

"All of my employers found me through friends and colleagues from my past, so I didn't have to job-hunt, per se. I'm well aware, though, that I couldn't do enough disguising of my résumé for people not to know that I have been around the block a few times," she says. "I doubt I could apply blindly online and get a response even if I thought a job was perfect for me."

Retiring was not on her radar. "I've done work for 50 bucks an hour and for $200 an hour. I'm just happy to roll my sleeves up and be engaged," she says. "It's far more fun than retirement could possibly be."

In September 2016, her peripatetic jobs came to a halt when she accepted a position as a general manager at wildbrine LLC, a food company that produces sauerkraut and salsa, among other products, in Santa Rosa, California. "Working in a blue-collar situation managing 50 just-above-minimum wage workers and developing specs for capital equipment is not even in the realm of possibilities of what I might have imagined, but here I am! Having a blast and learning tons," she says.

Getting Your Name Out There

The right kind of self-promotion is crucial to building a successful second act as a freelancer or contractor. While lining up a contract or part-time gig isn't all that different from finding a full-time job, the difference is that you have to do it over and over again. How good are you at selling yourself?

Here are nine tactics to help you promote yourself and your business and bring in new clients and projects.

Work the websites. Upwork.com can lead you to online positions, Freelancer.com to project-based work, and VirtualVocations.com to telecommuting jobs ranging from grant writing to graphic design to bookkeeping. On TaskRabbit.com, you can sign up for jobs ranging from handyman to personal assistant.

Setting up an account is free on these sites, but you usually pay a percentage of your earnings. Upwork, for example, charges fees of 20 percent, 10 percent, or 5 percent, depending on the total amount you've billed with the client.

Leverage social media. In addition to having a LinkedIn page, you might want Facebook, Instagram, Pinterest, and Twitter pages for your business. Canvass your peers to see which networks they use professionally. Photographers often showcase their work on Instagram. Pinterest is popular if you're in the retail or consumer goods business.

Mine your network. Let people know you're looking for temporary assignments. Be bold. Announce your services from time to time on Facebook or post word of a job you've just completed. Join industry groups on LinkedIn. Periodically send out mass e-mails to your contact list announcing your services. And continue to network the old-fashioned way, face to face.

Keep building your network. When you're engaged in a project or temporary assignment, collect names and contact information for all the people you work with. One project or temporary assignment often leads to others.

Be active in industry groups. If there's a certain industry you're interested in, join a local association or organization connected with it. Attend industry and professional meetings and conferences. Monitor the association job boards and let other members know you're open for business.

Reach out to nonprofits, too. They often hire project-based or contract professionals. You might even offer your services pro bono to get your name out there and gain references for future jobs.

Know what you're worth. Research the going rate for what you do. Many contract workers have websites where they post their rates. Or contact some of them in your field and ask. If they're reluctant to share, they might open up if you explain you're considering entering the field but don't want to undercut others on price.

Launch your own website. If you plan to make contract work your full-time occupation, you'll want to build a strong brand. It will help you build your clientele by establishing you as an expert in your field and someone who can be trusted.

The cornerstone in online branding efforts will be a website, blog, or combination of the two. You can post articles to demonstrate your insight into the industry, share a full portfolio of your work, and include testimonials from past clients and supervisors. Low-cost options such as GoDaddy, SquareSpace, Wix, or WordPress make it easy to customize your own site by adding photos and text to templates.

You can launch a single-page website with a professional photo, detailing your professional background and interests—kind of like a spotlighted resume—and build on it later. If you need something more complex, you can always hire a professional, but you can expect to pay much more.

After you have the basics set up, it's a good idea to post new content regularly. Regular blog posts will boost your site's ranking with search engines, making prospective clients more likely to view your page.

Don't be shy. Some people are naturals at selling themselves face to face. If you're not, consider taking a public-speaking class at a community college. Most courses cover techniques for such things as managing communication anxiety, speaking clearly, and tuning in to your body language. Sign up for an acting or improvisational comedy workshop; these can help you build your confidence and stage presence. Or join Toastmasters. Groups of about 20 people meet weekly for an hour or two. You learn how to focus your attention away from your own anxieties and concentrate on your message and audience. Finally, consider working with a personal career coach.

All of these steps will translate into enhanced creativity and communication in your future temporary workplace—and likely boost your general happiness, too. Good luck!

CHAPTER

22

Be Your Own Boss

■ ■ ■

Robin Bylenga has been in love with bike riding since she was a 10-year-old girl racing through sunflower fields in Lubbock, Texas, on her bright-blue 10-speed Schwinn. She rode with her arms outstretched and head flung back. "Pure freedom," she says.

For Bylenga, now in her 50s and the founder of Pedal Chic, a women's cycling and athletic boutique in Greenville, South Carolina, it hasn't always been a smooth ride.

When the former Southwest flight attendant and newly divorced mother of three children—then ages 1, 4, and 5—reentered the workforce and began to piece a career back together, she went through a series of sales jobs.

She worked as a commercial real estate broker and peddled L'Oreal hair products to beauty salons. But the overnight sales trips to cover her typical two-state territory took a toll with young children at home. To find her focus, she climbed on a bike for the first time in years. Something clicked. "I rode and rode and rode," Bylenga recalls.

And it was that simple passion that landed her a job selling something she held dear—pedal power—at a local bike store. The only travel involved: pedaling to the shop each day. "Women began to come into the store just to talk to me about their bikes, and to ask me more personal questions like what kind of bra I rode in, and what trails were good to ride with our kids," Bylenga says. "I made biking, which can have a pretty macho image, less intimidating for them." And she sold a lot of bikes.

It was her "aha!" moment. "This was what I was meant to do," she says. Bylenga spent a year researching the market and testing the waters for a business in biking. She started small. She invested $500 for a small inventory of women's biking apparel that she parlayed into $1,500 in sales at a local bike race.

Meantime, she tapped free resources such as the Clemson Regional Small Business Development Center (SBDC), a collaboration of the Small Business Administration (SBA) and local universities. The SBA's SCORE program connected her with a retired retail executive for advice. She also tapped her own network to find small business mentors.

Then Bylenga opened Pedal Chic, reportedly the country's first women's-only bike shop, and has been riding fast ever since. Bicycles generally range in price from $350 to $1,500, but she has sold a carbon fiber road bike with electronic shifters for a little over $5,000.

Her start-up costs for Pedal Chic were $50,000. Bylenga's primary financing came from a $40,000 local development loan offered through Michelin Development. Rate: 3.5 percent. The term was for five years, plus the first six months were interest-only.

The loan allowed Bylenga to sign a lease for Pedal Chic's 2,000-square-foot space on Main Street, to purchase additional inventory and, most importantly, to create two full- and three part-time jobs. She personally invested about $10,000—a combination of her own savings from the divorce lump settlement and a gift from her parents.

Pedal Chic takes a hybrid retail approach—60 percent bikes and bike gear and 40 percent women's apparel. It's a smart formula when it comes to making money. Gross sales margins on clothing are nearly double bike returns.

The word has spread quickly through some savvy marketing. The store is a leading supporter of the annual "You Go Girl" all-women's triathlon held in Greenville. A loyal and ever-growing following of women ages 35-plus stop by weekly for her planned group rides, some for the entire family. And she offers classes on bicycle maintenance, called "Women with Wrenches," taught by Pedal Chic's full-time female bike mechanic.

Bylenga also has how-to videos on YouTube. In one, she explains how to lube your bicycle chain. In a twist, there's a hot guy by her side who does nothing but smile and hand her rags.

Bylenga's bike shop is profitable and she is able to pay herself a salary. Most recently, the Pedal Chic brand was licensed. Now a full Pedal Chic line of products including bikes will be sold through her store, online, and through various other venues.

Women are "rediscovering the joy of biking they had in their childhood like I did," Bylenga says. The motivations vary, but fitness, social activity, and even the desire to be a green commuter are all part of the trend.

Best return on investment: "Every time I help another woman build up confidence and find a cadre of women to connect with through cycling, it's a payday," Bylenga says.

Whipping Up Chocolate . . . and Profits

While she was busy earning master's degrees in anthropology and gerontology, Cathy Churcher certainly never imagined that one day she would wind up working wrist-deep in creamy dark chocolate in the kitchen of her tiny, 400-square-foot shop, Chocolate Cravings, in Richmond, Virginia.

But Churcher, then 50, dipped into her childhood passion for chocolate and quit her $56,000 a year position as the director of admissions at the Bon Secours School of Nursing. "I stepped out in faith that I could make a go of it in a new career," she says.

In reality, Churcher's career shift had been in the works for years. For decades, she whipped up buttercreams and peanut-butter balls as gifts for friends and family. Encouraged by their accolades, she enrolled in culinary classes, earning her certificate as a professional chocolatier at Ecole Chocolat in Vancouver. She rented a professional kitchen space to whip up her treats after working hours. On weekends, she sold them at local farmer's markets. As the word of her delicacies spread, local stores and restaurants began buying her treats to sell to their customers.

Wrestling with how to manage a burgeoning business and whether or not she had the resources to turn it into a full-blown occupation, Churcher tapped the advice of a counselor at a local economic development group. The counselor helped her put together a business plan free of charge and apply for the proper business and health department licenses. She and her husband ran the numbers to see where they could trim costs to get by without her salary for a time. And, importantly, she strategically studied her local competitors long enough to see them come into (and go out of) business—and to find a niche for her products.

More and more people are starting businesses in their 50s. I suspect some of that is a result of feeling frustrated by the job hunt and burned out by rejection and deciding, what the heck, I have something I have always wanted to do and maybe the universe is trying to tell me something.

According to the 2016 Kauffman Index of Entrepreneurial Activity, people between the ages of 55 and 64 accounted for 24.3 percent of new entrepreneurs, up from 14.8 percent in 1997. In fact, over the past decade, the highest rate of entrepreneurial start-ups belongs to the 55-to-64 age group.

What It Takes to Be the Boss

Working as your own boss in your dream field sounds romantic, but in fact it's not always dreamy.

Money can be a big stumbling block. If you're starting your own business, there are start-up costs, and chances are you won't even be able to pay yourself a salary for the first year or so. You run the risk of doing some serious damage to your retirement savings if you need to dip into them to pay your bills, since you don't have as much time to rebuild as you might have when you were a decade or so younger.

The good news is that with years of experience, you're far more prepared to launch than a 20-something.

Starting a business later in life allows you to take advantage of the treasure trove of business experience you have built up, your network of connections, and your road-warrior-honed skills of how to be competitive and navigate your way from failures to success. And you've probably grown out of any impetuous streak you might have had in your youth. My guess is you will take the time to think it through before you make the leap.

I have interviewed hundreds of entrepreneurs and profiled some of their success stories in my book *What's Next?* and I am always struck by their confidence, tenacity, and hope. No one questions how challenging it can be, but for most people, the reward is an inner payout that blows right by the financial struggles and setbacks.

For the most part, we're not talking Silicon Valley start-ups here, but small shops that might employ a handful of helpers.

Entrepreneurs who succeed are generally the ones who have asked for assistance. You'll definitely need a list of professionals to help you, from a lawyer to a tax accountant. And like other second acts, it's always good to try out the job first as an apprentice or moonlight to be sure it's right for you. A great place to start your research is at AARP's Small Business website (aarp.org/work/small-business). You'll find helpful resources from building a business plan to funding advice and more.

AARP and the SBA have formed a multipronged collaboration to promote entrepreneurship. The partnership hosts Encore Mentoring events that offer counseling, training, and mentoring on small business creation. Through online educational resources and in-person events, budding entrepreneurs get help on assessing whether they're ready to start a business.

Your ultimate success in running a small business will come from having a clear vision of what it is you want from the very beginning. How much time can you really devote to it? How flexible do you want it to be? Is it too late to really make a go of it?

To get a lay of the land, I asked Elizabeth Isele, Founder and CEO of the Global Institute for Experienced Entrepreneurship, for her take on this growing trend.

"Talk about power and promise," Isele says. "Today's senior entrepreneurs are dynamic economic engines. As they launch new businesses and create jobs, they're revitalizing our economy. They are not, as some would have it, draining Social Security and Medicare reserves but are actually bolstering those funds with their increased tax dollars."

And then, when she noticed me flinch at the use of the word "senior," she says something that caught my attention. (As you have may have noticed, I try not to use the term "seniors." Though I'm over 50, I don't feel like a senior, and I bet you don't either.) "Come on now," she says quite seriously. "Kerry, when did the word 'senior' become a bad thing? When we were in high school and college, we couldn't wait to be seniors. When we went to work, one of our goals was to become a senior partner, or senior vice president, or senior something. It was a good thing. Being a senior meant you were someone to look up to, someone to respect, seek counsel from, someone whose experience was highly valued."

Ahh, so true, Elizabeth. And then she started spinning stories of successful senior entrepreneurs, from one-person e-commerce to Main Street small business, and from small-scale social enterprises to major cultural festivals. I was inspired. Senior entrepreneurs rock!

Senior-Junior Partnerships

Twenty-somethings and 50-somethings have something in common: it's hard to get traction in the job market. As a result, senior entrepreneurs and younger partners are increasingly teaming up to launch ventures.

Take Michael Lowe, for example. He was bored with retirement. He had enjoyed a three-decade legal career, most of it spent as a corporate lawyer for Verizon.

"I was just kind of hanging around the house," Lowe says. "I decided I might as well try something else."

He had a good rapport with his son-in-law, John Uselton, now in his 40s, a fellow enthusiast of home brewing, wine collecting, and distilling spirits—and the two of them decided to start a business. Their mutual passion for craft distilling eventually grew into New Columbia Distillers, the first microdistillery in Washington, D.C.

Start-ups like Lowe and Uselton's are so-called legacy partnerships. The partnerships are started at or near the older partner's retirement from a lifelong career, with two generations bringing complementary assets to a new business. The assets are typically capital and experience from the older partner and energy, technical expertise, or online marketing skills from the younger.

"Many seniors are creating legacy businesses alongside a younger member of their family," says Isele. "It's a winning formula for both generations and, contrary to popular opinion, seniors with their wealth of experience and resilience are much more risk adverse than their younger counterparts."

While there are no statistics to document these new generational pairings, the trend appears to be gathering momentum in the current economy. In some demographic groups, too, these multigenerational start-ups are leading the way, Isele adds.

For example, Hispanic entrepreneurs are creating more legacy businesses than any other demographic, according to Yanira Cruz, head of the National Hispanic Council on Aging. Often family members are working together to create small retail businesses like florist shops, restaurants, and other businesses in the food industry, and service businesses like cleaning companies.

"The culture has a lot to do with that approach," she says. "We're raised to take care of our elders, and a commitment to care for one another has been projected onto starting a business."

The No. 1 rule is having a clear idea of what each partner brings to the table. "We use a lot of what we learned in our backgrounds," Uselton says.

Working for ourselves is often what so many of us really want to do at this stage of our lives. It harks back to that entrepreneurial mindset that I think most of us have en*gin*dered in us, as my Irish grandmother, Ellen Nolan Hannon, would say.

I work for myself. My brother does. My father did—on a much larger scale. I suspect one or two of my eight nephews and nieces will, too.

Being an entrepreneur can produce teeth-grinding anxiety when you take on too much work, or when there is too little of it, or when your invoices seem to have slipped into a black hole.

It can be hard to juggle that whole work-life balance thing when your work is your life. I don't think I've ever met entrepreneurs who say they aren't working harder than they ever have, but . . . they are okay with that. I suspect it's because when it is your own business, your own money at risk, your own dream up for validation, your work becomes your life in many ways. It's who you are at this stage of your life. Of course, not everyone is hardwired for this kind of adjustment, but for those that are prepared, the ride can be truly worth every ounce of perspiration and aspiration.

The Going-Solo Economy

I spend a great deal of time in the small Virginia towns of Culpeper, Sperryville, and Warrenton, all about an hour-plus drive from Washington, D.C., and close to the breathtaking Shenandoah National Park. My husband and I have a tiny cottage out that way. The vistas of the Blue Ridge Mountains, rolling fields, and mountain streams are the lure. And of course, there's the awe of star-strewn night skies.

This is the land of small business and sole proprietors. Small business owners operate every place I shop or dine. I'm on a first-name basis with most of them. They are grocers, coffee roasters, innkeepers, organic farmers, veterinarians, antique dealers, silversmiths, winemakers, whiskey distillers, dairy operators, bakers, restaurateurs, and more.

There's a tack shop for the horsey set, with saddles and stylish riding boots, that smells enticingly of rich English leather and liniment. (As a horse-addled adult, I'm biased, of course.) One bakery, in particular, makes me instantly hungry just by opening the door. And don't get me started about Janet's mouth-watering pies at Roy's Orchard & Fruit Market in Sperryville. Then, too, dozens of artists have studios here and market their goods privately by word-of-mouth. Farmers raise sheep and cattle, and stable owners board and train horses for a living.

Despite the rise of big-box and online stores, this small-town Virginia world is a network and community of small business bravehearts with entrepreneurial drive and a belief that they will make it, and the lion's share are making it . . . for today. And that's what small business is often all about, the present. It's frequently tenuous, living on the edge.

It can be a struggle when the leaf peepers and park hikers are gone, and the short, cold days of winter set in. But year after year, the entrepreneurs keep at it. Of course, there are those who fall by the wayside, and we mourn the loss. We root for them to succeed and put our money where our mouth is by supporting them.

These towns depend on small business to thrive. More than a few of the owners are mid-life entrepreneurs, who have switched careers to do something they love.

Going solo isn't for everyone. You need business chops—an understanding of the whole kit from marketing to sales and finance, or the willingness to learn those integral facets. At the heart of it, though, is something that can't be taught. It's a dream, powerful self-motivation, and inner drive.

Here are some basic business steps I recommend to help you land among the winners.

Do the prep work. Find a mentor. Who do you know who might be able to guide you along your new path? You may have to study marketing, finance, and employment law. Sign up for a community college or certification program to get the necessary skills. You can begin by contacting your town's or county's Small Business Development Center.

Seek out virtual advice. A new virtual adviser, Alice (helloalice. com) is a platform that uses artificial intelligence (AI) to let female entrepreneurs connect with other business owners, government resources, potential funders, and mentors. Alice provides assistance from some of the top entrepreneurship sources in the country, including the Case Foundation, the Kauffman Foundation, and the SBA. Her promise: to "connect founders with the resources they need to scale."

By asking Alice, women looking to build businesses should be able to find answers to questions about financing, strategy, marketing, and legal needs. For starters, it's free (for now) and it's not technically restricted to women, although Alice is coded with women in mind. You enter your profile based on your industry, start-up stage, revenue, and location. Alice then curates your needs based on what you're looking for—say, a tech solution or an attorney—and the answers are different for every user. The goal is to connect entrepreneurs with resources they can't find in their location or that aren't on their radar.

Take inventory. The checklist for launching a company from the SBA (sba.gov) is a great place to begin. It helps you review your situation, identify a niche, analyze the market, and get a sense of your financial picture.

Write a business plan. There's no strict model to follow, but in general, a simple plan—which you'll have to submit to get a loan or other financing—should be about 20 pages. Here's what you'll need:

- An executive summary that explains what your company will do, who the customers will be, why you are qualified to run it, how you'll sell your goods and services, and your financial outlook.
- A detailed description of the business, its location, your management team, and your staffing requirements. You'll also need to include information about your industry and competition.
- A market analysis that targets your customers more specifically, including age, gender, and geographic location. The analysis also will describe your sales and promotional strategy to reach them.
- A realistic forecast of start-up outlays—cost of raw materials, equipment, employee salaries, marketing materials, insurance, utilities, and fees for attorneys and accountants—and how much you expect to sell and to earn.

Line up sources of funding. Here are some ways to find the money to get started:

- **Savings.** Most startups are funded with personal savings. (This is where a severance package comes in handy.) It's advisable to set aside at least six months of fixed living expenses, though. Try not to dip into your retirement savings—you'll be subject to withdrawal penalties and income taxes and lose the tax-deferred compounding that could serve you well in retirement.
- **Friends and relatives.** Money is often lent interest free or at a low rate. Be sure to put the terms in writing so that there are no misunderstandings about interest and repayment. Be forewarned: Money can wreak havoc on relationships should things not work out as planned. I want you to tread lightly if you think it might have the possibility of turning ugly.
- **Banks and credit unions.** A solid business plan and a shiny credit record are prerequisites. You might try a bank that's familiar with you or your industry, or one that is active in small-business lending. To find a bank that offers SBA-guaranteed loans, check the Local Resources section of the agency's website (sba.gov). An SBA-guaranteed bank loan can keep your down payment and monthly payments low. Keep in mind that a lender will still want you to put up collateral, usually in the form of a real estate asset. Plan to have some capital or equity that you personally put into the business. Lenders want you to have some skin in the game, so to speak. Business.usa.gov is the federal government's site for entrepreneurs seeking short-term microloans and small business loans. Search this site for info on all programs available in your state.
- **Angel investors and venture capital firms.** These individuals and firms invest in exchange for equity or partial ownership. But they are typically overwhelmed by requests for financing. Another source of venture capital is the SBA's Small Business Investment Company Program.
- **Economic development programs.** This type of financing will take a little homework, but it's worth pursuing. For example, if you're a woman, you might consider getting your firm certified as a woman-owned business. That can help you

qualify for money that's only available to companies with that designation.

- **Certification can also help you land government clients.** Small-business certifications and verifications confirm a company's status, like whether the principal owner is a minority group member or whether the firm is located in an economically disadvantaged area. The SBA's economic development department can help you determine if this might be an avenue for you. If you're a veteran, the Department of Veteran Affairs, for instance, can provide you with information on how to get certified.

- **Grants.** Grants.gov lists information on more than 1,000 federal grant programs. Female entrepreneurs should check out the SBA network of nearly 100 Women's Business Centers around the country. They offer state, local, and private grant information to women interested in starting for-profit or nonprofit businesses.

- **Online seed money.** Virtual fundraising campaigns on sites like Kickstarter, Indiegogo, and GoFundMe have been gaining in popularity with people raising money for a pet project or new business. But if you're trying to crowdfund money this way, you'll need savvy marketing and elbow grease to create a winner.

  Kickstarter is a crowdfunding website that entrepreneurs use to find people who'll invest small amounts of money in tech projects or creative endeavors like music or video games. Someone can donate anywhere from $1 to the sky's the limit. It's not an investment. Most successfully funded projects on Kickstarter (the largest crowdfunding site) raise under $10,000. But some projects have indeed crested far higher.

  Each of the big crowdfunding sites handles the funding process differently.

  On Kickstarter, when people donate, their credit cards are charged. Once you reach your goal, Kickstarter takes 5 percent of the amount raised and you pay 3 to 5 percent for credit card processing. If you don't bring in all the money you set as your goal by the deadline, the pledges are canceled, contributors aren't charged, and Kickstarter takes nothing.

Indiegogo charges a 5 percent fee on the funds you raise, plus you pay 3 to 5 percent for credit card or PayPal processing. Unlike Kickstarter, pledges aren't canceled if you don't reach your goal.

GoFundMe.com deducts a 5 percent fee and a 3 percent processing fee from each donation. All the remaining money you collect goes directly to you.

- **Home equity loans.** This may be an option because the funds are usually taken as a lump sum that you can pay off over time. If you have equity in your home and a credit score well above 700, it may be worth exploring. You may also qualify for a tax deduction on the interest on a loan up to $100,000. Consult a financial adviser. Just be certain that you'll be able to repay this kind of financing—your house is on the line.

And now the two sources of money you don't want to use:

- **Credit cards.** Avoid using plastic at all costs. Most cards carry double-digit interest rates, which is an outlandish price to pay for starting a business. Also, it's very easy to get yourself into trouble this way, given the financial ups and downs of a new venture.
- **Retirement savings.** Trust me, you don't want to dip into your 401(k) or IRA. Not only will you owe income taxes by taking money out, you'll lose the tax-deferred compounding and, if you're younger than 59½, you'll owe IRS withdrawal penalties. Worst of all, you'll hijack your future financial security. Please don't do that. No business is worth it.

Hire an accountant. It's critical to know which business expenses are deductible and more. Careful recordkeeping is essential, and having a pro to guide you will come in handy. I haven't met a new business owner who hasn't moaned about tax compliance worries, and it's more than simply withholding taxes for employees.

There's a broad sweep of taxes to consider, ranging from personal income tax to sales and payroll taxes. Hiring a knowledgeable tax professional makes sense. That can take some legwork. You need more than tax software to guide you, and someone who is adept at running individual tax returns isn't necessarily well versed in the intricacies of small business tax law.

Search for someone who is available to you all year round to answer the inevitable questions that arise. You might hire someone on a retainer basis, say, a couple of hundred a month, who can hold your hand and make sure the filings get sent in a timely fashion. Go to the source for more details: IRS Publication 334, "Tax Guide for Small Businesses" (https://www.irs.gov/publications/p334/). Useful information is available at the IRS Small Business and Self-Employed Tax Center (https://www.irs.gov/businesses/small-businesses-self-employed).

Don't neglect retirement savings. According to a recent BMO Wealth Management survey of 400 small business owners, only a fraction of America's entrepreneurs are prepared for retirement. A striking 75 percent of survey respondents age 18 to 64 have saved less than $100,000 for retirement. Those age 45 to 64 are only marginally more prepared: 32 percent have over $100,000 in retirement accounts and only 11 percent have more than $500,000. I was pleased, however, to see that 39 percent of business owners age 45 to 64—the ones closing in on retirement—had traditional IRAs or Roth IRAs, and 29 percent were saving in 401(k)-type accounts.

Why don't more small business owners save for retirement? "The business is their retirement plan," says David Deeds, the Schulze Professor of Entrepreneurship at the University of St. Thomas in Minneapolis. "The plan is that when they retire, they are either going to transfer the business to a family member in exchange for a share of future wealth or a buyout or they are going to sell it off and turn that into cash. There is a risk level to it," adds Deeds, who is also editor-in-chief of EIX, the Entrepreneur & Innovation Exchange, a social-media learning platform designed to improve the success rate of new business ventures. "If the business fails, your wealth goes away."

For small business owners, it's not that they don't want to save for retirement outside of their businesses. Their priority is to plow earnings back into the business to keep it growing, so they rarely pay themselves a big salary. "If you are a small business owner, much of your wealth is trapped in your business. The problem is in order to diversify that wealth, you have to remove that wealth from the business, and, in essence, remove some of the lifeblood from the business," Deeds says. "Taking money out impinges on growth prospects and it can make it hard to maintain the business."

The four main options: a SEP-IRA, a SIMPLE IRA, a Solo 401(k), and a SIMPLE 401(k). For all but SEP-IRAs, a business can be a sole proprietorship, a partnership, a limited liability company, or a corporation.

A SEP-IRA is a tax-deferred retirement plan like a traditional IRA and is great if you're the company's only employee (as I am). In 2017, you could contribute up to $54,000. The account is tax-free until you withdraw the money at retirement. Usually there is a penalty for removing the funds before age 59½, and you must start withdrawing the money at age 70½. One caveat: If you have employees, you generally must also fund SEP-IRAs for them.

A SIMPLE IRA is a retirement plan for business owners with 100 or fewer employees. Contributions are pre-tax and taken directly out of employee paychecks, similar to a 401(k). In 2017, your contribution couldn't exceed $12,500, or $15,500 if you're 50 or older.

A Solo 401(k) is for self-employed people without employees (except perhaps a spouse). In 2017, the IRS let you contribute, pre-tax, a $54,000 maximum in 2017, or up to $6,000 more if you're 50 or older.

A SIMPLE 401(k) is for businesses with 100 or fewer employees. You and your employees can borrow against the money in your 401(k) accounts and make penalty-free withdrawals due to financial hardship.

Check out 401(k) plans targeted to small businesses. Some 401(k) providers are actively targeting small businesses these days. Capital One, for example, launched Spark 401k, providing low-cost, all-ETF (exchange-traded fund) 401(k) plans for businesses with fewer than 100 employees. It offers access to retirement planning experts, too.

According to Capital One's research, 60 percent of small business owners don't think they have enough employees to offer a plan, which is a prevalent misperception, says Stuart Robertson, president of Capital One Advisors 401(k) services. "The truth of the matter is any size business, even an owner-only business, can have a 401(k) plan," he says.

Do the paperwork. The majority of small businesses require permits and licenses from your town, county, and state. These vary by location, and typically need to be renewed annually, so you will need to keep good records. Check out online resources for details. It's also smart to touch base with your town officials and local business owners to get a grip on the current local regulations.

Prepare to wait for income. You should expect that it will take three years or so before your business gets on its feet financially, but be prepared for it to take longer.

Don't Just Retire Abroad—Start Your Own Business There

When Dwight Stanford retired from his 25-year career as a surgeon in Kansas City, Missouri, he headed to Italy, more specifically a hilltop town named Offida. It wasn't on a whim. In 2006, he'd fallen hard for the Italian way of life after earning a master's degree in food science during a sabbatical there.

Today, the 59-year-old co-owns and operates a B&B in a 500-year-old farmhouse, as well as the Paolini & Stanford Winery, which produces 25,000 bottles of organic wine a year. On any given day, he might be out driving a tractor or preparing breakfast for B&B guests with the help of his fiancée, Maryse Pen. And just recently, he's been able to pay himself a small salary.

For many people, his story may seem like fantasy. But retiring abroad and opening a business there has, in fact, become increasingly common.

If opening a business in a foreign land sounds appealing to you, here are some steps that can help make it happen.

1. **Do your research**. International Living (internationalliving.com) magazine publishes an annual global retirement index that ranks the World's Best Places to Retire. For this year's 24 countries, which include Costa Rica, Ecuador, Mexico, Malta, Panama, Spain, Portugal, and Malaysia, its researchers crunched numbers on the cost of living, healthcare, housing, internet access, infrastructure factors such as international airports and, of course, weather.

Another resource is the Annual Retire Overseas Index, from the online publication Live and Invest Overseas (liveandinvestoverseas. com). This year's No. 1 place: the picturesque coastal region of Algarve, Portugal. International retirement expert Kathleen Peddicord and her team develop the annual ranking using statistics from public records, as well as sandals-on-the-street reporting by correspondents.

2. **Go for a lengthy visit.** Before settling on a place, spend a couple of months there to see if you really fit in. Befriend local expats to learn what brought them there and what kind of jobs they might have. Do your own sleuthing by talking to local businesspeople.

   Understand the local employment laws. Find out if the country allows foreigners to hold the kind of job you want and whether a work permit is required. Also, gauge competition for the job you're seeking; supply and demand applies as much here as anywhere.

3. **Leverage language.** If you speak a foreign language, or just studied one in high school, it can make sense to focus on places where it's spoken. And keep in mind that your English skills can open the door to a wide range of work that includes teaching English, interpreting and guiding English-speaking tourists, or operating a tourist-oriented art gallery, bistro, B&B, retail shop, or real estate agency.

4. **Become a virtual consultant.** Turn what you've done your entire career into a virtual consulting or project assignment–based business that you can do online. It's the ultimate telecommute, provided you have a good internet connection.

5. **Open a brick-and-mortar business.** This is more ambitious, but often it's doable. Patrice Wynne closed her independent bookstore, Gaia, in Berkeley, California, and retired with the goal of taking a break and enjoying the good life abroad. She discovered she wanted to keep working and remain creatively engaged.

   So Wynne, now in her 60s, opened Abrazos Boutique San Miguel, a 650-square-foot retail shop in the historic center of the Mexican colonial city San Miguel de Allende. It sells vibrantly patterned fabric aprons, handbags, and clothing sewn by local seamstresses.

   Hiring a bilingual person who can help steer you through operational challenges is essential for many expat small-business owners, Wynne says. Even if you're fluent in the language, you'll need a bilingual legal and tax adviser to grasp the ins and outs of applicable laws, employment regulations, and business contracts.

6. **Learn the local etiquette for business relationships.** Slow down. Some deals don't get done until you've had a meal together. In Mexico, for instance, even a simple business phone call takes extra time. You need to ask about family, health, and how the day is going.

7. **Start with a local job to get your feet wet.** While you map out your entrepreneurial venture, you might land a job to get a sense of the community.

For leads, check out ExpatExchange.com, a popular website on living abroad. "Expat retirees typically move to warm, beachfront areas such as Ecuador, Panama, Costa Rica, the Philippines, Thailand, the Dominican Republic, Mexico, and Belize," says founder Betsy Burlingame. "These areas are also popular tourist destinations, and expat retirees can often find work in businesses related to the tourist industry."

Other sites listed on the U.S. Department of State website for working overseas include:

American Citizens Abroad (americansabroad.org)
Escape Artist (escapeartist.com)
Expats Abroad (expats-abroad.com)
Going Global (goinglobal.com)
International Organizations Careers (iocareers.state.gov)
Jobs & Work Abroad (jobs.goabroad.com)
Kompass (kompass.com)
Transitions Abroad (transitionsabroad.com)

8. **Pay attention to taxes.** If you're going to earn even a small salary, consult with someone who knows international tax issues. Both the United States and your new country of residence could try to tax the money you earn.

As a U.S. citizen or resident alien, you are taxed by the United States on your worldwide income and must file an annual tax return with the IRS. However, you may be eligible for the foreign earned income exclusion, which is adjusted annually for inflation (which in 2017 exempted $102,100 of income per person from U.S. taxes). And if your foreign bank accounts hold a total of more than $10,000, with certain exceptions, you must file a disclosure form with the U.S. Treasury by April 15.

Finally, be open-eyed about the drawbacks. Your internet connection might flicker in and out. Siesta time? Even your bank may shut its doors. Local bureaucrats might want a little pocket money as thanks for filing your business paperwork.

And of course there's the possibility you'll get homesick. There's a lot to be said for living in the USA. But more than a few people have found fulfilling opportunities beyond its shores. You might become one of them.

Seven Tips from a Financing Whiz

Here are seven tips from Jeanne Sullivan, cofounder of the New York City–based venture capital firm StarVest Partners, for those who want to launch businesses and who need to attract money to their startup:

1. **Hone your story.** One way to get an investor or lender to open a wallet is to have the chutzpah to sell, sell, sell your vision in a snappy sales pitch. Short and sweet.

   "You need one or two lines that sum up your product or service," says Sullivan. "The key is to be able to get that company story out of your mouth in a clear, succinct, short pitch." You'll also want to include a cogent example of how a customer would use your product or service.

2. **Know your market.** To get a solid grip on the potential size of your customer base, Sullivan says, ask yourself: "How big is it? Is it crowded? What niche are you trying to serve?"

3. **Be sure you can reel off your business's current finances and financial needs.** Sullivan says an investor wants you to have "the street savvy on the financial details of your business" that allows you to discuss it easily.

   Says Sullivan: "It's important to be able to answer questions such as 'What are the capital needs of the business over time? What are the gross margins? What's your breakeven timeframe?'"

4. **Don't hesitate to ask people you know to invest.**

5. **Prepare for show and tell.** "If you're selling a product, get it in the hands of early pilot customers," says Sullivan. Then you'll have something real to discuss with an investor. "It is very hard to get funding before you build the product."

6. **Have a strategy for hiring your team.** "Outline the key people you need over the next 18 months and recruit them—knowing that they may work for you now for equity or part-time until you get some funding," Sullivan advises.

7. **Surround yourself with a useful board of advisers—a brain trust.** "A dynamic board early in your company's life adds gravitas," Sullivan says. "Those advisers can be formidable references for you with an investor. They can guide you and they may lead you to your first customers."

To find prospective board members, Sullivan says, tap your network of people who have experience with your type of business and invite about three to five of them to join your board. "Then, conduct either virtual or in-person meetings with them on a periodic basis to discuss two to three issues of key importance," says Sullivan.

One more thing I'd add to Sullivan's advice, based on what I've learned from entrepreneurs who've switched careers and started businesses in midlife: prepare to work harder than you ever have (most small business owners work more than 60 hours a week, according to a survey by small business loan provider Kabbage) and prepare for the inevitable setbacks.

But don't let that get you down. Most 50+ entrepreneurs I've met say they only wish they had done it sooner.

Afterword

Finding a great job is within your power. As you've read in this book, great jobs come in all different forms. At the root of what makes a job search successful—and a job *great*—is your attitude.

You have the ability to control how your mind confronts and responds to trying something new, to learning new skills, and to adapting to new work environments. At this stage in your life, you've proven time and again that you can do just that. You've worked alongside a diverse group of people in a variety of workplaces. You have swagger. And if you don't, then you should!

Even if you have had only one employer to date, which is less likely than it was in our parents' generation, you've taken on new job responsibilities along the way. You've pushed outside your comfort zone.

You aren't a novice. You come to the challenge of job seeking with an inner compass that has steadily given you direction. Your accumulated expertise allows you to quickly get up to speed in fields that may seem worlds apart from where you've started.

But even with all those arrows in your quiver, there is no getting around the fact that landing a great job is a process. It takes some detective work and preparation. Opportunities are rarely handed to you. You have to go out and do the legwork to achieve it.

I hope you come away from this book knowing the three major actions that will contribute to your success. Here's your recap:

1. **Pause and take the time to explore what you're good at and what you want to do.** What have you enjoyed in jobs and work experiences from your past? What are the pastimes you're passionate about, even those that sparked you as a child? Those personal questions will guide you to your next endeavor. They are your clues to what will make a job your great job. Dream a little. This could be the opportunity you've been waiting for to try something new.

2. **Do your homework.** Look into a wide variety of jobs, including by reading books like this. Learn about which jobs truly fit this stage of your life—from a financial, logistical, intellectual, physical, and psychological perspective. Check into all the resources available in your town for you to add new skills, volunteer, or moonlight.

3. **Network.** Ask people who know you well and people you've worked with over the years for advice on what kinds of opportunities they think you would be good at. Don't be bashful about asking if your contacts might be able to introduce you to someone who works for a company where you're keen on working, or has an opening you are eyeing. If they work for that firm, they might even be able to submit your resume directly through the employer's employee referral program. This is a win for them, too, because employers often offer cash incentives for employee referrals if the person is hired. And never forget to ask someone who else they suggest you talk to.

As I've said throughout this book, no two people are looking for the same ingredients in a job. Each person I interviewed had different skill sets, backgrounds, and goals. Many took the time to go back to school to prepare for a new kind of work. Others simply let their heart lead them to a job that makes clocking in turn them into a kid again.

There's no ideal starting point. You need to just press forward, pick up the phone, and call people who can share their network or expertise with you. Enroll in a class to add new skills. The very process of learning opens your mind to possibilities. It changes the way you see the world. You're engaged. Things shift.

Stay present. Living in the past and mourning your old job will make you feel rudderless and out of control. Concentrate on all the things you can do. Take action right now.

Focus on your own journey. Set small, daily achievable goals. And make notes at the end of the day of one or two things you accomplished. Refrain from comparing yourself to others who have already landed a great job, or aren't facing the same unique challenges you may be. Two great mental exercises I recommend to help you stay on course are meditation and visualization.

A vision board, whether you cut up images from a magazine or newspaper and glue them to posterboard, or pull them from Google Images and Pinterest to craft a virtual vision board on your computer, can help you create a blueprint for what you're seeking in your work life and a great job. Make one and look at it, look at it, look at it.

Stay positive. Reframe negative self-talk by shifting your thinking, for example, from "I'm too old to learn new things," to "I love to learn." Pessimism eats at your confidence. Be conscious of the language you use in your mind and make a pledge to replace it with positive words.

Stop complaining, being so tough on yourself, and blaming others for being in the situation you're in or for not hiring you. Focus your energy on what you do have sway over.

Follow my HOVER Approach. HOVER stands for the five core ingredients you must have, or will need to develop, to create change in your working life.

Hope is essential. When you have confidence that you can reach your goals, you will find a way to do so.

Optimism allows you to have a positive approach, which helps you keep pushing ahead even when there are roadblocks.

Value means knowing that you have something to offer—the skills and talent to get results and make progress, if you put out the effort.

Enthusiasm is the intangible "oomph" factor that provides the energy needed to make those necessary changes, both internally and externally.

Resilience, the knack for springing back in the face of adversity or failure, is indispensable to achieve happiness at work. Mental resilience allows you to show mettle in the face of adversity.

Finally, make these pledges to yourself:

- **I will be active online**. Build and maintain a strong online presence. Digital invisibility is a severe liability, indicating that you're out of date and unable to navigate the online world, a frequent stereotype about older applicants.

- **I will network, network, network**. Employers hire people they know, or people who know people they know. When reemployed workers were asked about the most effective steps they took in finding their current jobs, the overwhelming majority said networking. So do it the old face-to-face way, or do it online, but reach out to at least one person every day and ask for help and advice. Make it a point to tap your friends, relatives, former coworkers, social media connections, and anyone else you can think of.
- **I will not rely solely on job boards**. Cruising through job boards and applying online as you come across postings may give you a sense of accomplishment. But the sad fact is, many companies use talent-management software to screen resumes, weeding out droves without a human ever looking at them. As I have said repeatedly, most jobs are filled either internally or through referrals.
- **I will give my resume a facelift.** Trim your resume to two pages. Think advertisement, not obituary.
- **I will get my life in order.** Get physically fit. This will send a message subliminally that you're up for the job. Your age will become irrelevant; you'll have a certain vibrancy and energy that people want to be around.
- **I will learn something new.** Look at the specific requirements of the jobs you're applying for. If you don't have them, get them straightaway. A hiring manager who sees that you're taking classes or working toward a professional certification knows that you're not stuck in your ways. Plus, the very activity of learning will make you feel less stuck, more optimistic, and enthusiastic.
- **I will volunteer for a nonprofit or do pro bono work.** Volunteering can keep your skills current, allow you to network, and get your foot in the door at a future workplace. It can also fill gaps in your resume.
- **I will soul-search about what I really want in a job (and what I don't).** Focus your pursuit on workplaces you would truly like to join. Don't apply for open positions scattershot. To figure this one out, make lists: the best times in your working life, the things you really like to do, what you've excelled at, and what you really don't enjoy.

- **I will keep an open mind.** Above all, don't get trapped into thinking that you need an exact replacement for your last job. Consider a different profession in a different industry, making trade-offs about salary and flextime, stitching together a full-time position with part-time gigs. Don't pass up a golden opportunity just because it doesn't conform to your concept from 20 years ago of the perfect job. You can broaden your search by considering contract work or temporary assignments, which may lead to a full-time position. Who knows—you might find you like not being locked in somewhere long term.

This is *your* time to build a new life for new times.

Index